THE MIDDLE ENGLISH *PHYSIOLOGUS*

EARLY ENGLISH TEXT SOCIETY
No. 299
1991

THE
MIDDLE ENGLISH
PHYSIOLOGUS

EDITED BY

HANNEKE WIRTJES

Published for
THE EARLY ENGLISH TEXT SOCIETY
by the
OXFORD UNIVERSITY PRESS
1991

Oxford University Press, Walton Street, Oxford OX2 6DP

Oxford New York Toronto
Delhi Bombay Calcutta Madras Karachi
Petaling Jaya Singapore Hong Kong Tokyo
Nairobi Dar es Salaam Cape Town
Melbourne Auckland

Associated companies in Beirut Berlin Ibadan Nicosia

Oxford is a trade mark of Oxford University Press

British Library Cataloguing in Publication Data

The middle English physiologus.—(Early English Text
Society: Ordinary series: no. 299)
I. Wirtjes, Hanneke   II. Series
821.1

ISBN 0-19-722301-X

Set by Joshua Associates Ltd, Oxford
Printed in Great Britain by
Ipswich Book Company Ltd

PREFACE

Editing a Middle English text is uncomfortably like being pitted against the Hydra: only a Hercules would be capable of finishing the job. I can think of others whose efforts would have been more fruitful than mine. I myself had better acknowledge that it has been a privilege to be allowed to try and that it would be unwise to spend more time with the monster: I have cut off enough heads.

But is this new onslaught justified? There are several complete editions of the *Physiologus* (for which see the Bibliography), although they may no longer be readily available: Wright & Halliwell (1841), Mätzner (1867), Morris (1872, 1887), and Hall (1920) all present accurate texts. However, Wright & Halliwell, Mätzner, and Morris give the reader little help in their notes, and Hall, while he has a more extensive commentary, prints a diplomatic text which is awkward to use. Anyone trying to read the *Physiologus* in one of the available editions will, I think, find that it is a difficult text which deserves more attention than the earlier editors, who included it in anthologies of Middle English literature, were able to give it. It has been my aim to produce a separate edition of the *Physiologus*, with its own introduction, notes and glossary, in order to make the text accessible to the modern reader. I hope the reader will forgive my presumption in taking it upon myself to change the title of what used to be known as the *Bestiary*: my reasons are explained on p. lxxiii. Other, less drastic, changes include new suggestions to solve old cruxes. It is the work of earlier editors as well as that of Old and Middle English philologists since Hall that has enabled me to renew the attack: if more heads have grown back, the blame should be mine alone.

It is a pleasure to thank those who have helped me in my onslaughts. My first debt is to my parents, who have supported and encouraged me over the years. I have been fortunate in those who taught me. From my classics master, Mr R. J. Iwema, I learnt not only Latin and Greek but also the importance of intellectual rigour. Professor Johan Gerritsen I hold responsible for two of my abiding interests, mediaeval English and wine. Ever since my undergraduate days, his friendship has meant a lot to me. Miss Celia Sisam supervised the Oxford D. Phil. thesis on which the present edition is based, and she did so with exemplary scholarship and excellent whisky.

Professor Angus McIntosh has kindly dealt with queries about the dialect of the text, and Dr Malcolm Parkes gave his opinion on the date of the hand. My examiners, Professors E. G. Stanley and Janet Bately, suggested numerous improvements; Professor Bately also gave advice on how to turn the thesis into a book. Professor John Burrow generously read the typescript and corrected various errors. Finally, I should like to thank the Winston Churchill Birthday Foundation of the University of Bristol for a grant to cover part of the typing and Mrs Jan Tarling for her efficient way of dealing with what she rightly termed 'horrible work'. I have had all the help I could wish for, and I hope the Hydra is a little less dangerous as a result.

H.M.W.

CONTENTS

ABBREVIATIONS

Index   Carleton Brown and R. H. Robbins, *The Index of Middle English Verse* (New York, 1945); *Supplement* (Lexington, 1965)

Schneyer J. B. Schneyer, *Repertorium der lateinischen Sermones des Mittelalters* (Münster, 1969–80)

Thorndike L. Thorndike and P. Kibre, *Catalogue of Incipits of Medieval Scientific Writings in Latin*, 2nd ed. (Cambridge, Mass., 1963)

Walther H. Walther, *Initia carminum ac versuum medii aevi posterioris latinorum*, 2nd ed. (Göttingen, 1969)

Other abbreviations are listed at the beginning of the Glossary.

INTRODUCTION

1. THE MANUSCRIPT

The ME *Physiologus* survives in a single manuscript, British Library MS Arundel 292, which can be dated around 1300. It contains items in Latin, French and English and was probably written at Norwich.

The manuscript is parchment, 205 × 127 mm., and consists of (iv) + 116 + (iv) leaves. The flyleaves are s. xix paper; they have no watermarks. The first flyleaf at the beginning of the manuscript and the last flyleaf at the end are marbled on the recto and the verso respectively; the paste-downs, which are not conjugate with the fly-leaves, are of marbled paper of the same pattern. The verso of the last flyleaf at the beginning bears the coat of arms of Arundel. The original foliation, 1–116 in pencil in a modern hand, is correct, but it was changed in August 1885:[1] the blank leaf following f. 39 was overlooked, and f. 40 became f. 39. The leaves following the new f. 39 were renumbered accordingly. I have used the present, incorrect, foliation, which may be indicated as 1–39, [39²], 40–115, throughout.

The manuscript is tightly bound, which makes it difficult to work out the collation. The quiring, in so far as it can be established, is as follows: i², ii nine, iij¹², iv⁴ + 1 leaf after 27 (f. 28), v¹², vi⁸, vii⁸ + 1 leaf before 49 (f. 48), viij⁸, ix⁶ + 1 leaf after 67 (f. 68), x⁸, xi⁶ + 1 leaf after 80 (f. 81), xii¹⁰, xiij¹², xiv seven (f. 115). The quiring is obviously highly irregular, but the manuscript does not appear to be in booklets.[2] Hair faces flesh within the quire. The first quite is unsigned; quire ii is signed 'i' on the last verso (f. 11ᵛ), and quires iij–xi are signed 'ii' to 'x' at the bottom (middle) of the first recto and last verso. Quire xii is signed 'xii' in this same way; the final quires are unsigned. The quire signatures are contemporary. The gap in the signatures indicates that a quire is wanting. This quire may have contained the text 'De combustione ecclesie cath' sancte trinitatis Norwic'', which is listed in the old table of contents on f. 114ʳ.[3] This table of contents is in the hand of the main scribe. There are catchwords on ff. 47ᵛ and 96ᵛ in the bottom

---

[1] On the first flyleaf at the end of the book '116 ff.' is crossed out and replaced by '115 Folios. RPS. Aug: 1885 / examined by' in pencil.

[2] See below, p. xii.

[3] So N. R. Ker, 'Medieval Manuscripts from Norwich Cathedral Priory', *Transactions of the Cambridge Bibliographical Society*, I (1949–53), 1–28, p. 18.

right-hand corner. The one on f. 96ᵛ has been partly cut off. They are
not within a box or cartouche.

The written space is *c.*152 × 103 mm. The ruling is in pencil, 28
lines to a page. 27 lines are written: the top line is left blank. The prickings, round holes rather than slashes, are in the outer margins only,
one pricking for each line ruled and one for each of the two vertical
lines framing the written space. The prickings for the vertical lines are
at the bottom of the leaf.

The *Physiologus* is in the hand of the main scribe. This scribe,
scribe 1, is responsible for the whole manuscript, except a number of
later additions on f. 11ʳ and on ff. 68ʳ–71ᵛ. Scribe 1 writes a *textura
quadrata*: the main stroke of *t* protrudes above the headstroke; the top
compartment of *a* is closed up; the tironian note is used instead of the
ampersand; the feet of the minims have lozenge-shaped strokes.[1] C. E.
Wright assigns this hand to the second half of the thirteenth century,[2]
N. R. Ker to the end of the thirteenth century.[3] Dr M. B. Parkes,
whose judgement I shall follow here, dates the hand 's. xiii ex. or s.
xiii/xiv'.[4] If the text 'De combustione ecclesie cath' sancte trinitatis
Nowic'' was part of the original manuscript and if the title referred to
the great fire of 1272,[5] then we have a *terminus a quo* for the compilation
of the manuscript. Idiosyncratic features of the hand of scribe 1 are:
two forms of *g*, the normal hooked form for the stop and a hookless
form for all other phonetic values and a *p* (*wynn*) which is 'open at the
top and made in three strokes'.[6] *ð*, not *þ*, is used.

Later additions are in a variety of hands, each occurring only once.
Hand 2, f. 11ʳ, is a secretary hand, first half of the fifteenth century.
Hand 3, which appears on ff. 68ʳ–70ʳ, is anglicana, second half of the
fourteenth century. Hand 4, ff. 70ᵛ–71ʳ, is anglicana, middle of the
fourteenth century. Hand 5, f. 71ᵛ, is a mixed hand, second quarter of
the fifteenth century.[7]

[1] For a plate, see C. E. Wright, *English Vernacular Hands* (Oxford, 1960), p. 9.

[2] *English Vernacular Hands*, p. 8.

[3] 'Medieval Manuscripts from Norwich Cathedral Priory', p. 11.

[4] Opinion expressed to me on the basis of Wright's plate; Dr Parkes feels that s. xiii²
is too early for the *a* form in this hand (personal communication, September 30, 1987).

[5] The fire of 1272 is mentioned by Ker, 'Medieval Manuscripts from Norwich
Cathedral Priory', p. 5, and by H. C. Beeching and M. R. James, 'The Library of the
Cathedral Church of Norwich', *Norfolk Archaeology* 19 (1915), 67–116, p. 68.

[6] J. P. Gumbert and P. M. Vermeer, 'An Unusual *Yogh* in the *Bestiary* Manuscript—A
Palaeographical Note', *MÆ*, lx (1971), 56–7, p. 57, n. 6.

[7] So *The Oxford Book of Medieval English Verse*, ed. Celia and Kenneth Sisam (Oxford,
1970), p. 589.

The *Physiologus* is written out as prose. Lines of verse—or, in the alliterative portions, half-lines—are separated by a *punctus*; occasionally, the function of the *punctus* is syntactic rather than metrical.[1] There is no other form of punctuation in the *Physiologus*. The portions written by scribes 2–5 have no rubrication. In the rest of the manuscript, capitals are touched with red, and in the *Physiologus* the first letter after a *punctus* has red, whether or not it is a capital letter. Large capitals, which in the *Physiologus* mark off major divisions within the poem, are always in red, except in those parts of the manuscript which were added later. In the *Physiologus* the Latin headings are in red. The first letter of a new line in our poem often has the miniscule form, but a new section is always introduced by a large (two-line or larger) capital which catches the eye of the reader. There is no decoration in the manuscript.

The binding is nineteenth-century, leather over wooden boards. The tips and spine are in darker brown leather. The spine has five ribs, all genuine, and is decorated with horizontal gold-tooled lines, while diagonal gold-tooled lines mark off the tips. On the front and on the back are the arms of the Earl of Arundel and the words 'Bibliotheca Arundeliana', stamped in gold. The edges are not decorated.

The provenance is Norwich Cathedral Priory. The evidence for this is the press-mark 'C. x' on ff. 3^r and 114^v. N. R. Ker states that 'it looks entirely right as a Norwich mark, c. 1300'.[2] The lost item mentioned in the old table of contents, which relates to Norwich Cathedral, supports this.[3] When, at the Dissolution, the library collection was scattered, the manuscript left the library and eventually came into the possession of Thomas, Earl of Arundel (1585–1646). In 1666 his grandson, Henry Howard, afterwards Duke of Norfolk, gave most of Arundel's collection to the Royal Society (some of the manuscripts went to the Royal College of Arms). On f. 3^v there is a stamp, '*Soc. Reg. Lond / Ex dono HENR. HOWARD / Norfolciensis*'. In 1831 the Arundel collection of the Royal Society was transferred to the British Museum; in 1973 the Library Departments of the British Museum became part of the British Library.[4]

---

[1] e.g. in line 176, a *punctus* follows *forði*, which the *caesura* does not come till after *der*: *do we forði· so doð ðis der· ðanne be we derue*. For further examples, see the Commentary.

[2] 'Medieval Manuscripts from Norwich Cathedral Priory', p. 11.

[3] See above, p. ix.

[4] See Andrew G. Watson, *Catalogue of Dated and Datable Manuscripts c. 700 – 1600 in the Dept. of MSS, the British Library* (London, 1979), I, pp. 9–15; *Catalogue of Manuscripts in the British Museum*, ns I (London, 1834), pp. i–ii.

The contents of the manuscript are varied, and it is hard to say anything general about them, except that none of the original items appears inappropriate for the library of a religious foundation.[1] It is interesting to note that the *Physiologus* appears in the company of the fables of Odo de Cheriton, which is the item that follows it directly. Comparison of the collation and the contents of the manuscript shows that quires ii, v, ix, and xi originally had or still have blank last pages or leaves and that in quire xiij the end of a gathering coincides with the end of a text, but I am not sure that this warrants the conclusion that the manuscript was compiled from booklets, because the booklet theory does not explain why quires ii, ix, and xi consist of odd numbers of leaves and why so many of the remaining quires are aberrant.

The texts are listed in the order in which they were originally copied into the manuscript. An asterisk indicates a point in the folio sequence where there is an added item which will be described later.

*1. (f. 3^r) The Creed, ME verse
   Inc. I leue in godd almicten fader
   Expl. & eche lif i leue amen.
   (*Index* 1326)

2. (ff. 3^r–3^v) The Lord's Prayer, ME verse
   Inc. Fader ure ðatt art in heuene blisse
   Expl. Ooc fro iuel ðu sild us alle Amen
   (*Index* 787)

3. (f. 3^v) Hail Mary, ME verse
   Inc. Marie full of grace weel de be
   Expl. So be ðe bern ðatt is boren of ðe.
   (*Index* 2100)

4. (f. 3^v) In manus tuas, ME verse
   Inc. Louerd godd in hondes tine
   Expl. Louerd godd of soðfastheedd.
   (*Index* 1952)

---

[1] John Frankis, 'The Social Context of Vernacular Writing in Thirteenth Century England: The Evidence of the Manuscripts' in *Thirteenth Century England*, ed. P. R. Coss and S. D. Lloyd (Woodbridge, 1986), I, 175–84, compares Arundel 292 with other thirteenth-century anthologies and remarks that it 'reflects a fairly relaxed humane approach to piety' (p. 177). He concludes that what emerges from his study of these manuscripts is 'a picture of the clergy, at that date the literate section of the community, mediating vernacular writings, partly to other clergy and partly to the laity; in the latter case religious instruction shades off into the provision of entertainment' (p. 184).

5. (f. 3^v) 'Three things that make me fear', ME verse
   Inc. Wanne i ðenke ðinges ŏre
   Expl. i ne wot wider i sal faren.
   (*Index* 3969)

6. (f. 3^v) Meditation on death, ME verse
   Inc. If man him biðocte
   Expl. i wene non sinne sulde his herte winnen. prouerbium.
   memorare nouissima tua & in eternum non peccabis
   (*Index* 1422)

7. (ff. 4^r–10^v) *Physiologus*, ME verse
   Inc. Ðe leun stant on hille
   Expl. In cristes milce ure hope is best.
   (*Index* 3413)

(f. 11^v blank)

*8. (ff. 12^r–24^v) Fables of Odo de Cheriton, L prose
   Inc. Iverunt lingna ut ungerunt super se regem
   Expl. Illos autem qui nesciunt conspicere nisi terrena: proicit in
   tenebras exteriores.
   (printed *Fabulistes latins*, ed. L. Hervieux, IV, Paris, 1896; Hermann Oesterley, 'Die Narrationes des Odo de Ciringtonia',
   Jahrbuch für Romanische und Englische Literatur, ix (1868), 121–154)

9. (ff. 25^r–30^v) Debate between Mercy, Truth, Justice, and Peace, OF
   verse
   Inc. De quatre sorurs vus uoil dire. / Ke filies sunt deu nostre sire.
   Expl. Ke lunges auant furent dites. / E uerreiment en liure
   escrites.
   (printed *Libri Psalmorum versio antiqua gallica*, ed. M. Fr. Michel,
   Oxford, 1860, pp. 364–8)

10. (ff. 31^r–38^r) 'Dieu omnipotent', OF verse
    Inc. Deu le omnipotent. / Ki al cumencement. / Criat cel et terre.
    Expl. Pur lamur sa amie. / La pucele marie. / Amen dieu trestuz.
    (printed *Reimpredigt*, ed. Hermann Suchier, Bibliotheca Norman-
    nica, Halle, 1979)

11. (ff. 38^r–39^r) Part of a sermon by Stephen Langton, L prose
    Inc. Benedictione applica. benedicatur gens ecclesiastica. fugiat a
    nobis fraus diabolica. & maneat semper fides catholica.

Expl. Que portauit regem celorum et dominum. qui cum patre & spiritu sancto uiuit & regnat deus. amen.

(Schneyer, V, 468, item 32)

(f. 39ᵛ blank)

12. (ff. 40ʳ–60ʳ) Apollonius of Tyre, L prose
Inc. Fuit quidam rex antiochus nomine. a quo ipsa ciuitas nomen accepit antiochia.
Expl. Casus uero suos suorumque ipse descripsit. & duo uolumina fecit. vnum in templo diane ephesorum. & aliud bibliothece sue.
(printed Elimar Klebs, *Die Erzählung von Apollonius aus Tyrus*, Berlin, 1899)

13. (ff. 60ᵛ–67ᵛ) Fragment of Geoffrey of Monmouth's *Historia regum Brittanniae*, L prose
Inc. Cum Rex vortigernus inspexisset maximam cladem super eum uenturam
Expl. ambiguitate uerborum suorum. astantes in admiracionem commouit.
(corresponds roughly to Acton Griscom's text, London, 1929, VI. xvi to VIII. i, pp. 379, line 2 to 398, line 2)

*14. (ff. 72ʳ–86ʳ) St Patrick's Purgatory, L prose
Inc. Dicitur magnus sanctus patricius qui a primo est secundus
Expl. sacerdos autem uirginem quam quasi filiam nutriuit. deo seruituram in monasterio commendauit. explicit.
(printed E. Mall, 'Zur Geschichte der Legende vom Purgatorium des Heiligen Patricius', *Romanische Forschungen*, vi (1889), 139–97)

(f. 86ᵛ blank)

15. (ff. 87ʳ–104ᵛ) *Disticha Catonis*, OF verse with some L
Inc. Catun esteit paen. / Et ne saueit ren. / De crestiene lei.
Expl. Od deu eiens part. / E del pechur euerard. / A cit darmie deu merci. Amen.

16. (ff. 105ʳ–108ᵛ) De compositione chilindri qui dicitur orologium viatorum, L prose
Inc. Sumendum est lingnum maxime solidum.
Expl. & sic de aliis partibus intellige. & sic per umbram: scies altitudinem. Explicit composicio chilindri cum arte sua.
(Thorndike, col. 1536)

17. (ff. 108ᵛ–111ᵛ) De composicione quadrantis, L prose
Inc. Post chilindri composicionem.

Expl. et in tali gradu altitudinis erit stella in eadem hora: sic termi-
natur composicio quadrantis cum arte sua.
(Thorndike, col. 1062)

18. (ff. 111ᵛ–112ᵛ) De sortibus cum tabulis, L prose
Inc. Quia omnis presciencie uerissime perfecta comprehensio
Expl. Nouem & .9. minor vincit.
(Thorndike, col. 1226)

(f. 113ʳ blank, except for some pen-trials)

19. (f. 113ᵛ) Riddles, L verse
Inc. Tu qui lauas vnas herbas
Expl. Cauda canis sidetur que mox miles habetur.
(unidentified)

(f. 114ʳ contains a table of contents, in the hand of scribe 1; the remaining pages contain various scribbles and pen-trials)

20. (ff. 1ʳ–2ʳ) fragment of breviary, badly damaged and cropped by
binder

(f. 2ᵛ blank)

21. (f. 11ʳ) On the vanity of life, L verse
Inc. O caro carnea iam modo gloria postmodo uermis
Expl. Mutamt [*sic*] mores semper pignora prima memento.
(Walther, 12533)

22. (ff. 68ʳ–70ʳ) What to do in case of accidents at the Eucharist, L
prose
Inc. (S)i aperta quod absit neglicencia de corpore aut sanguine
christi acciderit
Expl. Tercia uiuentes hoc est in sanguine tincta
(unidentified)

23. (ff. 70ᵛ–71ʳ) The chorister's lament, ME verse
Inc. Vncomly in cloystre i coure ful of care
Expl. þanne sais oure mayster que vos ren ne vawt
(*Index* 3819)

24. (f. 71ᵛ) Satire against blacksmiths, ME verse
Inc. Swarte smekyd smeþes smateryd wyth' smoke
Expl. may no man for brenwaterys on nyht han' hys rest
(*Index* 3227)

2. LANGUAGE

In the following point by point discussion of the language of the Middle English *Physiologus*, lists of occurrences are complete unless otherwise indicated; abbreviations which are not self-evident are explained at the head of the Glossary, p. 49.[1] Whenever the Anglian dialect of Old English (abbreviated OA) shows developments different from West Saxon which are relevant to the text, Anglian is treated separately.

I. PHONOLOGY

A. Vowels in stressed syllables

1. ⟨a⟩ represents

(i) OE and ON *ă*: *draʒeð* (5, 192, 272), *makeð* (11, 45, 116 etc.), *naked* (82, 107, 108), *takeð* (61, 72) etc.;

(ii) OE *a/o* before a nasal (unless the nasal and a following consonant constitute a lengthening group[2]): *man* (1, 62; 66: *can*[3] etc.), *ðanne* (11, 56, 103), *wankel* (396) etc.;

(iii) OA *a* before *r* + consonant: *harde* adj. (175), *harde* adv. (177), *harm-dedes* (263), *narwe* (101) etc. and before *l* + consonant (unless *l* and the following consonant constitute a lengthening group): *falleð* (48, 82, 269; 469: *calleð*), *half* (406, twice), *walke* v. (130), *walke* n. (454) etc.;

(iv) OE *æ*: *after* (4, 497, 545), *at* (142, 235, 239 etc.), *craft* (99; 378: *maʒt*), *aʒte*, 'possessions' (421);

(v) OA *æ*: *chaueles*, 'jaws' (349), *sal* (13, 73, 89 etc.), *salt* (136) had OA *æ* because OA did not undergo palatal diphthongization; *waxe* (171); *waxen* (395) *waxeð* (110) presumably show breaking of *æ* to *ea*,[4] followed by Anglian smoothing, *ea* > *æ* (Campbell, §222);

---

[1] The discussion is confined to the language of the manuscript in which the *Physiologus* has come down to us: as will be shown in §§IV and V below (pp. xxxiv–lii), there is no way to determine the author's original language. For an earlier description of the language of the *Physiologus*, see Einar S:son Hallbeck, 'The Language of the Middle English Bestiary', D. Phil. thesis, Lund (Christianstadt, 1905).

[2] The *a* in *gangeð* (135, 155), *gangen* (98, 127, 370: *festen*), *gang[en]* (473, MS *gangande*: *standen*), *standen* (474: *gang[en]*) is attributed to early shortening by Lorenz Morsbach, *Mittelenglische Grammatik* (Halle, 1896), §90.

[3] Throughout, the colon is used to mean 'rhymes with'; for a detailed analysis of the rhymes, see part 3, 'Versification', pp. lii–lxviii.

[4] See A. Campbell, *Old English Grammar* (Oxford, 1959), §145.

(vi) OE $\bar{æ}^1$, shortened, in *blast* (485)[1] and in *togaddre* (425, 468).[2] *ðar* (7, 119, 161), *ðarto* (368), *ðarwiles* (164), and *ðarwið* (260) are not from OE $\bar{æ}^1$ but from OE *þār*, *þāra*, reinforced by ON *þar*;
(vii) OE *ea* in *bale* (151, 332).[3]

2. ⟨e⟩ represents
(i) OE and ON *ĕ*: *brennen* (218, 220: *rennen*; 372) *fele*, 'many' (261, 407), *meche*, 'mate' (524: *reche*), *set* pp. (190: *Fisiologet*) etc.;
(ii) OE *ē*: *feleð* (276, 374), *felen* (346), *her* adv. (16, 164, 209 etc.), *demen* (531), *deme* imperat. (128) etc.;
(iii) OA *ē* of various origins:
a. Primitive Germanic *æ* (corresponding to WS $\bar{æ}^1$: *dede* (71, 412, 413), *rede* (28: *ȝuðhede*), *slepen* (12, 401, 544), *slepeð* (467) etc.;
b. Primitive Germanic *ai* + *i* (corresponding to WS $\bar{æ}^2$): *del* 'part' (226), *fles* (102, 386), *imene* (217: *ouerwene*) etc.;
c. after palatal consonants, where WS would have palatal diphthongization, *ȝemen* 'take heed' (229), *ȝet* (32, 85, 86 etc.), *sep* (25, 426) etc.;
d. resulting from Anglian smoothing (Campbell §222): *heȝ* (14), *neȝȝen* 'approach', from the adj. *neh*, WS *neah* (108), *werk* (299—but this may derive from an Anglian smoothed form with *e*: Jordan, §66);
(iv) OE *ĕa*
a. resulting from *æ* < *a* (second fronting) followed by back umlaut, *æ* > *ea* (both characteristic of Mercian: Campbell §206): *heuekes*, 'hawk's' (599);
b. palatal diphthongization: *seftes* 'creatures' (313);
c. lengthened in late OE (Campbell §283): *ern* 'eagle' (62: *dern*), *ernes* (27);
(v) OE *ēa*: *heued* (116, 152), *lepeð* (200, 277), *ðewes* (126) etc.;
(vi) OE *ĕo*: *berȝes* (424—with possible smoothing in OA: Jordan, §66), *erðe* (16, 130, 566), *heuene* (39, 41, 129) etc.;
(vii) OE *ēo*: *brest* (105, 393), *deuel* (144, 284, 285 etc.),[4] *fend* (307) etc.;

---

[1] On the treatment of vowel quantity before *st*, see Richard Jordan, *Handbook of Middle English Grammar: Phonology*, tr. and rev. Eugene Joseph Crook (The Hague and Paris, 1974), §23, esp. n. 1. The same happens in *gast* (386: *stedefast*; 576: *vue*[*ma*]*st*), which is from OE *gǣst* with $\bar{æ}^2$, through shortening, followed by *æ* > *a*: see Jordan, loc. cit.
[2] *togiddre* (248) shows ME *e* > *i* before dentals: see Morsbach, §109, Jordan, §34. 1, and Karl Luick, *Historische Grammatik der englischen Sprache*, mit dem nach den hinterlassenden Aufzeichnungen ausgearbeiteten zweiten Kapitel von Friedrich Wild und Herbert Koziol, rpt. with an index by R. Hamer (Oxford, 1964), I. i, §379.
[3] OE *bealu* has the diphthong *ea* from inflected forms where it developed by breaking (owing to *bealw-*): Campbell, §209.
[4] The form *diuel* (19) shows ME *e* > *i*, but the change is rare before labials: Jordan, §34.

(viii) OE *y*: *stereð* 'stirs' (271), from OE *styrian*, could be an early example of lengthening in open syllables, i.e. the inflected *stireð* > *stēreð*; the text has *i* forms otherwise;[1]

(ix) the isolated form *steʒ* pret., 'ascended', (575) (OE *stāh*) is explained by S. T. R. O. d'Ardenne as due to rhyme association of this verb with *lihen* (AB spelling; OE *lēogan*, pret. sg. *lēah*, 'lie, deceive').[2]

3. ⟨i⟩ represents

(i) OE and ON *i*: *bi* (3, 19, 37 etc.), *bit* 'bites' (170, 182, 326 etc.), *drinken* (103, 224, 290 etc.), *ille* (362, 399) etc.;

(ii) OE *i* + palatal *g*: *bodi* (116, 151, 393 etc.), *oni* (331), *sti* (135: *bi*), *weri* (454: *ðerbi*) etc.;

(iii) OE *ȳ*. *fir* (109, 374), *kinde* (8, 27, 230 etc.), *mankin* (148: *win*; 511: *dim*), *ðirl* (100, 136) etc.[3]

4. ⟨o⟩ represents

(i) OE and ON *ŏ*: *blod* (327, 333, 438 etc.), *bone* 'request' (90), *costes* 'habits' (249, 585, 587), *dom* (177), *fox* (261, 307, 309 etc.), *of* (13, 76, 79 etc.) etc.;

(ii) OE and ON *ā*: *bon* 'bone' (438: *non*; 572: *onon*), *bro* 'brow' (535), *cloðed* (110), *cloðede* (146), *tokneð* (406), *tokned* (563) etc.;[4]

(iii) OE *a/o* befor a nasal in a lengthening group: *among* (130), *londe* (344, 554 both: *onde*), *song* (419: *ðerimong*; 597: *wrong*);

(iv) OA *a* before *l* + consonant if *l* and the consonant constitute a lengthening group: *biholdeð* (321), *biholden* (455), *cold* (438), *kolde* (429), *twifold* (281, 415) etc.;[5]

(v) OE *u*, perhaps, in *trostlike* 'confidently' (MS *trostlke*; 485, probably from OE **trust* adj.: see *OED* s.v.).

5. ⟨u⟩ represents

(i) OE and ON *u*: *buten* (101, 175), *dust* (5, 6), *kirke-dure* (119, 524),[6]

---

[1] On lengthening in open syllables, see below, pp. xlvii–xlviii.

[2] *þe Liflade ant te Passiun of Seinte Iuliene*, EETS, 248 (1961), 117 (p. 240); first proposed by Hallbeck, §15n. The form occurs in *Genesis and Exodus* as well: see the glossary to Olof Arngart's edition (Lund Studies in English 36, Lund, 1968), s.v. *steg*, where *stig* is the only form listed of the preterite (three occurrences, lines 319, 3527, 3599).

[3] *sundren* (518) is probably from OE *sundrian* rather than from OE *syndrian*.

[4] *oni* 'any' (331) has the vowel of OE *ān* (so *MED* s.v. *ani*).

[5] *helde* (152) and *helden* (121) are probably from WS *ea*, lengthened to *ēa* in lOE and becoming *e* in ME.

[6] On *dure*, which does not show lengthening of /u/ to /o:/, see E. J. Dobson, 'Middle English Lengthening in Open Syllables', *TPS* (1962), 124–48, pp. 129–32; see below, pp. xlvii–xlviii.

munen 'keep in mind' (249), *muneð* (172, 516), *uncuð* (348), *unkuð* (86), *vncuð* (413) etc.;

(ii) OE *ā*, probably the result of low stress: *nummor* (402) and *nummore* (179).[1]

6. ⟨ai⟩ represents OE *æ* + *g*: *dai* (21, 37, 133 etc.), *daies* pl., reformed from the sg. (97, 571),[2] *faier* (565), *fairere* (534), *mainles* (98) etc.

7. ⟨ei⟩ represents OE *æ* + *g*: *deies* gen. sg. (271), *breid* 'trick' (492), *breides* pl. (302).

8. ⟨y⟩ is not used except in *Moyses* (495), which represents Latin *Moyses*, from Greek *Mōysēs* (see *OED* s.v. *Moses*).

9. Vowels are not doubled to indicate length (see e.g. above, 2. ii, 4. ii); likewise, digraphs are not used to indicate length (see e.g. above, 2. iii, 5. i), except in *nout* (9, 531, 559). *nowt* (167, 185), *out* (464), *ovt* (518).[3]

B. *Vowels in unstressed syllables*

a. ⟨e⟩ is the vowel in unstressed syllables following the main stress: *abuten* (10, 127, 167), *abuuen* (15), *crede* (87), *hunger* (175, 268), *wankel* (396). Two words of OF origin are not in fact exceptions: *capun* (264: *tun*), where the second syllable has the main accent, and *dragunes* (559), where the second syllable may have had a secondary accent. In *tetoggeð* (279) and *tetireð* (279) the syllable preceding the main stress has *e* instead of *o*.

b. The treatment of medial *e* varies:

(i) it has been lost in *biforn* (52, 58, 236 etc.), *ikindled* (8; OE *gecynd* n. 'offspring'), *lendbon* (241; OE *lenden-bān*), *togaddre* (425, 468; OE *tō-gædere*), *togiddre* (248), *trendled* (537; OE *trendel* n., 'circle, ring');[4]

(ii) it is kept in *forloren* (59);

(iii) it is added, unetymologically, in *steuene* (503; OE *stefn*; but cf.

---

[1] *nummor* is the only form of the adverb used in *Genesis and Exodus*: see the glossary in Arngart's edition, which lists seven occurrences (lines 788, 1047, 1118, 1188, 1420, 1813, 3344).

[2] The plural *daʒes* (544) is from the OE pl. *dagas*.

[3] In 559, the MS reads *nout*, which spoils the rhyme (see the Commentary ad loc.); on *nout*, *nowt*, *out*, and *ovt*, see below, pp. xlix–l.

[4] Of these, *ikindled* and *trendled* are ME formations.

stefnes pl., 398), and in *sinezinge* (132; variant spelling *sinizing*, 225).[1] *betwixen* (258; MS *ben twixen*) may go back to *betweoxan* or it could be from OE *betweox*, with the extra syllable due to analogy with other prepositions in *-en*: see *OED* s.v. *betwixen, -twixe*.

C. Consonants

1. ⟨c⟩ and ⟨k⟩:

(i) initially the voiceless velar plosive, OE 'back' *c*, is usually ⟨c⟩ before a back vowel, e.g. *can* (68), *cunne* (6, 42, 113) *cold* (438), ⟨k⟩ before a front vowel or *n*, e.g. *kinde* (8, 27, 230 etc.), *kiðen* (27), *knoweð* (94), but *kolde* (429), *kam* (21, 310);

(ii) finally it is mostly ⟨c⟩: *boc* (308), *ilc* (225, 592), *swic* imperat. sg. (132), *swilc* 'such' (217), *wilc* (3) etc., but sometimes ⟨k⟩: *ilik* (301), *ilk* adj. (71, 523, 556), *ilk* pron. (596) *merk* (300), *swik* n. (302), *swilk*, 'such' (297), *werk* (299).

2. ⟨ch⟩ represents

(i) OE 'front' *c*, the voiceless palatal affricate: *chaueles* 'jaws' (349), *ches* 'chose' (524), *briche* 'helpful' (258, 530), *eche* 'eternal' (123) etc.;

(ii) OE *cc*: *fecheð* (157), *meche* 'mate' (524), *reche* imperat. (523) but OE *cc* is written ⟨cch⟩ in *dreccheð* (77), *feccheð* (264), *fecchen* (233).

3. ⟨3⟩ represents

(i) initially, OE 'front' *g*, the palatal semi-vowel: *zet* 'yet' (52, 85, 86 etc.), *zungling* 'young one' (486) etc.;

(ii) medially, between a back vowel and unstressed *e* (in OE between two back vowels) and between *l* and *r* and unstressed *e* (in OE *l* or *r* and a back vowel), OE *g*, the velar fricative: *drazen* inf. (384), *drazen* pres. ind. pl. (210, 345, 368), *sorzeden* (501), *folzen* (390, 579) etc.;

(iii) medially and finally, OE *h*, the palatal or velar fricative: *ni3t* (37, 133, 517 etc.), *no3t* adv. (108, 144), *no3t* n. (308), *fur3* 'furrow' (269) etc.

4. ⟨qu⟩ represents

(i) OE *cw*: *quenchet* (225), *quenching* (139), *quicke* (222). ⟨qw⟩ is used

---

[1] The added medial vowel in *sinezinge* and *sinizing* is explained by Professor d'Ardenne as due to rhyme association with OE *myngian/mynegian*: the rarity of the original form without the medial vowel may be the result, in dialects which have *i* for OE *y*, of the wish to avoid confusion with the verb from OE *singan*: see *Seinte Iuliene*, pp. 166–7.

in *qwemeð* (165; OE *cwēman*) and in *qweðsipe* (262; cf. OFris *quad*, MDu *quaed*, MLG *quât*, adj. s. + OE *-scipe*);
(ii) OE *hw*: *qual* 'whale' (535).[1]

5. ⟨s⟩ represents
(i) OE *s*: *sed* (158, 593), *sees* 'sea's' (359), *stedefastnesse* (126) etc.;
(ii) OE *sc*, initially and finally: *fis* (335: *is*; 341, 353 etc.), *sal* (13, 73, 89 etc.), *same* 'shame' (168, 298, 304: *name*), *sarpe* (279), *sipes* (363, 369, 397 etc.) etc., with the exception of *scrifte* (140), which has ⟨sc⟩.

6. ⟨ð⟩ represents OE *þ*, *ð*: *ðre* (435, 544, 571), *siðen* conj. (31, 32, 33 etc.), *teð* n. pl. (279) etc. ⟨þ⟩ is not used; *ð* is frequently assimilated to a preceding dental plosive or dental fricative: *atte* (119, 317, 524), *is te* (15, 80, 95 etc.), *&tus* (66, 106, 491 etc.), *bid tu* (133), *at tin* (142) etc.

7. ⟨p⟩ (*wynn*) is here printed ⟨w⟩; it represents:
(i) OE *w*: *walkeð* (103, 448, 554 etc.), *we* (25, 26, 154 etc.), *winter* (161, 162, 174 etc.) etc.;
(ii) OE *hw*: *wanne* 'when' (8, 333, 442), *wel* 'wheel' (537), *weðer* 'whether' (238, 464) etc., with the sole exception of *qual* (535: see 4(ii) above).

8. The OE clusters *hl-*, *hn-*, and *hr-* have invariably been simplified to *l-*, *r-*, and *n-* respectively, *lepeð* (200, 277), *lides* (13), *list* 'listen' (523), *listen* (63), *listneð* (268, 387), *louerd* (15, 74, 186 etc.), *louerdes* gen. sg. (259), *heuen-louerd* (149), *lude* (330, 546), *necke* (265), *rapelike* (156, 324), *raðe* (278, 292, 487), *rauen* (273), *rem* (11, 483, 548), *remede* (573), *remeden* (503), *remen* (483), *remeð* (470, 471, 478 etc.), *reming* (485), *reufulike* (471), *rewe* (177), *rewen* (388), *rof* (318), *hus-rof* (317).

9. Metathesis has occurred in *offriʒt* (562) and *ðrist* (201, 379); *atbresteð* (491), and *atbrosten* (404) are probably from ON *bresta*.

10. Metanalysis occurs only in *neilond* (339, 366).

11. Consonants are not doubled finally after short vowels: *al* (33, 44, 50 etc.), *God* 'God' (256), *it* (21, 28, 68 etc.) except in *all* (182) and *itt* (538).

---

[1] The spelling ⟨qu⟩ is characteristic of Norfolk: cf. below, §I. C. 7(ii), and for the localization of the text see below, §IV (pp. xxxiv–xl).

II. MORPHOLOGY

A. *Nouns*

The four-term system of OE (nom., acc., gen., dat.) has largely become a two-term system, with the gen. as the marked term.

1. In the sg. the form of the unmarked term usually derives from the OE nom., e.g. *ston*, OE strong masc. (21, 56, 100 etc.), *luue*, OE strong feminine (79, 514, 521), *name*, OE weak masc. (19, 95, 262 etc.), *sunne*, OE weak feminine (10, 43, 44) etc., but:

(i) there are occasional traces of a prepositional case:[1] *boke* (28, 190, 513; cf. *boc* nom., 308), *dede*, 'death' (22, 562; cf. *ded* nom., 364; but cf. also *to ded maken*, 112), *Gode* 'God' (78, 90: *fode*; cf. *God* nom., 256) etc.;

(ii) OE strong feminine nouns take -*e* in the nom. sg., irrespective of the original stem: *sowle* (524).[2] The -*e* appears also when the noun is the direct object: *aȝte* (421), *bote* (133), *bore* (75; 387: *sore*), *mede* (256: *nede*), *milce* (134), *siȝte* (81), *sinne* (183), *sonde* (382: *onde*), *soule* (151, 422);

(iii) in two cases etymological -*e* has been lost: *stel* (371; before a vowel; OA *stele*), *swik* (302: *ilik*; OE *swice*). *nos* (265) may show influence of ON *nös*;

(iv) *seppande* (313) is presumably influenced by pres. part. -*ande*. The -*e* in the first element of the compound *birde-time* (105) is a connecting vowel.[3]

---

[1] See Fernand Mossé, *A Handbook of Middle English*, tr. James A. Walker (Baltimore, 1952), §§55–6.

[2] OE strong feminines such as *sawol* (*ō*-stem) join Mossé's Type II, together with OE masculines such as *ende* (*ia*-stems). Mossé gives the paradigm:

sg.	nom./acc.	soule
	gen.	soules
	dat.	soule
pl.		soules

In the Midlands, which is where our text is from, the OE weak noun is part of Type II; the South has a separate Type II, with a gen. sg. in -*e* (*name*) and an -*en* plural (*namen*): Mossé, §55.

[3] OE *gebyrd-tima* is recorded only without the extra -*e* (see Bosworth-Toller, *Supplement* s.v.). Campbell mentions a form *gebyrdetid*, which is not recorded in Bosworth-Toller. He suggests that it is 'perhaps due to contamination with the *ia*-declension, which regularly has a connecting vowel in composition', §348, n. 2). Alternatively, *birde-time* could be a ME development: *MED* s.v. *birth(e)* n. has several instances of a nom. form *birde*.

2. The gen. sg. is normally formed by adding -(*e*)*s*: *belles* (484), *Cristes* (222, 594, 602), *ernes* (27), *hornes* (484), *prestes* (75) etc.[1] but:

(i) sometimes the ending is -*e*: *helle* (574), *heuene* (574), *soule* (139, 525);

(ii) there is no ending in *erðe* (566), in *nese* (2) if *nese* is from OE **neosu* (but cf. ON *nös*) and in *welle* (48) if *welle* is from OA *wella* (but cf. OA *well*).

3. The pl. follows the OE strong masculine, adding -(*e*)*s* to the stem: *briddes* (595), *limes* (31, 53, 117), *sinnes* (64, 140, 146), *sipes* (363, 369, 397) etc. with the exception of

(i) mutation plurals: *fet* (4), *men* (127, 130, 267 etc.), *sipmen* (400), *teð* (279), *wimmen* (516);[2]

(ii) plurals with ø ending (OE neuter *a*-nouns with long stems[3]): *der* (540), *ʒer* (434, 435: *her*), *sep* (25, 426) *ðing* (315);

(iii) -*e* plurals: *eldere* (150, 210);[4]

(iv) -*en* plurals (OE weak noun): *eʒen* (13, 34, 45 etc.), *willen* (458: *swiken*).[5]

4. There are no definite examples of the gen. pl.

B. Adjectives

1. Singular: adjectives ending in a consonant take the ending -*e* when occurring in weak position: *ðislittlewile* (173), *ðeoldelaʒe* (181), *ðeswetteste ðing* (344), *his beste wune* (457) etc. In strong position they do not add -*e*: *naked man* (108), *long liuenoðe* (173), *ilc siniʒing* (225), *a god stund* (271) etc.

2. Plural: if the stem does not end in a vowel, -*e* is often added in the plural: *oðre fules* (274), *mid here teð sarpe* (279), *harde sures* (175) etc., but: *mid oðer der* (540), *in hise sinnes dern* (64: *ern*).

[1] This would be Mossé's Type I, derived from the OE strong masculine (*a*-stem), for which he gives the paradigm (§55):

sg.	nom./acc.	ston
	gen.	stones
	dat.	ston(e)
pl.		stones.

[2] Campbell, §§620–7; Mossé, §58.   [3] Campbell, §§570, 573.

[4] *erðe* 'people of the earth' (130) is a collective sg., not a pl.

[5] This would be Mossé's Type III, which does not tend to appear north of the Thames: see Mossé, §55. Other former OE weak nouns take -(*e*)*s* e.g. *husbondes* (263; late OE *husbonda*).

3. When an adjective is used in the plural as subject complement, it frequently does not take an ending: *strong* (53: *wrong*), *siker* (178), *faȝen* (346: *draȝen*; 367: *draȝen*). *-e* in *bare* (107), *kolde* (429) may not have been sounded.

C. Adverbs

Adverbs formed from adjectives vary:

(i) some take the ending *-like*: *bitterlike* (326), *derflike* (275), *dernelike* (285: *biswike*), *gredilike* (202: *sikerlike*), *hardilike* (155), *laȝelike* (514), *liȝtlike* (277), *mildelike* (130), *rapelike* (156, 324), *reufulike* (471), *sikerlike* (80; 203: *gredilike*), *trostlike* (453; MS *trostlke*);

(ii) some take *-e*: *harde* (177), *heȝe* (504), *imene* (217: *ouerwene*), *iuele* (98), *longe* (569), *lude* (330, 546), *mirie* (398), *raðe* (278, 292, 487), *sore* (388: *lore*), *stille* (9, 21, 328 etc.), *wide* (342: *vnride*; 448: *unride*), *wille* (26);

(iii) a few take no ending: *fast* (142; from OE *fæste*), *wurðlic* (152: *ȝeuelic*, adj.).[1]

D. Pronouns

For convenience, possessive and demonstrative adjectives are included here.

1. Personal pronouns

first person	sg. nom.	*I* (27, 499, 518—all before a consonant)
		Ic (28, 166, 492, 550, 558—before a consonant or a vowel)
	obliq.	no examples
	poss.	no examples.
	pl. nom.	*we* (25, 26 (twice), 154 etc.)
	obliq.	*us* (25, 150, 172 etc.), *vs* (23)
	poss.	*ure* (20, 74, 149 etc.), *ur* (250, 596), *vre* (15, 186)
second person	sg. nom.	*ðu* (119, 120, 122 (twice) etc.), *tu* (118, 128, 133 etc.)
	obliq.	*ðe* (27, 144 (twice) etc.), *te* (125)

---

[1] Another example of an endingless adverb could be *hac* (592) if the conjecture that it is from the ON adj. *hak-r* and means 'ruthlessly, without hesitation' is correct: see the Commentary ad loc.

		poss.	ðine (134), ðin (137, 422), tine (140), tin (142), ði (141)
	pl. nom.		ȝe (63, 209)
	obliq.		ȝu (492, 516, 550 etc.)
	poss.		no examples.
third person	sg. masc.	nom.	he (1, 2, 3 etc.)
		obliq.	him (4, 7, 10 etc.)
		poss.	with sg. nouns: his (2, 5, 7 etc.); with pl. nouns: hise (4, 13, 31 etc.), his (34)
	fem.	nom.	ȝe (153, 157, 161 etc.)
		obliq.	hire (160, 162, 165 etc.), ire (159)
		poss.	hire (157, 160, 163 etc.)
	neut.	nom.	it (21, 45, 164 etc.), itt (538)
		obliq.	it (28, 68, 94 etc.)
		poss.	no examples
	pl. nom.		he (232, 233, 234 etc.)
	obliq.		hem (247, 278, 279 etc.)
	poss.		here (246, 278, 327 etc.)

it (399, 588) is an idiomatic use of the sg. rather than a pl.
Enclitic *is*, 'them', occurs in lines 6, 122, 266, and in *wes* (= *we is*), line 586.
Enclitic *it* occurs in ȝet (= ȝe it), line 170.

2. Demonstratives

adjectives	sg.	ðis (114, 115, 124 etc.), tis (62, 268); ðat (18, 48, 177 etc.), tat (14)
	pl.	ðise (350); no examples
pronouns	sg.	ðis (308, 406, 455); ðat (14, 139, 337 etc.), tat (84)
	pl.	no examples; ðo (383, 541)

3. Relatives
Relative pronouns are ðe (15, 19, 127 etc.) and ðat (11, 14, 36 etc.).

Syntactical note
As is generally, though not invariably, the rule in early ME in the East Midlands, ðe is used with animate antecedents (except in line 558, *For*

ðe swetnesse ðe Ic ȝu haue told, and line 173, ðis little wile ðe we on werld wunen) and ðat tends to be used with inanimate antecedents (but not exclusively so: A wilde der is ðat is ful of fele wiles (261), Ðis wirm bitokneð ðe man ðat oðer biswikeð (329), Cethegrande is a fis, / Ðe moste ðat in water is (335–6), Ðis fis ðat is unride (341), Ðe sipes ðat arn on se fordriuen (363— sipes meaning 'sailors'), So sep ðat cumen ut of folde (426)).[1] Both ðe and ðat are used in non-restrictive as well as in restrictive clauses.[2]

wos (564) is used as the gen. sg.[3]

ðat is also a compound relative, 'what, that which' (142, 160, 414) (Mustanoja, p. 190); wat occurs in this function at line 118 (Mustanoja, p. 194).

ðer (49, 396, 499) and ðar (119) appear as relative adverbs (Mustanoja, p. 202).

E. Verbs

1. Pres. ind.

sg. 1.   -e: haue (492, 558), rede (28), seie (499, 518, 550)

2.   -es: forbredes (122), forȝelues (123), forwurðes (123), hiȝtes (120, 142);
-est: hauest (122), hiȝtest (118)

3.   -eð: bereð (170, 182), falleð (48, 82, 269 etc.), hatieð (266— perhaps for hateð[4]), lepeð (260, 277), wakeð (24) etc.;
syncopated: abit (521), bihalt (463: biwalt[5]), bit (170, 182, 326 etc.), hitt (321), stant (1) etc.;
-(e)t: forsaket (70), quenchet (225), seit (518);
-es: bilimpes (242)

pl.   -en: beren (244), fallen (46, 274, 322), hatien (267), heren (26), waken (401);

---

[1] Angus McIntosh, 'The Relative Pronouns þe and þat in Early Middle English', EGS I (1947–8), 73–87, first observed this rule but it 'is not followed in the whole of the East Midland area' (p. 77). See also Tauno F. Mustanoja, A Middle English Syntax. I: Parts of Speech (Helsinki, 1960), 188–90; Kirsti Kivimaa, þe and þat as Clause Connectives in Early Middle English with Especial Consideration of the Pleonastic þat (Helsinki, 1966), 121–2. By contrast, in 'AB language' (the language of Ancrene Wisse and the 'Katherine Group'), þet simply competes with þe (Seinte Iuliene, §91).

[2] Mustanoja states that 'the tendency to confine that to defining (restrictive) clauses does not emerge until the rivalry between that and which begins' (p. 190).

[3] With animate antecedents, wos 'has been used as a relative since earliest ME' (Mustanoja, p. 200).

[4] See below, §II. E. 9.

[5] The MS reading biwarlt is clearly wrong: see the Commentary ad loc.

-e: *cume* (479), *fele* (494), *haue* (260)—both followed by the subject pronoun *we*; *haue* (594).[1]

In the sg., the endings *-e*, *-est*, and *-eð* (with or without syncopation) correspond to the OE (mainly WS) endings. The 2 sg. *-es* may go back to *-s* in Rushworth[1], where it appears besides *-st*.[2] The 3 sg. *-es* is unusual in the Midlands in ME, being a Northern ending (Mossé, §39);[3] *-(e)t* occurs in OE[4] and appears to be a Norfolk feature in ME.[5] In the pl. the ending *-en*, which is the OE subj. pl. ending, replaces OE *-aþ*, as is usual in the Midlands (Mossé, §39): variation with *-e* is common (Mossé, §39), but the three examples of *-e* ending followed by the subject pronoun *we* are better explained as deriving from OE (*we ridaþ*, *ride we*: Campbell, §730).

2. Pres. subj.

sg.   *-e*: *derie* (162), *falle* (443), *forwurðe* (171), *holde* (117), *rewe* (177) etc.

ø: *se* (108, 110), *ȝeld* (297)

pl.   *-n*: *gon* (26, 223)

The sg. ending *-e* is the same as in OE, as is ø when the stem ends in a vowel; this situation is characteristic of the Midlands (Mossé, §39). The form *ȝeld* (297) would seem to be an anomaly:[6] when the stem ends in a consonant, the pres. subj. sg. takes *-e* in all dialects of OE (Campbell, §735(b)), and in the ME only the North drops the *-e* (Mossé, §39). Instances of the pret. subj. are limited to *soȝe* (338) and forms of 'to be': in the sg., *were* (168, 277, 519) and *wore* (519: *more*), and in the pl., *weren* (562).

[1] *haue* could conceivably be an error for *hauen* caused by attraction to *be we* (590) and *do we* (592): the correct form *hauen* appears in *we hauen don wrong* (598).

[2] Campbell, §735(b). e.g. Rushworth[1], Matt. 8: 19, *ic wille folgian swa þu ganges & gæst* and cf. *gebiddes* (Matt. 4: 7) but *cymest* (Matt. 3: 14) (*The Gospel According to St Matthew in Anglo-Saxon, Northumbrian and Mercian*, ed. W. W. Skeat, Cambridge, 1887).

[3] Campbell explains the OE 3 sg. pres. ind. ending *-es* in the North as a falling together of 2 sg. and 3 sg. under the 2 sg. (*-es*): the confusion may have been aggravated by Scandinavian influence (§735(b)).

[4] Campbell takes the OE 3 sg. pres. ind. endings in *-it*, *-et* to be 'a genuine phonetic variant' (§735(b)) and notes that in eWS and in Rushworth[1] the examples are all from weak verbs but that Rushworth[2] has examples from strong verbs as well.

[5] Angus McIntosh, 'The Language of the Extant Versions of *Havelok the Dane*', *MÆ*, xlv (1976), 36–49, calls it 'unusual in most areas of ME' but 'of course extremely well attested in Norfolk' (p. 39); on the provenance of the *Physiologus*, see below, §IV (pp. xxxiv–xl).

[6] *ȝeld* could just possibly be an error for *ȝelt*, the syncopated form of 3 sg. pres. ind. (see §II. E. 1), because the sentence continues in the indicative: *& deuel ȝeld swilk billing / Wið same & wið sending / & for his sinfule werk / Ledeð man to helle merk* (297–300).

Syntactical note

The subjunctive is used in the following ways:

(a) optative: *& deuel ʒeld swak billing / Wið same & wið sending* (297), *Vre louerd Crist it leue us* (186) (Mossé, §126(a); Mustanoja, pp. 455–6);

(b) in adverbial clauses of condition: *bute he lif holde* (117), *if he naked man se* (108), *if he cloðed man se* (110), *oc if hire make were ded & ʒe widue wore* (519) (Mossé, §158; Mustanoja, pp. 469–70);

(c) in clauses of purpose: *ðat winter hire ne derie* (162), *ðat it ne forwurðe, ne waxe hire fro* (171), *ðat we ne gon to helle* (223) (Mossé, §154; Mustanoja, pp. 466–7);

(d) after a verb expressing thinking or believing: *he wenen ðat ʒe ded beð* (275), *Ðat tu wuldes seien ʒet / . . . Ðat it were a neilond* (337–9) (Mossé, §154. I(3); Mustanoja, p. 460; but cf. *A neilond he wenen it is*, 366, where *is*: *þis*);

(e) in a non-introduced clause of concession: *be it drie, be it wete* (552) (Mustanoja, pp. 468–9);

(f) in the preterite, in clauses of comparison: *so it same were* (168), *so ʒe ded were* (168), *also he weren of dede offriʒt* (562) (Mustanoja, pp. 464–5).

3. Imperat.

    2 sg. *-e*: *deme* (128), *feste* (126, 141), *herkne* (449), *newe* (125), *reche* (523) etc.;

           ø: *bid* (133), *feʒ* (141), *go* (138), *knov* (118), *let* (137), *list* (523), *swic* (132)

    1 pl. ø: *do* (151, 176, 592), followed by the subject pronoun *we*; *-e*: *bimene* (598), *leue* (528, 529), *luue* (525), *wende* (526) etc., all followed by the subject pronoun *we*; *-en*: *berʒen* (151)

    2 pl. *-eð*: *hereð* (35), *listneð* (268), *muneð* (516)

There are no examples of the third person pl. or the first and third persons sg.

Syntactical note

As in OE, the subjunctive is used in first- and third-person equivalents of the imperative, so the first-person plural forms, which end in *-e*, *-en* or ø, have endings that are characteristic of the subjunctive (see §I. E. 2; see also Mossé, §§94.VII, 127 and Mustanoja, pp. 474–5). The imperative pl. ending *-eð* (OE *-aþ*) is characteristic of the South and the Midlands in ME.

4. The infinitive usually ends in -en: beren (167; 439: stonden, inf.; 584: deren inf.), eten (171, 290), hunten (1), luuien (120), slepen (12, 544) etc. or -n if the stem ends in a vowel: don (183; 287 (MS ð̄on), 289), flen (235: ten, pres. ind. pl.), fordon (312: on). -e appears in biswike (286: dernelike) and chare (403: warre).

Variation between -en and -e is common throughout ME (Mossé, §94).

5. The present participle always ends in -ande: cripelande (99), fiȝtande (114), rennande (486). In addition to these, the MS has gangande (473) and sacande (479), both of which destroy the rhyme, which requires infinitives (the rhyme words are standen and maken respectively): gangande has accordingly been emended to gang[en], sacande to sa[ken]: see the Commentary ad loc.

In OE this ending is attested in Rushworth[1] (scattered instances only, mainly in gangande, 'going': Campbell, §735(j)). In ME it occurs in the North and North Midlands (see Mossé's map, p. 78) and as far south as Norfolk.[1]

6. The past participle of weak verbs ends in -(e)d: cloðed (110), eried (207), lered (209), seid (492: breid, n., 'trick').

Past participles of strong and weak verbs do not take a prefix, with the sole exception of ikindled, 'born' (8); idiȝt (320) is an adjective, 'ready', rather than a past participle.

Past participles of strong verbs are listed under 8, below.

7. The preterite indicative of weak verbs is formed by adding a dental suffix: dennede (18), filstnede (22), likede (16), remede (573) etc. (all third person sg.; there are no examples of the first and second persons singular); remeden (503), sorȝeden (501), suggeden (501), plural.

For the strong verbs see 8, below.

8. All the OE classes of strong verbs are represented. Deviations from the OE patterns are marked with an asterisk and discussed below: preterites (sg. unless otherwise indicated):

I ros (22, 573), steȝ (575)*
II ches (524), flet (338: ȝet), broken, pl. (211)
III wan (568: man), wurð (508)*

---

[1] See below, §IV, 'Provenance' (pp. xxxiv–xl).

IV *come* (18), *kam* (21, 310)*, *cam* (506), *bar* (19)
V *lai* (21, 569)
VI *sop* (313), *stod* (499: *god*)
VII *slep* (571), *fel* (493)

past participles:

I *fordriuen* (363: *liuen*), *sinen* (10), *writen* (513)
II *forloren* (59: *biforn*)
III *bunden* (393), *doluen* (20), *forbroiden* (96)*, *forwurden* (96)*
IV *broken* (122), *forbroken* (96)
V *sen* (154)*
VI *sapen* (536)
VII *biholden* (455), *fallen* (512), *waxen* (395)

wurð has the vowel of the pret. pl., *broken* of the pp. In *forbroiden*, OE *g* has become vocalized (through analogy with the infinitive and the preterite singular); *forwurden* has the vowel of the OE preterite plural and of the lOE and ME infinitive; *kam* and *cam* have taken the vowel of the majority of class IV verbs; *sen* is probably a contracted form of Anglian *gesegen* (Campbell, §743). For *steʒ* see above, §I. A. 2(ix). For the conjugation of modal and irregular verbs see the appropriate entries in the glossary.

9. Weak verbs that go back to OE weak verbs in *-ian* do not generally keep the *i* where OE had it except in isolated cases: *derie*, pres. subj. sg. (162), *luuien*, inf. (120; cf. *luuen*, inf., 251), *hatieð* pres. ind. 3 sg. (266; unhistorical), *hatien*, pl. (267; cf. *haten*, 263), *eried* (270).
The preservation of *i* is characteristic of a number of Southern and South Western dialects (Mossé, §94(V)),[1] but the number of instances in our text is too small to be significant.
The *i* in *hatieð*, 'hates' (OE *hataþ*), is unhistorical; perhaps *hatieð* is the result of attraction to *hatien* in the next line (267).

III. VOCABULARY

The vocabulary of the *Physiologus* consists of three major elements: Anglo-Saxon, Scandinavian, and French. By far the largest part is Anglo-Saxon, but a considerable number of words, often nouns and verbs denoting ordinary things and activities and also prepositions

---

[1] Such as AB language (see *Seinte Iulien*, §§105 ff.), Laʒamon's *Brut* and the *Kentish Sermons*.

and conjunctions, is from Scandinavian, as is to be expected in a text from an area that formed part of the Danelaw.[1] French borrowings are fewer and different in character: as is generally the case with French loanwords in early ME, they tend to be incidental, filling a specific lexical gap (names of animals for instance), and not denoting everyday objects and activities. Consequently, they are mostly nouns not verbs, and never, at least in this early text, prepositions or conjunctions.

A minor source is Continental (non-Scandinavian) Germanic: a few words, no more than five or six, are probably not from OE or ON, but from some branch of Germanic (High or Low German or Frisian)—it is impossible to be more specific. In at least one case, however, it is doubtful if the word is really a Continental borrowing or if it is from OE but just happened never to be recorded: there is nothing about the noun *smel*, 'smell' (2), to suggest that it cannot have been from an OE word, and the absence of parallels in cognate languages indicates that it is unlikely to have been a Continental borrowing: see *OED* s.v. *smell* sb. and v. Perhaps the same is true of *snute*, 'snout' (488), but at least we have a close parallel here, Middle Dutch *snute*, 'snout' (and see *OED* s.v. *snout* sb.). Three other words are definitely not from OE or ON: *qweðsipe*, 'wickedness' (262; cf. Chaucer, *Canterbury Tales, Cook's Prologue*, A. 4357 'But "sooth pley, quaad pley," as the Flemyng seith', and also B. 1628;[2] Middle Dutch *quaed*, Middle Low German *quât*, Old Frisian *quad*); *slumeren*, 'slumber' (401), for which cf. Middle Low German and Middle Dutch *slumeren*.[3]

The remaining words are more complicated: *taunede*, 'showed' (567) has parellels in Continental Germanic languages, Middle Low German, and Middle Dutch *tonen*, Middle High German *zounen* (all meaning 'show'), but none of these explains the vowel of ME *taunede*; *OED* s.v. *tawne*, *taune* v.[1] postulates an unrecorded OE verb **ætawnian*. It should be noted that the verb is rare in ME[4] and that it presents the only example in this text of the spelling *au* where the second element is vocalic. Perhaps OE **mire* would best account for *mire*, 'ant' (153, 172, 180), but the word is attested in Middle Dutch

---

[1] On the provenance of the ME *Physiologus*, see below, §IV (pp. xxxiv–xl).

[2] References to Chaucer are to *The Riverside Chaucer*, ed. Larry D. Benson (Oxford, 1988).

[3] It is possible to read *swak*, 'weak', rather than *swilk*, 'such', at line 297, and this would be a Continental Germanic borrowing (cf. Middle Low German *swak*), but the only ME text in which it is certainly recorded is *Genesis and Exodus*: see the Commentary ad loc.

[4] The only other text known to me in which this verb appears is *Genesis and Exodus*: see Arngart's glossary s.v. *taunen*.

(*miere*) and Middle Low German (*mire*), so the ME noun may well be a borrowing. The same could apply to *gres*, 'grass' (159: *es*; 431: *mandragores*), which appears in Old Frisian as *gers*, but *MED* records an isolated OE instance of *gres* from the Anglian dialect s.v. *gras* which is a possible ancestor.

The French loans are not numerous: no more than 25 words, some of which had entered the language during the OE period.[1] Pre-Conquest loans are: *capun*, 'capon' (264), *coc*, 'cock' (264), *leun*, 'lion' (1, 9, 12 etc.),[2] *panter* (533, 539, 560), *turtres*, 'turtle-dove's' (513),[3] *market* (331), *funt-fat*, 'font' (82).[4] French loanwords that are not recorded until ME are *cete*, 'whale' (349) and *cethegrande*, 'whale' (335), *dragunes*, 'dragons' (559), *bec*, 'beak' (32, 51, 52 etc.), *grace* (93), *Iesu* (72), *caue*, 'cave, hollow' (162, 170, 182), *cul*, 'choice' (541), *fin*, 'excellent' (580), *gin*, 'trick, trap' (464), *hardilike*, 'vigorously' (155—ending ME), *Inde* (423), *rime*, 'rhymed verse' (513), *robbinge*, 'robbing, stealing' (592—ending ME), *simple*, 'free from guile, honest' (590), *spuse*, 'spouse' (525), *uenim*, 'venom' (104, 204). *haleð*, 'drags' (160, 266), came into OF from Germanic (see *OED* s.v. *hale* v.¹). Although they are few, these French loanwords nevertheless form a significant part of the vocabulary of the *Physiologus*: several names of animals are French (*capun*, *cete/cethegrande*, *coc*, *dragunes*, *leun*, *panter*) and the name of the source, when it is mentioned, is French: *Fisiologet*, 'little Physiologus' (191). *crede* [OE *crēda*, L *crēdo*] (87), *pater noster* (87), and *satanas* (70) are pre-Conquest loans from Latin sources.

None of the French borrowings can be traced back to Central French (*francien*); all the OF words that have demonstrable dialectal affiliations are from Anglo-Norman: *capun* and *dragunes* show AN *u* for *o*; *spuse* has *u* for earlier close *ō* (a Western feature imported into AN[5]) and shows absence of prosthetic *e* (Pope, §1106); in *capun* and *market* velar articulation of Latin *c* is retained before *a* and *e* respectively (Pope, §1091); *gin* is aphetic for *engin* (Pope, §1137); in *uenim* final *n* has become *m* by dissimilation;[6] *cul*, as A. J. Bliss shows, is from the AN verb *cuillir*.[7]

---

[1] See Bosworth-Toller and *OED* s.vv. and the appropriate entries in the Glossary.

[2] OE borrowed *leo* from Latin; the spelling *leun* is Norman French: see *OED* s.v. *lion*.

[3] *turtres* is probably from Latin; the ME form could be a re-borrowing from OF: so *OED* s.v. *turtur*.

[4] The compound is recorded in OE, spelt *font-fæt* (Bosworth-Toller, *Supplement* s.v.): the *u* in *funt* may be from Norman French *funz*.

[5] Mildred K. Pope, *From Latin to Modern French* (Manchester, 1934), §1083.

[6] Mary S. Serjeantson, *A History of Foreign Words in English* (Manchester, 1935), Appendix D, p. 300. [7] 'Three Middle English Studies', *EGS*, ii (1948–9), 40–54, p. 54.

The Scandinavian element is considerably larger and it includes conjunctions and prepositions: *fro*, 'from' [*frá*] (22, 105, 109 etc.), *oc*, 'but' [*ok*] (104, 109, 130 etc.), *til*, 'till' [*til*] (10, 21, 41 etc.), *ðoȝ*, 'although' [*þó*, earlier *þoh] (17, 53, 248 etc.). The nouns, verbs, adjectives, and adverbs borrowed from ON are not learned terms: *bone*, 'prayer' [*bón*] (90), *brennen*, 'burn' [*brenna*] (218, 220, 371), *brenning* (100), *derue*, 'strong' [**derf-*, cf. *djarfr*] (176), *feȝ* imperat. sg., 'cleanse' [*fǽgja*] (141), *festeð*, 'fastens' [*festa*] (317, 389), *festen* (369), *feste* imperat. sg. (126, 141), *fikeð*, 'struggles' [ON *fíkja*: see *OED* s.v. *fike* v.[1]] (475), *gapeð*, 'opens his mouth' [*gapa*] (342), *heil*, 'healthy' [*heill*] (49, 245, 354), *hileð*, 'conceals' [*hylja*] (461), *ille*, 'bad' [*illr*] (362, 399), *ket*, 'flesh' [cf. *kjöt*] (295), *kirke*, 'church' [*kirkja*] (67, 121), *kirke-dure*, 'church-door' (119, 524—first element), *laȝe*, 'weak' [*lágr*, 'low'] (383), *lat*, 'pretends' [*láta*] (286, 287), *lateð*, 'abandons' [*láta*] (239), *leiðe*, 'hideous' [*leiðr*] (314), *mikel*, 'great' [*mikell*] (200, 260, 377), *mikle* (384, 385, 479 etc.), *mikel* adv., 'hard' [from preceding] (153), *mirke*, 'dark, dim' [*myrkr*] (69), *merk* (300), *munen*, 'keep in mind' [*muna*] (249), *muneð* (172, 516), *oc*, 'also' [*auk*] (45, 189), *onde*, 'breath' [*andi*] (272, 343, 381 etc.), *otwinne*, 'in two' [*twinnr*] (170, 182—second element), *rapelike*, 'hurriedly' [*hrapaliga*] (156, 324), *reisen*, 'raise' [*reisa*] (490, 495), *reiseð* (11), *reisede* (511), *rennen*, 'run' [*renna*] (221), *renneð* (156, 324), *rennande* (486), *scaðe*, 'injury' [*skaði*] (397), *skemting*, 'enjoyment' [*skemta*, v.] (291), *skies*, 'clouds' [*ský*] (40), *sloð*, 'slays' [*slá*] (288), *swi*[*ð*]*eð*, 'singes' [*sviða*] (44—MS *swideð*), *takeð*, 'takes' [*taka*] (61, 72), *tunder*, 'tinder' [*tundr*] (371), *ðeðen*, 'from that place' [*þeðan*] (320, 530), *vncost*, 'evil nature'[1] (131), *unskil*, 'excess' [OE *un-* + ON *skil*; cf. ON *úskil*] (290), *wille*, 'astray' [*villr*] (26).

On loans recorded already in OE are: *costes*, 'habits' [*kostr*] (249, 585, 587), *laȝe*, 'law' [*lagu] (12, 181, 183 etc.), *laȝes* pl. (120), *laȝelike*, 'faithfully' (514), *wrong*, 'crooked' [**wrang-*] (32, 52), *wrong*, n., 'wrong' (598). (See *OED* s.vv. *cost* sb.[1], *law* sb.[1], *wrong* a. and adj.; *MED* s.vv. *cost* n. (1), *laue* n.).

In some cases it is impossible to say whether a word is from OE or ON: *boðe*, 'both' [ON *báðir*, OE *bā þā*] (37, 133, 267 etc.), *boðen* (158, 213, 476), *frame*, 'benefit' [ON *frami* and OE *fremman*, *framian*, vv. and OE *fram*, adj. 'forward': see *OED* s.v. *frame*, n.[1]] (19).

The large Scandinavian element in the vocabulary of the *Physiologus* indicates that the text is not from the South or the South West; a few

---

[1] *vncost*, 'evil nature' (131) is probably a ME formation from *un* + *cost*: it is not recorded in OE.

OE words suggest that the language of the *Physiologus* is descended from an Anglian form of OE. Distinctively Anglian lexical items include *liuenoðe*, 'provisions' (173), *sending*, 'disgrace' (298), *turtres*, 'turtle-dove's' (513): *lifnoð* glosses *victus* in the Lindisfarne Gospels,[1] *scendung* glosses *improbitas* in Lindisfarne and the Durham Ritual (Wenisch, p. 315), and *turtur* appears in Lindisfarne and Rushworth[2], where a WS gloss would have *turtle* (Wenisch, p. 305). *bilirten*, 'deceive' (270) is descended from *belyrtan*, which is recorded only in Lindisfarne, where *bisuicen & bilyrtet* glosses *inlusus* (Matt. 2: 16).[2] The only other ME examples listed by *MED* s.v. *bilirten* are from *Ancrene Wisse* and *Genesis and Exodus*, both of which are from Anglian dialect areas. These are the only words that point to specific dialects of OE: as far as I know, there are no Kentish or WS words in the text. Unfortunately I have not been able to assign any of these 'Anglian' words to a subdivision of Anglian (such as Mercian).

Vocabulary is not a precise guide to the provenance of the *Physiologus*. However, these words may be associated with East Anglia: *taunede*, 'showed' (567), does not occur elsewhere except in *Genesis and Exodus*, which is an East Midland text;[3] *cliuer*, 'expert in seizing' (146) may be an East Anglian, or perhaps even Norfolk, dialect word: see the commentary ad loc. But these stray pieces of speculation cannot be used as evidence: the best they can do is confirm conclusions drawn from phonology and morphology.

IV. PROVENANCE

The ME *Physiologus* is an East Midland text. The North is excluded by the rounding of OE *a* to *o* (§I. A. 4(ii)), the appearance of OE *hw* and *w* (§I. C. 7(ii)), the *h*-forms in the third person pl. personal pronoun (§II. D. 1), the absence, with one exception, of the ending -(*e*)*s* in the third person sg. pres. ind. (§II. E. 1), and, finally, the use of -*en* endings in the pl. pres. ind. (§II. E. 1).

The South West is excluded by the appearance of OE *a/o* before a

---

[1] Franz Wenisch, *Spezifisch anglisches Wortgut in den nordhumbrischen Interlinearglossierungen des Lukasevangeliums* (Anglische Forschungen 132, Heidelberg, 1979), p. 316. But *liuenoðe* could be from ON *lifnaðr*.

[2] So Bosworth-Toller, *Supplement* s.v. *belyrtan*; Wenisch does not mention the word, but Hildegard Rauh, *Der Wortschatz des altenglischen Uebersetzungen des Matthaeus-Evangeliums* (D. Phil. thesis, Berlin, 1935), which Wenisch supersedes, confirms that *belyrtan* is a *hapax legomenon* (p. 41).

[3] *swak*, 'weak', could be added to this list if *swak* is read for *swilk* at line 297: see p. xxxi, n. 3 above and the Commentary ad loc.

nasal (unless the nasal and a following consonant constitute a lengthening group) as *a* (§I. A. 1(ii)), the absence of palatal diphthongization (§I. A. 1(v), with one exception: see §I. A. 2(iv.b)), and breaking (§I. A. 1(iii) and §I. A. 4(iv) with exceptions, for which see §I. A. 1(vii) and p. xvii, n. 3 and p. xviii, n. 3), *e* as the reflex of OE *ĕo* (§I. A. 2(vi, vii)), the reflex of OE *ў̆*, which is *i* (§I. A. 3(iii)), the appearance of *s* for OE *sc* (§I. C. 5(ii)), the frequent adverbial ending *-like* (§II. C(i)), the third person sg. feminine personal pronoun *ʒe* (§II. D. 1), the *-es* endings (beside *-est*) in the second person sg. pres. ind. (§II. E. 1), and the ending *-ande* in the pres. part. (§II. E. 5).

The West Midlands are excluded by *a* for OE *a/o* (§I. A. 1(ii)), *ĕ* for OE *eo* (§I. A. 2(vi, vii)), *i* for OE *ў̆* (§I. A. 3(iii)), *s* for OE *sc* (§I. A. 5) and *ʒe*, 'she' (§II. D. 1).

The South East is excluded by the absence of breaking (§I. A. 1(iii) and §I. A. 4(iv)), by *i* for OE *ў̆* (§I. A. 3(iii)), by the frequent adjectival ending *-like* (§II. C(i)), by *ʒe*, 'she' (§II. D. 1), by the ending *-es* for the second person sg. pres. ind. (§II. E. 1), the ending *-ande* for the pres. part. (§II. E. 5), and the absence of a prefix in the past part. (§II. E. 6). It follows that the *Physiologus* cannot be from anywhere except the East Midlands.

Within this general area, three features of its language point to Norfolk: first, the use of *ic*, beside *i*, for the first person sg. personal pronoun (§II. D. 1);[1] secondly, the sporadic occurrence of the ending *-et* in the third person sg. pres. ind. (§II. E. 1);[2] thirdly, the isolated example of the spelling *qu-* for the reflex of OE *hw-* (§I. A. 4(ii)).[3] However, before we can proceed to examine the evidence for a Norfolk provenance, we need to establish in what relation the surviving manuscript stands to the author's text and whether the language of the *Physiologus* as we have it is uniform. The former will be dealt with at greater length in the next section,[4] where I shall argue that the *Physiologus* as we have it is a letter-by-letter copy of an earlier exemplar and that it is not close to the author's original. The latter is more difficult to establish since mixed forms may be part of the

---

[1] The value of *c* is /k/, not /tʃ/: see §I. C. 1(i). The occasional use of *ik* for *I*, only before a vowel or h, is characteristic of Chaucer's Reeve, a Norfolk man (*General Prologue*, I. 620): see *The Reeve's Prologue*, I. 3867, 3888.

[2] Angus McIntosh, 'The Language of the Extant Versions of *Havelok the Dane*', *MÆ*, xlv (1976), 36–49, calls it 'unusual in most areas of ME' but 'of course extremely well attested in Norfolk' (p. 39).

[3] 'The Language of the Extant Versions of *Havelok the Dane*', p. 42 and p. 49, n. 13.

[4] See below, §V (pp. xl–lii).

language of an author or scribe. The text does not contain forms which are incompatible with an East Midlands provenance; for any signs of contamination from other East Midlands dialects we should examine spoilt rhymes.

Leaving aside half-rhymes and impure rhymes which may not be the result of scribal interference but due to the poet himself,[1] the following rhymes may have been spoilt by copyists: *ðere: nummore* (178–9), *to Gode ward: forðwarð* (228–9), *riche: ilike* (423–4), *bihalt: biwarlt* (463–4), *gangande: standen* (473–4), *sacande: maken* (479–80), *ðoʒt: ovt* (501–2), *briche: ʒeuelike* (530–1), *nout: oʒt* (559–60), *vuenest: gast* (575–6), *laʒt: hac* (591–2). Two of these, *forðwarð* and *biwarlt* are simple mechanical errors, and the sense of lines 591–2 is obscure,[2] so none of these is useful. *gangande* and *sacande* involve the substitution of a later construction (*come* with pres. part.) for an earlier one (*come* with inf.)[2] and do not indicate a scribe of different geographical origin. It could be claimed that *ðere: nummore* makes an acceptable rhyme, but emendation to *ðore*, which goes back to OE *þāra*, is to be preferred because it makes a perfect rhyme. Also, *ðore* appears to be an East Midland form in early Middle English: of the early instances of *þor(e)* that *OED* cites s.v. *there* two are from *Genesis and Exodus*, two from *Havelok*, and one from Robert Mannyng of Brunne (the one exception is a quotation from the South Western *Harrowing of Hell*). In the case of *ðoʒt: ovt* and *nout: oʒt* the substitution of forms without the spirant spoils the rhyme; loss of spirant is a change that is not limited to any particular area of the East Midlands.[3] Here again, the scribal alteration points to a later stage in the development of the language, not to a difference in dialect. The *n* in *vuenest* is a mechanical error (wrong number of minims) for *m*; the ending *-mest* in *vue[m]est*, from OE *mæst*, has not undergone early shortening, but for the sake of the rhyme we need a form that has. Orm has *masst* and *vue[ma]st* is well attested.[4]

The two remaining spoilt rhymes, *riche: ilike* and *briche: ʒeuelike*, might, at first sight, reveal something about the degree of uniformity of the language of Arundel 292, but on further examination turn out not to. Clearly, *riche* and *briche* require rhyme words in *-iche*, and *-liche* for '-ly' is held by Professor McIntosh to be characteristic of Suffolk

---

[1] See below, part 3, 'Versification' (pp. lii–lxviii), esp. p. lxiv.
[2] See the Commentary ad loc.
[3] For a fuller treatment of the loss of *ʒ* from the cluster *ʒt*, see below, pp. xlix–l.
[4] *st* is a cluster that is capable of causing shortening but does not always do so: see Jordan, §23, esp. Remark 1; for *vuemast* see *OED* s.v. *uvemast*.

rather than Norfolk.[1] The surviving text of the *Physiologus* has *-like* throughout, never *-liche*.[2] The occurrence of *-like* in rhyme at lines 285–6, *dernelike*: *biswike*, rules out the possibility that the author's form was *-liche* and that all instances of *-like* are scribal. Either the author's form was *-like* but he used *-liche*, a form from a neighbouring dialect with which he was familiar, because he needed it for the rhyme, or the author had both *-like* and *-liche* in his own dialect. The second possibility can be paralleled from the work of scribe D of the Cleopatra text of the *Ancrene Riwle*, which Professor McIntosh assigns to North West Norfolk.[3] It follows that the presence of *-liche* forms in the archetype cannot be taken as a sign that there are traces of Suffolk language or that the *Physiologus* originally belongs somewhere near the border with Suffolk.

Otherwise the language is, to a large extent, uniform. The only notable exceptions are in the verb system. The inf., which normally ends in *-(e)n*, ends in *-e* in two instances where the rhyme requires it: *biswike* (286: *dernelike*) and *chare* (403: *warre*).[4] In the pres. ind. the second person sg. takes *-es* (five examples) or *-est* (two examples); the third person sg. takes mostly *-eð* and syncopated forms are frequent, but there are three instances of *-(e)t* and one of *-es*.[5] Since the infinitives in *-e* are conditioned by the rhyme, it is reasonable to assume that they go back to the author; we have no means of determining which of the present indicative forms are authorial and which are scribal. What is certain is that none of these is impossible in Norfolk in the late thirteenth and early fourteenth centuries.[6]

Granted that there is no firm evidence of serious admixture of other dialects, we need to take into account the evidence provided by Arundel 292 itself. The manuscript is from the Library of Norwich Cathedral Priory: it has a press-mark 'C.x' on ff. 3ʳ and 114ᵛ which N. R. Ker associates with Norwich, *c.* 1300,[7] and the old table of

[1] 'The Language of the Extant Versions of *Havelok the Dane*', p. 42 and p. 49, n. 13.

[2] See above, §II. C.

[3] Ed. E. J. Dobson, EETS 267 (1972); scribe D's language is assigned to North West Norfolk in 'The Language of the Extant Versions of *Havelok the Dane*', pp. 38–9. Because of the scarcity of material for Norfolk in early ME, Professor McIntosh's localization is perhaps unwarrantably precise; yet it is clear that scribe D is not from further south, since Dobson places him tentatively in South Lincolnshire (p. clx). Scribe D contributed corrections to the text of *Ancrene Riwle* as well as three short lyrics and a sermon; his work is discussed below, pp. xxxix–xl and in §V.

[4] See above, §II. E. 4.   [5] See above, §II. E. 1.

[6] Note that all these endings can be paralleled from *Genesis and Exodus*. See Olof Arngart's edition (Lund Studies in English 36, Lund, 1968), pp. 31–2.

[7] See above, part 1, 'The Manuscript', p. xi.

contents, which is in the hand of the main scribe, lists an item, now lost, 'De combustione ecclesie cath' sancte trinitatis Norwich''.[1] This does not necessarily mean that the manuscript was written at Norwich, but, given the local interest suggested by the lost item, it does seem probable.

If the manuscript is from Norwich, it does not automatically mean that the language of the *Physiologus* as we have it can be assigned to Norwich, although this is of course possible. Arundel 292 may have been written by a scribe who had come from elsewhere in Norfolk and had not accepted the spelling conventions of Norwich. Another explanation might be that Arundel 292 was written at Norwich but was copied letter by letter from a manuscript that originated from somewhere else in Norfolk. We cannot hope to resolve this question beyond doubt, because there are not enough surviving early ME texts from Norfolk to establish dialect criteria for different parts of the county. Nevertheless, Professor McIntosh suggests that the *Physiologus* is from West Norfolk, not far from the Suffolk border, SW of Oxborough. His method is as follows:

For the later Middle English period it is possible . . . to associate a large number of literary texts with West Norfolk. The further step of linking certain earlier texts (such as A [i.e. the Laud text of *Havelok*]) with this same complex is less straightforward because they invariably display some characteristics which are no longer in evidence in the later period and which it would therefore be fruitless to attempt to 'match' neatly with those of any later texts no matter when these were written. It is then a question of discounting such features and—concentrating on those which have not become obsolete in later ME—of seeking to discover which later texts show the most striking affinities with the earlier ones. If it proves possible to single out a considerable number of such texts and to provide good grounds for associating all of these with one area, then it is reasonable to assign the earlier texts to that same area rather than anywhere else.[2]

---

[1] See above, part 1, pp. ix–x.

[2] 'The Language of the Extant Versions of *Havelok the Dane*', pp. 36–7; a map of West Norfolk and those parts of Lincolnshire, Ely, and Suffolk bordering on it appears on p. 45 of the article (no scale is given). It should be stressed that Professor McIntosh's proposed localization is tentative: 'A comparison of [the *Physiologus* and *Genesis and Exodus*] with the later W. Norfolk material suggests that they probably belong some little distance east of A [the Laud text of *Havelok*] and B [the fragments of *Havelok* preserved in Cambridge University Library Additional 4407, Art. 19]. The absence of early texts ascribable to central Norfolk makes it difficult to establish any eastern limit to the area within which all five texts [the fifth being Cleopatra D] are likely to fall. Besides, dialectal characteristics separating west from east Norfolk are much less pronounced than those which distinguish north from south. All that can be said is that there are

Looking at Professor McIntosh's map of Norfolk and the surrounding counties, we notice at once how little material there is for East Norfolk. This is bound to make it difficult to disprove a Norwich provenance for the surviving text of the *Physiologus*: Professor McIntosh has not localized a single text further east than Oxborough. Also, all the texts localized in Norfolk on other than linguistic grounds are from the late fourteenth and fifteenth centuries, which is considerably later than the *Physiologus*. Given the limitations of his evidence, I doubt if the *Physiologus* should be placed in such a small area of West Norfolk, particularly since the surviving manuscript is from Norwich. Mentioning the Norwich press-marks, Professor McIntosh admits that 'in the absence of early material from E. Norfolk, it would be rash to insist that the characteristics which the *Bestiary* [i.e. the *Physiologus*] displays could not have been current there in the thirteenth century'.[1]

Even though the exact provenance of the *Physiologus* may be in doubt, comparison with *Genesis and Exodus* and with scribe D of the Cleopatra text of *Ancrene Riwle* shows extensive linguistic similarities, which go well beyond the shared East Midland character of the three texts. All these have the following features in common:[2]

(1) use of *hem*, *here* forms (as distinct from those in *þ-*) in the oblique of the third person pl. of the pers. pron.: see §II. D. 1; Arngart, p. 30 and his glossary s.v. *he* pr. pl.; Dobson, p. cliv;

(2) use of *werld/werlde* for 'world', to the exclusion of *world*, *word*: see the Glossary s.v.; Arngart's glossary s.v.; Dobson, p. clvii (Cleopatra D also has *uerdlike* and *werdlike* from **werd*);

(3) use of *-like* for '-ly': see §II. C(i);[3] Arngart, p. 30; Dobson, p. 111 (f. 57ᵛ: *bitterlike*, *redilike*, *opinlike*);[4]

quite clear differences marked, roughly speaking, by the Ely–Norfolk border which place the group firmly in Norfolk rather than further west and that comparison with a large number of other rather later texts favours west rather than east or even central Norfolk. As for the characteristics distinguishing north from south, the consensus of evidence would seem not only to forbid S. Lincolnshire on the one hand and N. Suffolk on the other, but would fairly strongly indicate that the language of A, B, [the *Physiologus*] and [*Genesis and Exodus*] is to be associated with some area not very far north of the Suffolk border.'

[1] 'The Language of the Extant Versions of *Havelok the Dane*', p. 48, n. 11.

[2] Cleopatra D and *Genesis and Exodus* are suitable for comparison with the *Physiologus* because they are relatively free from textual corruption and, as far as can be ascertained, do not show admixture of other dialects: see below, pp. xlii–xliii.

[3] But two rhymes require *-liche*: see above, pp. xxxvi–xxxvii.

[4] But *-liche* does occur in a sermon in scribe D's hand preserved in MS Trinity College Cambridge B. 1. 45, which is in the same dialect and uses the same spelling system (Dobson, pp. cxliii–iv), *blepeliche* (f. 41ᵛ: Dobson, p. clvii).

(4) use of *swilc* 'such': see Glossary s.v.; Arngart's glossary s.v.; Dobson, p. clv. The *Physiologus* and *Genesis and Exodus* also share *ilc/ilk*, 'each' and *wilc*, 'which' (interr.), spelt *quilc* (pl. *quilke*) in *Genesis and Exodus*: see the glossaries;

(5) use of *-et* in the third person sg. pres. ind.: sporadic in the *Physiologus* (see §II. E. 1), frequent in *Genesis and Exodus* (Arngart, p. 31) and regular in Cleopatra D (Dobson, pp. cxlix and clix).

Naturally, there are differences as well as similarities. The most striking difference is the pres. part. ending *ande* (§II. E. 5): Cleopatra too has *-inde* or *-ende* (Dobson, p. cl), *Genesis and Exodus* either *-ende* or *-ande* (Arngart, p. 32: the two occur equally often). Although *-ande* is normally associated with the North,[1] Professor McIntosh assures me that *-ande* forms are common in Norfolk.[2] Clearly, then, these three texts belong to roughly the same area of the East Midlands, almost certainly Norfolk. However, Professor McIntosh's proposed localization SW of Oxborough, near the Suffolk border, seems to me to be more precise than the evidence warrants. Until further proof is available, a Norwich provenance remains a possibility for the extant version of the *Physiologus* or of earlier versions.

V. DATE AND TRANSMISSION

Two kinds of evidence are available for determining the date of the text of the *Physiologus* as represented by its sole surviving manuscript, one kind internal, i.e. linguistic, and the other external, i.e. codicological. Not all of the codicological evidence is equally precise. First, the hand of the scribe can be dated *c.* 1300.[3] Secondly, the volume has press-marks assigned to Norwich, *c.* 1300 by N. R. Ker.[4] Thirdly, an item in the old table of contents may refer to a fire that took place in Norwich Cathedral in 1272, but this is the least reliable piece of evidence of the three.[5] On balance, codicological evidence would suggest that the manuscript of the *Physiologus* was written *c.* 1300, but this tells us nothing about the date Theobald's *Physiologus* was originally translated into English, except that it cannot have been much after 1300.

The evidence afforded by the text itself is of a different nature in that it is more complex and difficult to interpret. It cannot give us a

---

[1] See Mossé's map, §93 (p. 78).
[2] Personal communication, 7 August 1985.
[3] See above, p. x.
[4] See above, p. xi.
[5] See above, pp. ix–x.

clear-cut *terminus ante quem* or *terminus a quo* because linguistic changes are hard to date even within half a century; nevertheless, the language of Arundel 292 may provide some indication as to whether this manuscript is a faithful representation of the author's original or whether it is at several removes from it.

What needs to be investigated first is: could the scribe of Arundel 292 have been a letter-by-letter copyist? The practice of copying an exemplar *litteratim* was common in the early ME period: well-known examples are the *Lambeth Homilies*[1] and the Cotton MS of *The Owl and the Nightingale*, which preserved the two spelling systems of its copy text.[2] The evidence from Arundel 292 suggests that our scribe may have been in the habit of copying letter for letter rather than 'translating' his copy text into his own dialect. The other ME pieces in the hand of scribe 1, who was responsible for the *Physiologus*, are verse paraphrases of the Creed, the Lord's Prayer, the Hail Mary and *In manus tuas*, and two short lyrics.[3] All these were copied as one continuous text, and, when broken up into verse lines, they occupy a total of 58 short lines. They are in an East Midland dialect; in Professor McIntosh's opinion, the dialect is substantially the same as that of the *Physiologus*.[4] The differences between these six pieces, which are items 1–6 in the manuscript, and the *Physiologus* are in spelling:

(1) items 1–6 have *ct* where the *Physiologus* has *ȝt*: *almicten* (1), *boctest* (41), *noct* (33);

(2) final *-t* and *-d* are often doubled: *bikennedd* (5), *deadd* (9, 12, 41), *godd* (1, 36, 39, 42), *ðatt* (2, 5, 38), but *ðat* (55; 45: MS *dat*), *itt* (24, 25, 28), but *it* (26) etc.;

(3) final *-f* is doubled in *off* (12, 19);

(4) vowels are occasionally doubled: *hijs* (14), *leet*, 'let, allow' (33), *ooc* (34), *soðfastheedd* (42);

(5) final *-k* appears in *wilk* (46), *swilk* (297), and *ik* (4), but *ic* (28);

(6) a digraph *ea* is used in *deadd*, 'death' (9, 12, 41);

(7) *sc* appears medially in *bliscedd* (24, 37).

---

[1] See Celia Sisam, 'The Scribal Tradition of the *Lambeth Homilies*', *RES* NS ii (1951), 105–113; on the subject of letter-by-letter copying in ME generally, see Michael Benskin and Margaret Laing, 'Translations and Mischsprachen in Middle English Manuscripts', *So Meny People Longages and Tonges: Philological Essays in Scots and Mediaeval English Presented to Angus McIntosh*, ed. Michael Benskin and M. L. Samuels (Edinburgh, 1981), 55–106.

[2] See Eric Gerald Stanley's edition, 2nd edn. (Manchester, 1970), p. 7.

[3] For texts see the Appendix below, pp. 47–8; also Max Garrett, 'Religious Verses from MS Arundel 292', *Archiv* LXVI Jahrgang, CXXVIII Band (1912), 367–8.

[4] Personal communication, October 31, 1985.

(1) *ct* is a rare spelling, which also appears in *Genesis and Exodus* and *Havelok*.[1] (2) The spelling *deadd*, 'death', suggests that these doubled consonants were probably not intended to indicate a preceding short vowel, as they are in the *Ormulum*. Regular *-dd* in *Godd* and *deadd* may have served to distinguish those nouns from the adjectives *gōd* and *dēad*, but since the poems have no examples of the adjective *god* and of uninflected *dead* (the plural *dede* occurs at line 16) this cannot be proved. (4) Doubling of the vowel probably does not indicate length: the vowel in *hijs* is short, while the long vowel in *Gost* (5) is represented by single *o*. (5) final *-k* where the *Physiologus* has mostly final *c* is more likely to be a difference in spelling than to indicate a difference in pronunciation.[2] (6) Since the digraph *ea* appears only in *deadd*, it cannot be proved to indicate a long vowel. (7) *bliscedd* does not occur in the *Physiologus*, and neither does any other form of the verb (its OE etymon is *bletsian*, influenced by *blissian*), so no direct comparison can be made; also, the value of *sc* is uncertain, but note that the first occurrence (24) rhymes with *blisse*. *sc* does not occur medially in the *Physiologus* to represent either OE *ts* or OE *ss*.

Clearly, then, the scribe uses two different spelling systems, one for items 1–6 and another for the *Physiologus*. The most likely explanation for this is that he reproduced the spelling of his exemplars. Items 1–6 and the *Physiologus* may have come from different exemplars or they may have come from one manuscript which was copied by two different scribes who did not have the same system of orthography. If the *Physiologus* and items 1–6 are the product of letter-by-letter copying, perhaps even by a succession of scribes, then there is a likelihood that the texts as we have them contain elements that belong to an earlier state of the language and not to *c.* 1300, the date of the surviving manuscript. It follows that the text of Arundel 292 cannot be dated on linguistic evidence. However, what we can do is to compare it with other Norfolk texts of a similar date in order to assess whether our text of the *Physiologus* represents earlier language and what conclusions can be drawn as to the transmission of the poem.

The most suitable texts to compare with the *Physiologus* and items 1–6 are *Genesis and Exodus*, which survives in a single manuscript, Corpus Christi College Cambridge MS 444, and those portions of British Library MS Cotton Cleopatra C. vi for which the scribe known as scribe D was responsible, viz. his corrections to the text of the

---

[1] Arngart, p. 17; Jordan, §17, n. 1.
[2] In the *Physiologus* final *-c* denotes /k/: see above, §I. C. 1(ii).

Ancrene Riwle and the short additional items in his hand, three lyrics and a sermon. A third early Norfolk text cannot be used for this purpose: although Professor McIntosh has now convincingly demonstrated that the main manuscript of *Havelok the Dane*, Bodleian Library MS Laud 108, was written in Norfolk, the various stages that the text of the poem has evidently passed through and the fact that the poem was originally composed further north render the text of MS Laud 108 unsuitable for detailed orthographical, morphological, and phonological comparison.[1] The textual history of Cleopatra D is simple: scribe D's alterations to the text of the *Ancrene Riwle* may reasonably be expected to represent his own pronunciation, spelling, and grammar. Dobson states that the forms and spellings of the sermon are scribe D's: there are only slight variations between his usage in Cleopatra and that in a second copy of the same sermon in his hand in Trinity College Cambridge MS B. 1. 45 (p. cxlvii). Dobson dates scribe D's work 'after 1284, though perhaps before 1289' on external evidence (p. cxlvii), and Professor McIntosh has assigned the dialect to Norfolk.[2]

No detailed work has been done on the transmission of *Genesis and Exodus*. The manuscript belongs to the first quarter of the fourteenth century;[3] Professor McIntosh has located the poem in Norfolk.[4] Professor Arngart discusses the traditional date of composition, *c.* 1250, saying that 'this dating on the whole agrees with the stage of linguistic development it reveals, assuming it to be in the E. Midl. dialect' (p. 45). To judge by the small number of textual corruptions, the extant copy preserves a good text, carefully transmitted; nevertheless, the manuscript is some fifty years or more later than the original, so the comparison of its language with that of the *Physiologus* and items 1–6 should be undertaken with caution.

The first point of comparison is orthography, viz. the use of the older graphs, *ð*, *þ*, *ȝ*, and *p*, and also the adoption of the changes in the spelling of the East Midlands dialects that took place during the thirteenth and fourteenth centuries. The *Physiologus* and items 1–6 use the same selection of older graphs: *þ* is not used, *ð* being the only graph representing the alveolar fricatives;[5] *p*, not *w*, is used for /w/;[6]

---

[1] 'The Language of the Extant Versions of *Havelok the Dane*', pp. 36–40; *Havelok*, ed. G. V. Smithers (Oxford, 1897), p. lxxxix.
[2] 'The Language of the Extant Versions of *Havelok the Dane*', pp. 38–40.
[3] Arngart, p. 11.
[4] 'The Language of the Extant Versions of *Havelok the Dane*', p. 41.
[5] See above, §I. C. 6.   [6] See above, §I. C. 7.

ȝ represents OE 'front' g and OE h.[1] *Genesis and Exodus* has mostly ð (or d by mistake[2]) for the alveolar fricatives, rarely *th*, while ðh is common medially and initially and *t* finally.[3] The same hooked two-compartment letter which in the *Physiologus* and items 1–6 represents only /g/ is used for both 'yogh' and velar stop; with rare exceptions, p is used for /w/ in *Genesis and Exodus*, but the scribe occasionally confuses p and þ, writing, for instance, *pligt* for *þligt*.[4] Cleopatra D normally uses þ, never ð, for the alveolar fricative; *th* and *tþ* are also used, while *t* and *d* occur finally, mostly in verbs.[5] Dobson suggests that *d* for /θ/ finally 'may be due to AN influence, but it seems likely that misunderstanding of earlier English ð plays a part' (p. clix). Cleopatra D does not use p or ȝ. /w/ is written *w* or *uu*, and *u* regularly after consonants; *u* and *v* are occasionally found in other positions (p. clviii). As for ȝ, the scribe has *i* or *j* (occasionally *y*) for the semi-vowel, the spirants having become vocalised (p. clviii). On f. 8ᵛ he has added a Latin note on the spelling of the main scribe: 'Hec sunt signa posita in hoc libro anglico. *p. ȝ. p. p. p* et istud ponitur pro duplici .v. þ: sicut þorn. hec ȝ: pro i'. The letter ð, which is used by the main scribe, is not mentioned by D; Dobson assumes that he did not understand it (p. xii, n. 2).

Scribe D's comment may suggest that the graphs p and ȝ had become obsolete and ð, which he does not include in his note, incomprehensible. Compared with Cleopatra D, the *Physiologus* seems old-fashioned. p for /w/ is exceptional at this date: it was being replaced by *w* from the twelfth century onwards[6] and ð becomes increasingly rare towards the end of the thirteenth century,[7] but as *Genesis and Exodus* has both p (wynn) and ð it would be rash to say that the *Physiologus* must be archaic in its use of these letters. The *Physiologus* is exceptional, however, in using p, ȝ, and ð with so few errors[8] and

---

[1] See above, §I. C. 3.

[2] *d* spellings of this kind are frequent in *Genesis and Exodus* (Arngart, p. 16), just as they are in the *Physiologus*. In my opinion, they are errors for ð, because in the type of hand in which both texts are written, a *textura quadrata*, the difference between ð and *d* is no more than a cross-bar: see below, Commentary to line 21.

[3] Arngart, pp. 15–16.   [4] Arngart, p. 12.   [5] Dobson, pp. clviii–clix.

[6] A notable exception is its sporadic use in the Laud text of *Havelok*: Jordan, §16; Smithers, p. lxxxviii.

[7] Karl Brunner, *Abriss der Mittelenglischen Grammatik*, 4th ed. (Tübingen, 1959), §5; Jordan says that it 'is retained until the end of the 13th cent.' (§16).

[8] Errors of *d* for ð have been noted (above, n. 2); otherwise, the text has one example of ȝ for g, ȝinȝen (228), for ȝingen, 'rejuvenate', and one of g for ȝ, maig (352) for maiȝ, 'can', the explanation being that in this scribe's hand ȝ is simply g with a hook added: see above, part 1, 'The Manuscript', p. x.

generally without employing alternatives. Considering that the scribe
uses *ð* and *p* in the same way in items 1–6 (where *ʒ* occurs only in *steʒ*;
these texts have *ct* where the *Physiologus* uses *ʒt*[1]), this exceptional
practice is perhaps more likely to be an idiosyncracy on the Arundel
scribe's part than to derive from his exemplars. What we have here is a
conservative scribe who retains *p* and *ð* without adopting newer
spellings.

Professor McIntosh has outlined some of the changes in orthography that were introduced into the East Midlands dialects in the
thirteenth and fourteenth centuries, and a number can be added to his
list.[2] It is instructive to examine how far the *Physiologus*, items 1–6,
Genesis and Exodus, and Cleopatra D have absorbed the following new
spelling conventions (asterisks indicate changes listed by Professor
McIntosh):

    (1) *o* for /u/;
*(2) *ou*, *ow* for /u:/;
*(3) doubling of *o* to indicate length;
    (4) use of the digraph *ea* for /ɛ:/;
*(5) *ay* for earlier *ai*;
*(6) final *-k* for final *-c*;
*(7) *wh* or *w* for earlier *hw*;
    (8) doubling of final consonants.

(1) Cleopatra D frequently writes *o* for /u/;[3] it is rare in *Genesis and
Exodus*[4] and does not occur in the *Physiologus*[5] and in items 1–6. (2) *ou*
and *ow* appear occasionally in *Genesis and Exodus*,[6] frequently in Cleopatra D,[7] and not at all in the *Physiologus*[8] and in items 1–6. (3) Doubling of *o* to indicate length is common in *Genesis and Exodus*[9] but absent
from Cleopatra D (e.g. *lok*, f. 23ᵛ, *blod*, *dom*, *wok*, f. 57ᵛ) and the
Physiologus;[10] it does occasionally appear in items 1–6. (4) *Genesis and
Exodus* frequently uses the digraph *ea* to denote /ɛ:/;[11] the example
from items 1–6, *deadd*, is uncertain,[12] and Cleopatra D and the *Physiologus* do not use *ea*.[13] (5) *ay* for *ai* is often used in *Genesis and Exodus*,[14]
but never in Cleopatra D, the *Physiologus*[15] and items 1–6. (6) Final *-k*

---

[1] See above, p. xli.
[2] 'The Language of the Extant Versions of *Havelok the Dane*', p. 37 and pp. 47–8, n. 3.
[3] Dobson, p. clx.   [4] Arngart, p. 13.
[5] See above, §I. A. 4.   [6] Arngart, p. 13.
[7] *stroutende*, *tou* (f. 23ᵛ), but *tu* (f. 23ᵛ), *ful* (f. 57ᵛ), and see Dobson, p. clx.
[8] See above, §I. A. 9.   [9] Arngart, p. 13.
[10] See above, §I. A. 9.   [11] Arngart, p. 13.
[12] See above, p. xlii.   [13] See above, §I. A. 9.
[14] Arngart, p. 13.   [15] See above, §I. A. 6.

for final *-c* appears occasionally in the *Physiologus*[1] and in items 1–6,[2] more commonly in *Genesis and Exodus*,[3] and regularly in Cleopatra D, which has no instances of *-c*. (7) *w* for earlier *hw* is regular in the *Physiologus*, with the exception of *qual*, 'whale' (535),[4] and items 1–6, whereas Cleopatra D has mostly *hw*;[5] *Genesis and Exodus* has the characteristically Norfolk spelling *qu*, sometimes *quu*, rarely *w*.[6] (8) Doubling of final consonants is limited to *off* (four occurrences; the usual spelling is *of*) in the *Physiologus*[7] and does not occur at all in Cleopatra D, but it is common in *Genesis and Exodus*,[8] where it does not necessarily indicate a short vowel: the same applies to items 1–6.[9]

Taking into account that these are texts of widely differing length, comparison of their spelling systems shows that *Genesis and Exodus* is the most advanced,[10] the only change for which it has no evidence being (7), where it usually has the Norfolk spelling *qu(u)*. Cleopatra D is more old-fashioned, with no more than three newer spellings being employed regularly, (1), (2), and (6). The *Physiologus* consistently exhibits (7) only, with the one exception noted, and has rare occurrences of (6). The four instances of (8) in the *Physiologus* are not significant statistically. In addition to (7), (8), too, is well-attested in items 1–6, and these texts have examples of three more innovations, (3), (4), and (6), although (4) is uncertain. This makes the *Physiologus* a more conservative text than the other three in its orthography, but the spelling of items 1–6, while it is different from that of the *Physiologus* in many respects, is not much more advanced. However, the evidence offered by six short pieces which total no more than 58 lines in length is hard to evaluate against that provided by the 4,162 lines of *Genesis and Exodus*. Nevertheless, the conclusion that the spelling of the *Physiologus* is conservative for a text that was copied *c.* 1300 is justified; the obvious explanation for the 'archaic' appearance of the poem is that the scribe took over the spelling of his copy text. Comparison of the morphology and the phonology of the *Physiologus*, *Genesis and Exodus*, and Cleopatra D shows that these aspects of the language of the *Physiologus* are also less advanced than is usual for a Norfolk text of the period.

---

[1] See above, §I. C. 1(i).   [2] See above, p. xli.
[3] Arngart, p. 15.   [4] See above, §I. B. 4(ii).
[5] All the instances of *w* are taken from Trinity College MS B. I. 45: see Dobson, p. clvii.
[6] Arngart, p. 18.   [7] See above, §I. B. 11.
[8] Arngart, pp. 13–14.   [9] See above, pp. xli–xlii.
[10] Professor McIntosh notes, 'It may be observed that [*Genesis and Exodus*]'s orthographical characteristics are perceptibly less archaic than those of the [*Physiologus*]' ('The Language of the Extant Version of *Havelok the Dane*', p. 48, n. 3).

The morphology of the *Physiologus* is less obviously conservative than its spelling, because, although by the late thirteenth century the morphological changes that took place during the early ME period, such as simplification of the nominal inflexions and the breaking down of the weak/strong distinction in the adjective (the latter also a matter of syntax) were well under way in the Midlands, the rate of change was not such that the morphology of a text can form a basis on which to date the text even within a fifty-year period. Thus there are no significant differences in the way nouns, adjectives, and adverbs are treated in the *Physiologus*, items 1–6, *Genesis and Exodus*, and Cleopatra D. The *Physiologus* and items 1–6 show no morphological differences, but there are a number of interesting differences between the pronouns found in Arundel 292 and those in *Genesis and Exodus* and Cleopatra D: the *Physiologus* has *h* forms throughout in the third person pl. of the personal pronoun (items 1–6 have no instances).[1] Cleopatra D has as many occurrences of *þei* (*tei*) as of *he* but only *h* forms in the genitive and the oblique; *Genesis and Exodus* uses the neuter sg. *it* as often as *he* in the nominative and has one example of *þei*; it uses *h* forms in the other cases.[2] The total absence of *ð* forms from the *Physiologus* indicates an earlier stage of development than that of *Genesis and Exodus* and Cleopatra D.

The phonology of the text is a somewhat better guide to the state of its language, because the late thirteenth century was a period of considerable phonological change. There are no significant differences in phonology between the *Physiologus* and items 1–6, but comparison with *Genesis and Exodus* and Cleopatra D is helpful. Four sound changes should be examined in dating the text of the *Physiologus*:

(1) lengthening in open syllables;

(2) coalescence of *ai* and *ei*;

(3) vocalization of OE *g* between back vowels (in ME, a back vowel and *e*) or between *l/r* and a back vowel (ME *e*) to *w*;

(4) disappearance of the spirant from the cluster *ʒt* (OE *ht*) following a front or back vowel (confined to the East Midlands).

(1) Lengthening in open syllables is difficult to date. Jordan puts it in the first half of the thirteenth century because 'on the one hand Orm still clearly marks the shortness with a little curl, on the other hand

---

[1] With the exception of two occurrences of *it* (399, 588) in the nominative: see above, §II. D. 1. Mustanoja, *A Middle English Syntax*, sees this usage as an aspect of formal *it* (anticipatory subject) (p. 132).

[2] Arngart, p. 30.

MS Cambridge Gg 4. 27 of KH [*King Horn*] (about 1260) in v. 1264 rhymes *name*: *blame*'.[1] Dobson dates it 'after rather than before 1225' in the South and in the Midlands,[2] but since rounding must have taken place before lengthening in open syllables (if this was not so, the result would have been forms like *nome* from earlier *name* throughout the South and the Midlands) and rounding is usually dated first half of the thirteenth century,[3] Dobson's dating must be rejected as too early because it does not allow for enough time to elapse before rounding is completed. It seems best to adopt the conventional dating for the lengthening of vowels in open syllables, viz. the first half of the thirteenth century. *Genesis and Exodus* definitely shows lengthening in open syllables.[4] The snippets of verse in Cleopatra D (on f. 23ᵛ) unfortunately do not contain rhymes that could prove lengthening; the prose could not provide any evidence. The *Physiologus* poet is generally careful in his rhymes,[5] so they can be used for this purpose. There are no rhymes which depend on lengthening not having taken place; equally, there are no rhymes which depend on lengthening. The only possibility could be *Gode*: *fode* (90–2), but perhaps the two sounds would be close enough to make an acceptable rhyme even without lengthening. Otherwise, the *Physiologus* has no instances which could prove lengthening proper; the isolated form *stereð*, 'stirs' (271)—the verb normally has *i* in this text—could be the result of the later lengthening of *i* to *e* /eː/, which began in the North in the thirteenth century and spread southward.[6] This would, however, be an early example of the change because it did not reach the East Midlands until the second half of the fourteenth century. *Genesis and Exodus* has *i*, and otherwise *e* forms do not, as far as I know, appear before Chaucer: see *OED* s.v. *stir*. But it would be rash to draw any firm conclusions from a single instance; since neither form of lengthening can be proved beyond reasonable doubt, lengthening in open syllables cannot be used as a criterion for dating the text of the *Physiologus*.

(2) The falling together of *ai* and *ei* is dated second half of the thirteenth century by Jordan; in Luick's opinion it was completed by the end of the thirteenth century.[7] Dobson's statement that in Cleopatra D 'the beginning of confusion between the two sounds ...

[1] Jordan, §25, n. 4.
[2] 'Middle English Lengthening in Open Syllables', *Transactions of the Philological Society* (1962), 124–48, p. 133.
[3] Jordan, §25, n. 4.   [4] Arngart, p. 25.
[5] See below, part 3, 'Versification', p. lxiv.
[6] Jordan, §26 and see above, §I. A. 2(viii).   [7] Jordan, §95; Luick, §408, Anm. 1.

indicates a date approaching 1300' (p. clxi) is confirmed by his external evidence for the date of Cleopatra D. *Genesis and Exodus* has
numerous examples of *ei* rhyming with *ai*, proving that the two diph-
thongs have coalesced, although they are mostly kept apart in spelling.[1] With Arundel 292 it is difficult to say whether there is merely 'the
beginning of confusion' or whether the two sounds have fallen
together: the appearance of *dei* (517) and *deies* (271) as well as *dai* (21,
37, 133 etc.) and *daies* (97, 571) implies some degree of coalescence,[2]
but since the rhymes offer no help in this case it is impossible to determine if the *ei/ai* variation was introduced by a copyist or if the two
sounds had already become one in the author's dialect.

(3) The vocalization of *g* is dated thirteenth century by Luick,[3] and
Jordan states that it took place from 1200 onwards,[4] but this date is
probably too early: Jordan adds that the change first started in
Worcestershire, in which case his evidence is probably the Worcester
Tremulous Hand, which he dates 'about 1200'[5] but which has now
been shown to be early thirteenth century.[6] In view of this and in view
of his mention of the Nero text of *Ancrene Riwle* as consistently ex-
hibiting the vocalization of *g*, we can safely assign the change to the
early thirteenth century. It should then be expected in late thirteenth-
century texts; *Genesis and Exodus*[7] and Cleopatra D[8] do indeed show it,
but there is no evidence of it in the *Physiologus*.[9]

(4) Loss of the spirant from earlier *ȝt* has received little attention in
the handbooks: Luick and Morsbach do not give a date, and Jordan
says that the change took place in the course of the fourteenth century.[10] Yet loss of the spirant is general in Cleopatra D, and his work is
definitely earlier than 1300.[11] *Genesis and Exodus* has forms with the
spirant appearing besides forms without, e.g. *ðowgte* as well as
ðowtes.[12] The spirant is generally retained in the *Physiologus*, e.g. *siȝte*
(81, 527), *ðoȝt* (444, 501); the only exceptions are *ovt* (502, 518), *out*
(464), *nout* (9, 531, 559), *nowt* (167, 185). These also have forms with *ȝ*:
noȝt (108, 128, 144 (twice)), *oȝt* (560). The rhyme *ðoȝt: ovt* (501–2)[13]
tells us nothing about whether the author's form had a spirant or not,

[1] Arngart, p. 20.   [2] See above, §I. A. 6–7.
[3] Luick, §402, Anm. 1.   [4] Jordan, §95.   [5] Jordan, p. 9.
[6] N. R. Ker says that the duct of the 'tremulous' hand was formed in the late twelfth
century, but he dates the 'tremulous' hand as we know it to 1225–50: 'The Date of the
"Tremulous" Hand', *Leeds Studies in English*, vi (1937), 28–9.
[7] Arngart, p. 21.   [8] Dobson, p. clviii.
[9] See above, §I. C. 3(ii) (p. xx).   [10] Jordan, §196.
[11] Dobson, p. cxlvii.   [12] Arngart, p. 24.
[13] See above, p. xxxvi, and see the Commentary ad loc.

although the noun *ðoȝt* does not appear without *ȝ* (see the Glossary
s.v.); yet the rarity of *ȝ*-less forms strongly suggests that they are
scribal. There are no rhymes which confirm forms without the spirant.

It is hard to decide how to interpret (2), and (1) does not prove the
absence of lengthening in the text of the *Physiologus* as it has come
down to us; but failure to show (3) and the rarity of forms that show (4)
are certainly exceptional in a late thirteenth-century Norfolk text.
Perhaps the Arundel scribe's habit of copying *litteratim* could account
for this.

Considering the evidence provided by orthography, morphology,
and phonology, it would seem that in some respects the text of the
Physiologus as we have it does not represent the language of *c.* 1300, the
date of the manuscript. When the text of the *Physiologus* is compared
with the other ME pieces in the hand of the Arundel scribe, the
conclusion must be that the scribe was in the habit of copying his
exemplars letter by letter, but that his practice of copying *litteratim* did
not extend to the graphs he used, since the graphs *ð*, *ȝ*, and *p* (*wynn*)
are employed both in the *Physiologus* and in items 1–6, and nearly
always correctly. The scribe's habit of copying *litteratim* explains why,
compared with other Norfolk texts of the period, the spelling of the
Physiologus has a conservative appearance and why the text shows little
or no evidence of a number of the linguistic changes which took place
during the thirteenth century. In all likelihood, the scribe did not, with
a few exceptions perhaps, bring the language of his copy text up to
date.

If the date of the sole surviving manuscript, *c.* 1300, determines the
terminus ad quem for the date of the extant text of the *Physiologus*, the
terminus a quo is determined by the language in which it has come
down to us, provided that my hypothesis concerning the Arundel
scribe's habits is correct. Bearing in mind that a text cannot be dated
with any great degree of precision on the basis of its language, we can
probably assign the surviving text of the *Physiologus* to the latter part of
the thirteenth century. It is unlikely to date from before 1200, as it
shows rounding of earlier *ā* to open *ō*,[1] and the beginnings of confusion between *ai* and *ei* make it unlikely that it dates from before
1250. Failure to show the change of /γ/ to /w/ and the state of the

---

[1] See above, §I. A. 4(ii); it was completed in the Midlands in the course of the thirteenth century according to Jordan (§44), Luick (§369), and Morsbach (§135, Anm. 1).
Jordan says that the change was general in the South Midlands in the second half of the
thirteenth century (§44).

text's spelling and morphology would indicate a date in the second half of the thirteenth century, early rather than late within this fifty-year period.

The presence of numerous corruptions in the *Physiologus* indicates that, although we are dealing with a copy that represents the language of a time up to half a century before the date of the manuscript, we do not necessarily in Arundel 292 possess a text that is close to the author's original. Often the corruption is a simple matter of a rhyme being destroyed because a stribe substituted a later form for the poet's earlier one.[1] When this happens, there is no way of telling at which point in the transmission the error arose, but it involves no more than one copyist making the actual mistake. A number of corruptions can be explained only, if at all, by assuming that more than one copyist was involved. An example is *mid he brest ouel* (404), which should perhaps read *mid here best ouel*, 'with their best efforts, with all the strength they have' (*ouel*, from OE *afol*, 'strength').[2] A possible explanation for how the corruption arose is that the abbreviation for *re* was accidentally omitted by a scribe, thus rendering the phrase unintelligible. A later copyist, taking *he* to be a personal pronoun and possibly not understanding the rare word *ouel*, inserted an *r* into *best* in order to turn it into a verb. Alternatively, *brest* for *best* may not have been the result of *he* for *here* but instead came about through attraction to *atbrosten* in the same line. Either way, the likelihood is that more than one scribe was involved. The surviving text contains other examples of corruptions which can be explained only from the interference of two copyists,[3] and it is improbable, though not impossible, that only one intermediary between archetype and extant text should have caused the degree of corruption manifest in Arundel 292.

Granted that the *Physiologus* is the product of a string of copyists, at least one of whom, the Arundel scribe, copied his exemplar *litteratim*, and granted that the text as we have it represents the language of the second half of the thirteenth century, can we hazard a guess as to when the poem was first composed? Its date of composition is usually given as 'before 1250', but no reasons are ever stated.[4] The only clues the manuscript provides are corruptions which are the result of a copyist

[1] For examples, see above, p. xxxvi.
[2] See the Commentary ad loc.
[3] The meaningless *onder steuene* (503) should perhaps be emended to *o[re] steuene*, 'with a single voice': for an attempt at explanation, see the Commentary. Other examples include lines 591–2, for which (and for further instances) see the Commentary.
[4] e.g. in the Bibliography to *MED*.

substituting a later form for an earlier one, but these depend on changes such as the disappearance of the spirant from the cluster *ȝt* and the replacement of *come* followed by an infinitive with *come* followed by a present participle which can only be dated roughly.[1]

Our conclusion must be negative: it is possible that the *Physiologus* was first composed before 1250, but this cannot be proved. It is not possible to determine how many layers of transmission there are between the author's text and the surviving manuscript, but the degree of corruption we find in Arundel 292 suggests that the *Physiologus* had passed through the hands of several copyists before it reached our scribe. What is clear is that the Arundel scribe was not in the habit of 'translating' his copy text into his own dialect but instead aimed to copy his exemplar letter by letter, as other scribes may have done before him. This process of copying *litteratim* explains why a text that has come down to us in a manuscript of around 1300 is written in the language of the previous half-century.

3. VERSIFICATION

The ME *Physiologus* shares with its source, Theobald's *Physiologus*, a remarkable variety of metres. Theobald states his intention in the Prologue:

Temptans, diversis si possem scribere metris (I. 5).[2]

He writes in quantitative metres only, avoiding the post-classical accentual verse, and barring occasional lapses, shows reasonable skill. The metres used are the following:[3]

(1) hexameter for the Lion, the Sirens, the Onocentaurs (these last left out by the ME poet) and the Panther:

Tres leo naturas et tres habet inde figuras (I. 1).

What distinguishes these verses from classical hexameters is the presence of internal rhyme (*naturas*: *figuras*). They are known as leonine hexameters; whether the name derives from this section of Theobald's poem or whether the choice of leonine hexameters for

[1] See the Commentary to line 473.
[2] All references to Theobald's *Physiologus* are taken from *Theobaldi 'Physiologus'*, ed. P. T. Eden (Mittellateinische Studien und Texte 6, Leyden and Cologne, 1972).
[3] See Eden, p. 25, n. 4; for metrical lapses, see Eden, p. 27, n. 6; p. 33, nn. 1 and 2; p. 61, n. 1.

the Lion is a metrical joke on the part of the poet (cf. his use of adonics for the Turtle Dove) cannot be determined;[1]

(2) elegiac couplets for the Eagle, the Ant, the Fox, the Stag, the Whale, and the Elephant, but again Theobald uses internal rhyme:

Esse ferunt aquilam super omne volatile primam

Que se sic renovat, quando senecta gravat (II. 1–2);

(3) sapphic stanzas for the Serpent; the rhyme scheme is irregular:

Jam senex serpens novus esse gaudet

Atque jejunans macie perhorret

Pellis effeta tremit: ossa nervis

Sola manetis (III. 1–4).

(4) hypercatalectic dactylic trimeters for the Spider, the lines rhyming in twos or threes:

Vermis araneus exiguus (VII. 1).

(5) adonics for the Turtle Dove (i.e. dactyls alternating with spondees; in this case, the lines divide into four feet); end rhyme is irregular:

Turtur inane nescit amare (XIII. 1).

None of these metres are of course rare: hexameters, elegiac couplets, sapphic stanzas and adonics can all be found explained in the standard mediaeval textbook on Latin metre, Bede's *De arte metrica* (Bede even recommends the use of internal rhyme for hymns written in the dactylic hexameter);[2] hypercatalectic dactylic trimeters would have been familiar from some of Prudentius' hymns.[3] What is unusual

---

[1] For the suggestion that the term may derive from the section on the Lion, see Léon Hermann, 'Thiébaut de Vernon', *Le Moyen Age*, l (1940), 30–43, p. 42. Cf., however, Du Cange, *Glossarium mediae et infimae latinitatis*, editio nova aucta a L. Favre, 10 vols. (Niort, 1883–7), s.v. *léonini*, where 'leonine' is tentatively derived from the name of the poet Leo, fl. in the reign of Louis VII (1137–80) or Philip Augustus (1180–1223).

[2] Ed. C. B. Kendall and M. H. King, *Bedae Venerabilis opera*, Pars I, *Opera didascalia* (Corpus Christianorum, series latina 123A, Turnholt, 1975), 59–141, p. 113: 'Optima autem uersus dactylici et pulcherrima positio est, cum primis penultima ac mediis respondent extrema, qua Sedulius frequenter uti conseuit' (followed by examples).

[3] So Eden, p. 25, n. 4 and Max Manitius, *Geschichte der lateinischen Literatur des Mittelalters*, 3 vols. (Munich, 1931), III, 732, n. 8. For an example see Prudentius' *Hymnus in honorem passionis Eulaliae Beatissimae Martyris, Peristefanon III* in *Aurelii Prudentii Clementis Carmina*, cura et studio Mauricii P. Cunningham (Corpus Christianorum, series latina 126, Turnholt, 1966), pp. 278–85; the first 40 lines are no. 21 in *The Oxford Book of Medieval Latin Verse*, ed. F. J. E. Raby (Oxford, 1959).

about Theobald's poem, however, is that the poet should have chosen
to write in a variety of metres. A parallel would seem to be Boethius'
De consolatione philosophiae, and the author of the gloss that was added
to the *Physiologus* in the thirteenth or fourteenth century asserts, 'Et
nota quod auctor iste sequitur Boetium . . . ponendo diversa genera
metrorum.'[1] But it cannot be proved that Theobald was indeed following Boethius, and it should be noted that his selection of metres is
not the same as Boethius': Boethius never has internal rhyme, does
not use hypercatalectic trimeters and has a far greater variety of
metres.[2] Also, from antiquity onwards the mixture of prose and verse
found in Boethius has been recognized as a separate form, the *prosimetrum*, so that a learned imitator of Boethius would have been likely
to preserve his alternation of prose and verse.[3] The most likely conclusion, then, is that Theobald's *Physiologus* is a genuine metrical experiment, as its author implies in the Prologue, and one that is apparently
without a parallel in Mediaeval Latin literature.

The metrical form of the ME *Physiologus* is similarly unique. Four
different metres are used:

(1) alliterative long lines for the Lion, the Serpent, the Ant, and the
Spider and for the *naturae* of the Fox and the Siren;
(2) couplets, mostly four-stress but frequently three-stress, rhyming
aabb, for the Stag, the Whale, the Elephant, the Panther, and the
Dove (the Dove is not in Theobald) and for the *natura* of the Eagle
and the *significaciones* of the Fox and the Siren;
(3) common metre for the *significacio* of the Eagle;[4]
(4) septenaries for the Turtle Dove.

Comparison of the metres used by Theobald and those used by his
translator shows at once that the ME poet merely attempts to match

---

[1] The gloss has not been edited; the quotation is from Manitius, III, 733.

[2] For a survey of the metres used in the *Consolatio*, see Joachim Gruber, *Kommentar zu
Boethius 'De consolatione philosophiae'* (Texte und Kommentare 6, Berlin and New York,
1978), pp. 19–24.

[3] On the history of the *prosimetrum* see Gruber, pp. 16–19, and Udo Kindermann,
'Laurentius von Durham "Consolatio de morte amici": Untersuchungen und kritischer
Text' (D. Phil. thesis, Erlangen, 1969), pp. 56–82. Lady Philosophy's words at IV, pr. 6,
'Sed video te iam dudum et pondere quaestionis oneratum et rationis prolixitate fatiga-
tum aliquam carminis exspectare dulcedinem; accipe igitur haustum, quo refectus firm-
ior in ulterioria contendas', should not be taken at face value but seen in the context of
the *prosimetrum* (Boethius, *Philosophiae consolationis libri qvinqve*, ed. Karl Büchner, 2nd
edn., Heidelberg, 1960).

[4] The term is from hymnody: see Derek Attridge, *The Rhythms of English Poetry* (London and New York, 1982), pp. 86–7. The measure is perhaps better known as the ballad
stanza.

Theobald's variety—although he uses four, not five, different kinds of metre—and does not aim to render a particular metrical form in his source by means of a single ME form: hexameters are represented by alliterative long lines (the Lion and the *natura* of the Siren) or four-stress couplets (the Panther and the *significacio* of the Siren); elegiac couplets by alliterative long lines (the Ant and the *natura* of the Fox), four-stress couplets (the Stag, the Whale, and the Elephant, the *natura* of the Eagle and the *significacio* of the Fox) or common metre (the *significacio* of the Eagle); sapphic stanzas by alliterative long lines (the Serpent) and adonics by septenaries (the Turtle Dove). The only case in which a particular ME metre matches a single Latin one appears to be that of the Turtle Dove, but this may well be accidental; also, the ME poet's alliterative lines occasionally turn into septenaries, so that septenaries are not in fact confined strictly to the Turtle Dove.[1]

The range of metres of the ME *Physiologus* is not paralleled elsewhere in early mediaeval English verse. There are sporadic instances of poets using two metrical forms within the same poem, and Schipper quotes an interesting example of a fragmentary piece from MS Harley 913, known as 'Christ on the Cross', in which the description of Christ's torments is in alliterative long lines and the exhortation to sinful mankind in four-stress couplets.[2] Another poem from the same manuscript, likewise fragmentary, on the Seven Deadly Sins, is also written in two metres, tail-rhyme for the introduction, four-stress couplets for the disquisition on the sins.[3] These, however, are the only two instances known to me where the change in metre indicates a transition within the poem: in the remaining examples the change appears to be arbitrary. R. M. Wilson draws attention to the unusual

---

[1] On alliterative long lines in the *Physiologus* lapsing into septenaries, see below, p. lxvi.

[2] J. Schipper, *Altenglische Metrik* (Bonn, 1881), pp. 179–80. The poem, which is not, *pace* Schipper, from MS Harley 2277 but from MS Harley 913 (Brown/Robbins, *Index* 1943) is printed in *Early English Poems and Lives of the Saints*, ed. Frederick J. Furnivall (Berlin, 1862), pp. 20–1, and in *Die Kildare-Gedichte*, ed. W. Heuser (Bonner Beiträge zur Anglistik 14, Bonn, 1904), pp. 125–9. It is also printed in *Religious Lyrics of the XIVth Century*, ed. Carleton Brown, 2nd edn., rev. G. V. Smithers (Oxford, 1956), pp. 1–2, under the title 'Respice in faciem Christi', from two different manuscripts: MS Bodley 42 (a shorter version) and St John's College Cambridge MS 15. Robbins suspects that the lyrics in his collection 'printed as "of the beginning of the century" have been carried over from the closing decades of the thirteenth' (p. xii). Furnivall dates the Harley version 'before 1300' (p. iij). In their notes, Robbins and Smithers observe that archaic words have been replaced in the Harley text.

[3] Brown/Robbins, *Index* 3400; printed in *Early English Poems and Lives of the Saints*, pp. 17–20, and in *Die Kildare-Gedichte*, pp. 116–24.

versification of *Dame Sirith*, which has tail-rhyme stanzas for the first
132 lines, followed by eight four-stress couplets and finally an irregular alternation of the two, but 'with apparently no change in the
subject-matter to correspond with the change in verse'.[1] The *Proverbs
of Alfred* presents a similar case: the poem is mainly in alliterative long
lines, but parts of it are in rhyming couplets, again for no apparent
reason. (A complication is that the rhyming couplets are not invariably
of the regular four-stress kind, and hence the distinction between lines
with internal rhyme in the alliterative portion and rhyming couplets
with ornamental alliteration is not clear-cut.[2])

In his metrically highly unusual poem, then, the author of the ME
Physiologus is plainly not drawing on a native tradition, and there does
not appear to be any poem in Old French or in Mediaeval Latin apart
from Theobald's *Physiologus* that could have prompted the translator's
metrical experiment in Middle English. Like those of his sources, the
metres used by the English translator are not rare in themselves:
numerous parallels can be found in early ME literature. His innova-
tion, which has, as far as I know, left to trace in later ME verse (Henryson occasionally shifts from rhyme royal to '*Monk's Tale* stanza' for the
moralitas of a fable, but there is no connection between Henryson's
Fables and the ME *Physiologus*), is in the variety of metrical forms he
uses.

Irregularities in the verse make it hard to establish precise metrical
rules for alliteration, use of internal rhyme in the alliterative sections,
and the required number of stresses in the alliterative portions as well
as in the sections in couplets.[3] Further difficulties are presented by the
state of the text, which is demonstrably corrupt in some places. In the
sections in couplets, rhymes can often be restored,[4] but when the line
is obviously corrupt in the alliterative parts, rules of alliteration are
frequently not definite enough to provide a firm basis on which to
emend,[5] a position that is quite different from that of the textual critic
of Latin and Greek or Classical OE verse.

---

[1] *Early Middle English Literature*, 3rd edn. (London, 1968), p. 238.
[2] *The Proverbs of Alfred*, ed. Olof Arngart, II, *The Text Edited with Introduction, Notes and
Glossary* (Acta Reg. Societatis Humaniorum Litterarum Lundensis XXXII, II, Lund,
1955); see esp. the section on metre, pp. 225–32.
[3] See below, pp. lvii ff.
[4] See above, pp. xxxvi–xxxvii.
[5] As, for instance, in line 5: see the Commentary ad loc.

ALLITERATIVE LINES

The alliterative long line of the *Physiologus* is in all essentials the same
as that used in Laȝamon's *Brut* and in the *Proverbs of Alfred*. It is not
subject to the strict rules of classical OE prosody; its relation to the
looser OE verse found in the *Anglo-Saxon Chronicle* and to the poems
of the Alliterative Revival has been written about extensively.[1] The
basis principles are: the half-line has a fixed number of metrically
stressed syllables (generally two), but the number of non-accented syllables varies; half-lines are linked by alliteration, but they may be
linked by rhyme (including assonance or half-rhyme) instead or by
both rhyme and alliteration or not have any linking device at all; the
first beat of the second half-line, which is the 'head-stave' in OE verse,
does not necessarily determine the sound on which the line alliterates;
enjambment, which is frequent in OE, is rare.[2]

When it comes to drawing up more precise rules for the metre of the
Physiologus, two things need to be taken into account. First, the state of
the text: because the sole surviving witness is corrupt, it is not always
possible to discover on what sound a line is meant to alliterate. Take,
for instance, line 404, which, in the manuscript, reads *Ofte arn atbrosten
mid he brest ouel* and which does not make sense as it stands. If it is

---

[1] A possibility that has been advanced more than once is that the early ME verse of
Laȝamon's *Brut* is descended from the loose OE verse represented by the *Chronicle*
poems through the intermediary of lost popular oral poetry. This view is expounded
most clearly by Dorothy Everett, 'Laȝamon and the Earliest Middle English Verse', in
her *Essays in Middle English Literature*, ed. Patricia Kean (Oxford, 1955), 23–45. Angus
McIntosh, 'Early Middle English Verse', *Middle English Alliterative Poetry and its Literary
Background*, ed. David Lawton (Cambridge, 1982), 20–33, draws attention to the similarities between the homilies of Ælfric and Wulfstan and early ME alliterative verse. N. F.
Blake's term for the intermediary style between verse and prose found in these homilies
is 'rhythmical alliteration' ('Rhythmical Alliteration', *Modern Philology*, lxvii (1969–70),
118–24); he says, 'in those parts of the country . . . where there was no tradition of rhythmical alliteration and where sermons were usually based on French models (as, for
example, the Kentish sermons), would-be poets were inevitably forced to rely upon
French or Latin forms . . . [alliteration] could never have become the organizing prin-
ciple for their structural forms' (p. 120). Because it does not take account of the non-
West Midland provenance of the *Physiologus* (Norfolk) and the *Proverbs of Alfred*
(Sussex, in the opinion of Arngart, ed. cit., II, 57–64), Professor Blake's theory will not
explain the use outside the West Midlands of an alliterative line which is essentially the
same as Laȝamon's. See also R. M. Wilson, *Early Middle English Literature*, pp. 13–17
and 171–2, and Thorlac Turville-Petre, *The Alliterative Revival* (Cambridge, 1977),
pp. 6–25.
[2] See Dorothy Everett, 'Laȝamon and the Earliest Middle English Alliterative
Verse', pp. 26–7. Professor McIntosh points out that the term 'alliterative' as applied to
this type of verse is misleading ('Early Middle English Alliterative Verse', pp. 20–1).

emended, tentatively, to *Ofte arn atbrosten mid he[re] best ouel*, meaning, 'Often, with all the strength they have, they escape', does the line alliterate on the vowels or on *b*? But the text does not have many lines such as this one. Secondly, and more importantly, not all lines in the alliterative parts of the *Physiologus* have alliteration: some have internal rhyme and others have no connecting device at all. Thus we may be tempted to seek an alliterative pattern in a line which was not intended to have any alliteration. As a result, it is difficult to determine with certainty which sounds alliterate and which do not. This *caveat* having been stated, the alliterative sections of the *Physiologus* can now be examined in detail and compared with other ME poems in long alliterative lines.

In classical OE verse the number of beats per half-line is invariably two, but this may not be so in the *Physiologus*. For instance, the first half-line of the poem could be stressed

$$\times \; / \times \quad \times \quad \times \quad / \times$$
Ðe leun stant on hille

(i.e. like an OE type A line) or

$$\times \; / \times \quad / \quad \times \; / \times$$
Ðe leun stant on hille.

The existence of four possible three-beat half-lines which bear the alliteration on all three beats points to the existence of a three-beat half-line in the *Physiologus*:

Driueð dun to his den, ðar he him berȝen wille (7)
Seftes sop ure Seppande, sene is on werlde (313)
Ðis wunder wuneð in wankel stede, ðar ðe water sinkeð (396)
Ðe sipes sinken mitte suk, ne cumen he nummor up (402).[1]

Since both Laȝamon's *Brut* and the *Proverbs of Alfred* permit three-beat half-lines,[2] we should probably allow them in the *Physiologus*.

Since by no means every line in the alliterative portions of the poem has alliteration, alliteration cannot be a *sine qua non*, e.g.:

[1] Two other half-lines that could be analysed as *aaa* do not in fact have three stresses bearing the alliteration: in line 175 a *punctus* follows *hauen* in the manuscript, giving *We sulen hunger hauen· & harde sures buten we ben war here*. This means that the first half-line, *we . . . hauen*, has two beats, *aa*. Line 176, *Do we forði, so doð ðis der, ðanne he we derue*, is perhaps better described as a septenarius (see below, p. lxvi).

[2] See Kurt Brandtstädter, 'Stabreim und Endreim in Layamon's Brut' (D. Phil. thesis, Albertus-Universität zu Königsberg in Pr., Kirchhaim N.I.., 1912), esp. pp. 23–4; also Herbert Pilch, *Layamons 'Brut': eine literarische Studie* (Heidelberg, 1960), pp. 135–56; *The Proverbs of Alfred*, II, 225–32, esp. p. 226.

Driueð dun to his den, ðar he him berȝen wille (7)
Ðis wirm bitokneð ðe man ðat oðer biswikeð (329).

Both these lines make sense and have the requisite number of beats, only their half-lines are not connected by alliteration (although line 7 has alliteration within the half-line). If lines without alliteration are acceptable, it follows that it is impossible to draw up firm rules as to what does and does not constitute alliteration. Common sense would suggest that, as in OE, single consonants alliterate with each other and that any vowel alliterates with any other vowel, but the *Physiologus* does not have any certain examples of vocalic alliteration.[1] Vocalic alliteration is rare in Laȝamon but 'fairly frequent' in the *Proverbs of Alfred*.[2] The difficulty is in the consonant clusters.

The rules for classical OE verse are plain on this point: the consonant clusters *sc*, *sp*, and *st* alliterate only with themselves, not with each other or with *s*. One line in the *Physiologus*, however, alliterates only when *s* is taken to alliterate with a cluster containing *s*:

Mirie ȝe singeð, ðis mere, & haueð manie stefnes (398),

and a number of other lines have an extra alliterating syllable if the restrictions of OE verse do not apply:

Stille lið ðe leun, ne stireð he nout of slepe (9)
Oc or sei ðu in scrifte to ðe prest sinnes tine (140)
Sipmen here steringe forȝeten for hire stefninge (400).

In some cases it should be remembered that in the Norfolk dialect in which this text is written OE *s* and OE *sc* have coalesced.[3] This may well affect lines 140 and 400; it is definitely relevant in the following:

Seftes sop ure Seppande, sene is on werlde (313)
Sipes ȝe sinkeð & scaðe ðus werkeð (397).

(In line 397 *scaðe* is probably from ON *skaði*, so is likely to have been pronounced with initial /sk/.) In Laȝamon *sp*, *st*, and *sc* do not alliterate with each other, while there is confusion over *s* and *sc* alliterating; in the *Proverbs of Alfred sc* alliterates with itself only and *st* alliterates with *s* as well as with itself (the text has no instances of *sp* in alliterating position).[4]

---

[1] If my emendation of line 404, *Ofte arn aþrosten mid he[re]* [MS *he*] *best* [MS *brest*] *ouel*, is accepted, the line could be regarded as alliterating either on *b* or on the vowels: see above, pp. lvii–lviii.

[2] Brandtstädter, p. 29; Arngart, II. 227.

[3] See above, part 2, §I. C. 5(ii) (p. xxi).

[4] Brandstädter, p. 29; Arngart, II. 227.

Another point at which the verse of the *Physiologus* differs from classical OE verse is that in the lines of the *Physiologus* that can be taken to alliterate, the first beat of the second half-line does not necessarily determine the sound on which the line alliterates: out of *c.* 100 lines that have alliteration to link their half-lines, approximately one third lack alliteration in this position, e.g.:

> ʒet is wunder of ðis wirm more ðanne man weneð (169)
> He wullen on ðis foxes fel & ʒe it wel feleð (276)
> On brest & on bodi oc al ðus ʒe is bunden (393).

This is not uncommon in the *Proverbs of Alfred* and is also permitted in Laʒamon's *Brut*.[1] When it comes to giving figures for the various patterns of alliteration found in the *Physiologus*, we should remember that there is uncertainty about which sounds alliterate, so figures quoted are no more than approximate. Also, a number of lines defy any attempt at classification into alliterative patterns, e.g.:

> Mirie ʒe singeð, ðis mere, & haueð manie stefnes (398).

Does this line alliterate on *m*, giving *aa/ax*, or can we assume that *s* alliterates with *st*, in which case we have 'double' alliteration and three beats in the first half-line?

The most frequent patterns of alliteration are *aa/ax* and *aa/xa*, which account for half the total together. The next most common are *ax/ax* and *xa/ax*, but it should be noted that out of the eighteen examples of *ax/ax* eleven occur in the section on the Serpent, which is the part of the text that is most highly corrupt. Less frequent (fewer than seven examples each) are *ax/xa*, *xa/aa*, *ax/aa*, and *xa/xa*. 'Double' alliteration, *ab/ab* or *ab/ba*, occurs no more than twice, in line 2 and, depending on an emendation in the second half-line, in line 5 (*Ðraʒeð dust wið his stert ðer he [dun] steppeð*).[2] Examples of all beats alliterating are rare (323 and possibly 101 and 176). Compared with classical OE verse, which has either *ax/ax* or *aa/ax*, this variety of alliterative patterns is bewildering; yet it is familiar from the *Proverbs of Alfred* and Laʒamon's *Brut*.

A large number of lines in the alliterative sections (*c.* 34) join their half-lines by means of rhyme. In the majority of these (*c.* 24) the rhyme is pure; approximately ten lines use assonance or inflectional rhyme instead. Out of all these lines with internal rhyme, only four use

---

[1] Arngart, II. 227–30; Pilch, pp. 163–5.
[2] See the Commentary ad loc.

alliteration, too, as a connecting device, but alliteration within the half-line is common in lines with rhyme. For instance:

Marie bi name, ðe him bar to manne frame (19: alliteration + rhyme)
Til ðe sunne haueð sinen ðries him abuten (10: inflectional rhyme)
Listneð nu a wunder ðat tis der doð for hunger (268: assonance).

A few lines in the alliterative parts of the *Physiologus* are still un-accounted for and should be mentioned briefly here, to be considered more extensively under their proper heading, for these lines can be read as seven-beat lines and should therefore be regarded as sep-tenaries rather than as long alliterative lines.[1]

RHYMING COUPLETS

The poem is written out as prose in the manuscript,[2] and as a result the distinction between alliterative sections and parts in four-beat rhyming couplets is not as immediately obvious as it would be in a modern printed edition. This is of some importance, for to a mediae-val eye and ear the difference between a line from one of the 'allitera-tive' sections, which has internal rhyme but no alliteration, and a rhyming couplet may well have been less apparent than it would be to us. Compare, for instance:

Ðis lif bitokneð ðe sti ðat te neddre gangeð bi (135),

which scans perfectly as a four-beat couplet if *bitokneð* is given four syllables, and

Twifold forbisne in ðis der
To frame we muȝen finden her (281–2),

which is from a section in four-beat couplets but which could be read as an alliterative line of the *ax/aa* pattern. The manuscript punctua-tion, a *punctus* marking the end of a four-beat line and the *caesura* in a long alliterative line, reinforces this similarity.

These examples suggest that the distinction between verse in the early ME alliterative mode and four-beat rhyming couplets is not absolute. Professor McIntosh proposes to replace the traditional terms 'accentual' (to describe alliterative lines) and 'syllabic' (to describe verse in couplets) by 'heteromorphic' and 'homomorphic'. In heteromorphic verse, 'the basic "foot" units have a number of different

---

[1] See below, p. lxvi.   [2] See above, part I, 'The Manuscript', p. xi.

forms (in a manner brought out for Old English by the various clas-
sifications from Sievers onwards) and ... it is usual for these to succeed one another in no fixed order';[1] in homomorphic verse, the lines
have 'only one basic foot unit' and 'lines and larger entities are made
up of a continuous succession of examples of this unit'.[2] But is this, at
least in the case of the *Physiologus*, not to exaggerate the differences
between the two? For the 'feet' of the alliterative sections of the
Physiologus cannot usefully be divided up into types,[3] and in the rhyming parts the verse is too irregular to justify the assertion that there is
only one basic foot-unit. Take, for instance, this passage from the
natura of the Whale, which is typical of all the sections in couplets in
the poem:

> Đis fis ðat is vnride,
> Đanne him hungreð, he gapeð wide.
> Vt of his ðrote it smit an onde,
> Đe swetteste ðin ðat is o londe.
> Đerfore oðre fisses to him draȝen.
> Wan he it felen, he aren faȝen (341–6).

Of these lines, 341 has only three beats, and 345 could be read as
having five; the remaining lines have the prescribed four beats, but
none of them has the expected eight syllables: they all have ten or
eleven syllables, and while elision has to be assumed two unstressed
syllables still follow a beat in many cases, as in

> / × × / × × / × / ×
> Vt of his ðrote it smit an onde.

Both these types of line, the 'short' one that has no more than three
beats and the 'long' one that contains 'feet' that consist of three
syllables rather than two, are so common throughout the poem that
the term 'homomorphic' does not apply to the rhyming couplets of the
Physiologus.

It is useful to compare these parts of the *Physiologus* with the verse of
other early ME poems in short rhyming couplets. The versification of
Havelok the Dane has been studied in detail by G. V. Smithers. Like the
sections in rhyming couplets in the *Physiologus*, the lines of *Havelok*
have four beats, but they are far more regular in that the number of
syllables per line is usually eight (there is a lower limit of seven, for a

---

[1] 'Early ME Alliterative Verse', pp. 21–2. [2] Ibid., p. 22.
[3] As Professor Arngart does for the *Proverbs of Alfred*, ed. cit., II, 226; the verse of
the *Physiologus* is simply too irregular to be reduced to a manageable number of
patterns.

line that begins with the first on-beat, and an upper limit of nine, for a
line that begins with a metrically unaccented syllable and which has
feminine rhyme).[1] Metrical accents and linguistic stresses generally
coincide: on-beats on linguistically unstressed syllables are avoided,
as are on-beats on successive syllables.[2] All these things are marks of a
skilful poet. The verse of the greatest poem in early ME, *The Owl and
the Nightingale*, also in four-beat couplets, is similar to that of *Havelok*
and displays an at least equal degree of competence: see the discussion
in E. G. Stanley's edition.[3] It is to the versification of poems such as
these that Professor McIntosh's term 'homomorphic' can be applied
meaningfully.

However, the *Physiologus* poet did not write this kind of regular
verse, and approximately a quarter of his lines in the sections in rhyming couplets have three beats rather than four. What is interesting is
that he is capable of sticking to the four-beat pattern if he wants to: he
does so in two of the shorter sections, that on the Dove, which is
entirely in four-beat couplets, and that on the Panther, which has only
two three-beat lines (544–5) out of 52. The two shorter lines in the
Panther draw attention to the central concern of this part of the poem,
Christ's Resurrection:

> In his hole siðen stille
> Ðre daȝes he slepen wille;
> Ðan after ðe ðridde dai
> He riseð & remeð lude so he mai (543–6).

Three-beat lines are more frequent in the longer sections, such as
those on the Stag, the Whale, and the Elephant, which suggests that
one object of varying the number of beats is to relieve the potential
monotony of the regular four-beat line. But throughout the sections in
couplets, the poet uses three-beat lines to draw attention to a moral
point or a surprising turn in the narrative, e.g. the sailors' being
unaware that their island is really a whale (339–40):

> Ðat tu wuldes seien ȝet
> Ȝef ðu it soȝe wan it flet
> Ðat it were a neilond
> Ðat sete one ðe se-sond (337–40).

---

[1] 'The Scansion of *Havelok* and the Use of ME *-en* and *-e* in *Havelok* and by
Chaucer', *Middle English Studies Presented to Norman Davis in Honour of his Seventieth Birthday*, ed. Douglas Gray and E. G. Stanley (Oxford, 1983), 195–234, p. 199.

[2] 'The Scansion of *Havelok*', p. 202.

[3] 2nd edn. (Manchester, 1970), pp. 35–40.

Their misapprehension is to cost them their lives, just as we forfeit eternal salvation if we put our trust in the Devil.

The *Physiologus* shares the use of three-beat lines within four-beat sections with the text that is linguistically its closest parallel, *Genesis and Exodus*,[1] but *Genesis and Exodus* does not have the very long lines that the *Physiologus* also employs at high points in the narrative:

He suggeden & sorȝeden & weren in ðoȝt (501),

in which the first three beats are followed by three syllables that do not take the beat, and

ȝef him ðat biforn teð bilimpes for to tirȝen
Alle ðe oðre cumen mide & helpen him for to herien (242–3),

which are perhaps best read as septenaries.[2] Yet the poet does not show himself to be equally skilful everywhere: it is hard to see what the point is of the two long lines (210–11) at the beginning of the *significacio prima* of the Stag, which are not pleasing to the ear. Perhaps it is to highlight the immediately following catalogue of sins which is in three-beat lines and hence would have stood out sufficiently anyway. But on the whole the verse in these sections is certainly not inept.

The poet is generally careful about his rhymes. Rhymes spoilt by copyists have been discussed;[3] otherwise, lines 27 and 246 stand alone and lines 226–7 and 355–6 lack rhyme, without there being a break in the text. Rhymes are mostly pure, but examples of assonance and of inflectional rhyme are frequent, e.g. *wadeð*: *lateð* (238–9), *mikel*: *litel* (507–8), *skemting*: *foxing* (291–2), *gredilike*: *sikerlike* (202–3), *reisen*: *forðen* (495–6). Half-rhyme is rare: instances are limited to *fel*: *al* (409–10), *smel*: *oueral* (547–8), *wisedom*: *man* (283–4—the form *mon* is not part of the dialect in which this text is written[4]), *wine*: *birdene* (253–4). Feminine rhyme is common, as in *hornes*: *ðornes* (206–7), *ouerwene*: *imene* (216–17), *kinde*: *minde* (429–30, 587–8). A word ending in -*e* is not generally allowed to rhyme with a word ending in a consonant, so -*e* is probably syllabic in the *Physiologus*. Exceptions are *dimme*: *him* (34–5), *wille* (noun): *unskil* (289–90). Words in -*e* occasionally rhyme with words in -*en*: *swiðe*: *siðen* (196–7), *winnen*: *ðerinne* (357–8), *laȝe* (adjective): *draȝen* (383–4), *wise* (noun): *risen* (471–2), *hole*: *ðolen* (569–70), again suggesting that final -*e* is always pronounced, except, of course, when it is subject to elision.

---

[1] Arngart, pp. 47–50, esp. p. 49. [2] See below, p. lxvi.
[3] See above, part 2, 'Language', §IV, pp. xxxvi–xxxvii.
[4] See above, part 2, 'Language', §I. A. 1(ii) (p. xvi).

COMMON METRE

Apart from two places in the section on the Elephant (otherwise in rhyming couplets) where the poet lapses into common metre, lines 447–50 and 455–8, common metre is confined to the *significacio* of the Eagle. It is rare in ME: none of the major poems in mediaeval English literature, early or late, is in common metre, but instances of it can be found in the various collections of ME lyrics edited by Carleton Brown and R. H. Robbins.[1] The origins of this measure are obscure.[2]

The versification of the *significacio* of the Eagle is generally regular. Two lines do not scan as four-beat lines:

His muð is ȝet wel unkuð (86)
Bidden bone to Gode (90),

and

& tus his muð riȝten (91)

is awkward as a three-beat line, but for the rest every line in the section has the required number of beats. With the exception of lines 70 and

---

[1] *English Lyrics of the XIIIth Century*, ed. Carleton Brown (Oxford, 1932) has only two examples of poems in common metre, items 27 and 40; *Religious Lyrics of the XIVth Century*, ed. Carleton Brown, 2nd edn., rev. G. V. Smithers (Oxford, 1957) has nine, items 21, 56, 57, 58, 63, 71, 72, 74, 133 (56–8, 63, 71, 72, 74 are all from the same manuscript, Advocates' MS 18. 7. 21); *Secular Lyrics of the XIVth and XVth Centuries*, ed. R. H. Robbins (Oxford, 1955) has four, items 142, 144, 179, and 180; *Religious Lyrics of the XVth Century*, ed. Carleton Brown (Oxford, 1939) has seven, items 17, 20, 93, 95, 132, 163, 189 (17 is macaronic and 95 and 189 have refrains that are not in common metre). Beatrice H. N. G. Geary, 'A Study of 15th Century English Lyric Verse from MSS. and Editions' (B. Litt. thesis, Oxford, 1933) counts 14 examples for the whole of the fifteenth century (p. 145) out of the 164 examined (p. 164).

[2] Two lines of septenaries with their first half-lines rhyming would equal a four-line stanza in common metre. This leads Geary to remark: 'Since the stanza is derived from the old septenary, the division of the lines at the caesura giving the 4- and 3-stress lines, one of the points of interest in connexion with it is the continuance of its relation with the 7-stress line rhyming in couplets.' But the question that needs to be asked is whether or not common metre is an early ME development. The *septenarius* is a Mediaeval Latin form and is rare in Old French (see Adolf Tobler, *Vom französischen Versbau alter und neuer Zeit*, 3rd edn., Leipzig, 1894, pp. 103–4). Common metre does not occur in Old French; I have not been able to find any examples of it in Mediaeval Latin (there is no mention of common metre in Dag Norberg, *Introduction à l'étude de la versification latine médiévale*, Stockholm, 1958, pp. 73–7 and 112–17), so the conclusion must be that common metre developed in ME. We do not know if the ballad stanza developed out of the common metre stanza or if it was a separate form. J. W. Hendren, *A Study of Ballad Rhythm with Special Reference to Ballad Music* (Princeton Studies in English XIV, Princeton, 1936), merely says: 'The precise formal analogy between [common metre or septenaries—he does not distinguish the two] and its melody in folk song indicates that, somehow or other, the two must have developed together' (p. 60).

72 and 78–82, where there may well be a textual problem,[1] rhymes are pure, with only two instances of feminine rhyme, *listen*: *Gristen* (63: 65) and *riȝten*: *Driȝtin* (91: 93), and one example of *equivocatio* at lines 72: 74, *Crist*: *Crist*.

SEPTENARIES

The only chapter that is entirely in septenaries is the one on the Turtle Dove. Yet septenaries also appear in sections that are otherwise in long alliterative lines or in rhyming couplets. Places in alliterative sections where the poet lapses into septenaries are: Lion, *significacio* 25–6; Serpent, *significacio* 124; Ant, *significacio* 176–87; Spider, *natura* 326; Siren, *natura* 402. The section on the Stag, which is in four-beat couplets, contains four lines in septenaries, viz. 242–3 and 259–60. The sudden shift in metre may well have been deliberate in the Lion, the Serpent, the Ant, and the Stag (259–60): the two lines at the end of the chapter on the Lion certainly emphasize the moral lesson to be learnt by the reader:

He is hirde, we ben sep, silden he us wille,
If we heren to his word ðat we ne gon nowor wille (25–6).

Yet the lines from the Stag (242–3), the Spider, and the Ant do not seem to have a similar purpose: perhaps the last two should be regarded as long alliterative lines with aberrant scansion.

Poema Morale and the *Ormulum* are the only other important ME poems which are in septenaries. For the rest, this metre is restricted to a number of lyrics; it is rare in lyrics dating from after the fourteenth century.[2] Like *Poema Morale*, these lyrics rhyme in pairs. Old French has very few examples of this metre; the likelihood is that the poet derived his use of it from earlier ME verse or direct from Mediaeval Latin, which is where the metre originates.[3]

In his discussion of the metre of the *Physiologus*, Hall classes as septenaries only those seven-beat lines which rhyme in pairs.[4] The

[1] See the Commentary ad loc.
[2] Geary, 'A Study of 15th Century English Lyric Verse', does not find any examples in the fifteenth century (p. 164); there is, however, one instance in Carleton Brown's *Religious Lyrics of the XVth Century*, viz. item 3. *Secular Lyrics of the XIVth and XVth Centuries* has none; *Religious Lyrics of the XIVth Century* has 16 (items 12, 14, 18, 28, 34, 42, 55, 62, 64, 65, 81, 83–6, 135), and *English Lyrics of the XIIIth Century* four (items 25, 28, 55, 59).
[3] See above, p. lxv, n. 2.
[4] *Selections from Early Middle English*, ed. Joseph Hall (Oxford, 1920), p. 592. Hall does not see rhyme as a *sine qua non*: in his account of the versification of *Poema Morale*, he says, 'The Septenarius is a . . . metre of seven feet, with or without rhyme' (p. 327).

result is that he limits the *septenarius* to lines 176–87, 259–60, 513–20, and 523–32 (he appears to have overlooked 25–6 and 242–3): thus the last two lines of the *natura* of the Turtle Dove are not counted as septenaries, despite the fact that they can be read as having seven beats (though it is possible to scan them as eight-beat lines). They are clearly of a different character from the normal alliterative line:

> Buten one goð & one sit & hire olde luue abit:
> In herte haueð him niȝt & dai, so he were o liue ai.

Surely the poet's intention was to write an entire section in seven-beat lines.

The section on the Turtle Dove and the other long passage in septenaries, part of the *significacio* of the Ant, are competent examples of the metre, but occasionally a line does not scan:

> & wende we neure fro him ward, be dai ne be niȝte (526),

though here the problem could be solved by adding the propositional ending -*e* to *dai*[1] and allowing a beat to fall on *ne*. However, putting a metrical stress on a conjunction would create a wrenched line, so the improvement would in fact be small. Other lines that are one beat short are:

> Ðe mire suneð ðe barlic ðanne ȝe fint te wete (180);
> It be[t] [MS *ben*] us e[rð]liche [MS *ebriche*] bodes &
>   bekneð [MS *bekned*] euelike (184);
> Nu & o Domesdei & tanne we hauen nede (187).

184 is highly corrupt; in the case of the other two lines, a little ingenuity would put things right, but would this be justified if out of thirty-two lines—not counting septenaries within sections in other metres—four want one stress?

Most of the lines in these two passages rhyme in pairs, except, in the Turtle Dove, lines 521–2[2] and 515–16, and in the Ant, lines 176–7. Hall proposes emendations for the last two pairs,[3] but if three pairs of lines out of sixteen fail to rhyme, perhaps we should take it that rhyme is not absolutely necessary. Not all of the rhymes are pure: *wete*: *moten* (180–1) is a half-rhyme (in *nummore*: *ðere*, 178–9, *ðere* should be emended to *ð[o]re*, however[4]). Feminine rhymes include *euelike*:

---

[1] On the use of the prepositional case in the *Physiologus*, see part 2, 'Language', §II. A. 1(ii) (p. xxii). The text has no examples of *dai* in the propositional case.
[2] See above pp. lxvi–lxvii.
[3] For *derue* (176) he proposes *glewe* 'wise, prudent' (p. 605); for *siðen* (515), he reads *seden*, 'separate, depart' (p. 621).   [4] See below, part 2, 'Language', §IV, p. xxxvi.

ʒeuelike (184–5), *fede*: *nede* (186–7), *rime*: *lif-time* (513–14), *fleʒeð*: *leʒeð* (517–18), *wore*: *more* (519–20).

The problems posed by the sections in septenaries are typical of those that confront the editor of the *Physiologus* throughout the poem. Lines in alliterative sections do not necessarily have alliteration; septenaries do not always have seven beats and do not always rhyme in pairs; in four-beat couplets the number of beats varies, as does the number of syllables; and in rhyming sections generally the rhyme sometimes fails. Although the versification is irregular, the poet is obviously not without skill and often changes the metre in mid-section for a specific purpose. Our conclusion must be, then, that we should not emend simply because the verse is irregular: as long as the text makes sense and scribal interference cannot be proved beyond reasonable doubt, what we are inclined to perceive as irregularity should rather be seen as a genuine feature of the prosody of the *Physiologus*. The unfortunate implication of this is that when the text makes little sense or none at all, as happens for instance at lines 115 and 404, prosody does not give the firm guidance that it gives the textual critic of *Beowulf* or Horace.

4. BEASTS AND BESTIARIES

Aristotle's great work of zoology is known to us under its Latin title, *Historia animalium*. But the word *historia*, which Latin borrowed from Greek, goes back to Aristotle himself when he describes the nature of his undertaking:

And, after all, this is the natural method of procedure—to do this only after we have before us the ascertained facts about each item, for this will give us a clear picture of the subjects with which our exposition is to be concerned and the principles upon which it must be based.[1]

It is to be a *historia*, a systematic investigation. The object of the enquiry is not a zoological classification, but a study of the different properties of animals and an explanation of the causes of these differences:

What has just been said has been stated thus by way of outline, so as to give a foretaste of the matters we have to examine; detailed statements will follow later; our object being to determine first of all the differences that exist and the actual facts in the case of all of them. (491. a. 7–12)

[1] 3 vols., ed. and tr. A. L. Peck (London and Cambridge, Mass., 1965–), 491. a. 12–14.

This does not mean that the *Historia animalium* does not contain errors which are the result of credulity, such as the belief that animals can be impregnated by the wind (541. a. 26–31), but Aristotle's aim is to observe, to describe, and to explain: the *Historia animalium* is in fact a scientific treatise.

Pliny's *Naturalis historia* is not based on scientific observation: it is essentially a compilation from the writings of earlier authors, as Pliny himself tells us in his Preface.[1] Even if independent investigation is not Pliny's object, he is nevertheless concerned with factual description.[2] Yet many of the things he describes as facts are actually fiction.

When the *Physiologus* came to be written, the approach was radically different. The *Physiologus* is the product of a Christian culture, although its orthodoxy is not beyond dispute.[3] Nature is not studied for its own sake but for what it can tell us about God's purpose and about how we should conduct our lives. Nature has become a metaphor, a book to be studied by all good Christians.[4] This way of looking at the natural world has its roots in the Judaeo-Christian method of biblical exegesis practised in Alexandria, and it is incompatible with

[1] '$\overline{XX}$ rerum dignarum cura—quoniam, ut ait Domitius Piso, thesauros oportet esse, non libros—lectione voluminum circiter II, quorum pauca admodum studiosi attingunt propter secretum materiae, ex exquisitis auctoribus centum inclusimus XXXVI voluminibus, adiectis rebus plurimis, quas aut ignoraverunt priores aut postea invenerat vita' (*C. Plini Secundi Naturalis Historiae Libri XXXVII*, ed. C. Mayhoff, 5 vols., Leipzig, 1892–1909 I, Praef. 17). Book I is taken up with a list of contents and an enumeration of the sources of each Book.

[2] Lynn Thorndike comments, 'He writes not as a naturalist who has observed widely and profoundly the phenomena and operations of nature, but as an omnivorous reader and voluminous note-taker who owes his knowledge largely to books or hearsay, although occasionally he says "I know" instead of "they say," or gives the results of his own observation or experience' (*A History of Magic and Experimental Science during the First Thirteen Centuries of our Era*, 2 vols., London, 1923, I, 48).

[3] The earliest reference to the Latin version of the *Physiologus* is in the *Decretum Gelasianum*, supposedly of 496, in which it is condemned as heretical, but this document is now no longer thought to be genuine: the relevant material is collected in Giovanni Orlandi, 'La tradizione del Physiologus e i prodomi del bestiario latino', *Settimane di studio del Centro italiano di studi sull'alto medioevo*, xxxi (1985), 1057–106, at p. 1066, n. 30.

[4] Witness the familiar lines from Alan of Lille's *Anticlaudianus*:

> Omnis mundi creatura
> quasi liber et pictura
> nobis est in speculum;
> nostrae vitae, nostrae mortis,
> nostri status, nostrae sortis
> fidele signaculum.

(*The Oxford Book of Medieval Latin Verse*, item 242, lines 1–6).
On Nature as a book, see further Ernst Robert Curtius, *European Literature and the Latin Middle Ages*, tr. Willard R. Trask (London, 1953), pp. 319–26.

the Aristotelian approach, which strives to observe differences (*dia-phorai*) and essential characteristics (*symbebēkota*), and tries to seek out their causes (*aitiai*); an exclusively allegorical mode of thought, which sees the world in terms of symbols rather than causal relationships, is not concerned with truth in the objective, scientific, sense and hence makes the development of science impossible.[1]

Although it is not known when the *Physiologus* was first composed, it is almost certain that the text was originally written in Greek, probably in the second century AD, in or near Alexandria. There is no general agreement on the date and place of composition of the original Greek *Physiologus*. The first definite mentions of the *Physiologus* are in the *Hexaemeron* of Pseudo-Eustace and in the writings of Ambrose and Epiphanius, which implies a *terminus ante quem* of the last quarter of the fourth century.[2] Friedrich Lauchert has no doubt that the text was written in Alexandria, probably in the first third of the second century,[3] but M. R. James proposes a later date, 'perhaps in the fourth century—very likely in Egypt, in some community of monks'.[4] Max Wellmann places the origin of the Greek *Physiologus* some time between 254–5 (the date of Origen's death) and 380, but probably towards the end of the period, and suggests that it was written in Caesarea, where Origen had moved his school in 230–1.[5]

[1] The point is made by Rosemary Freeman, *English Emblem Books* (London, 1948), with reference to the disappearance of allegory and the development of science in the second half of the seventeenth century: 'In a world in which the importance of things was estimated by their significance rather than by their nature, no scale of strictly scientific value could be evolved. The study of cause and effect is merely hampered by the perception of symbolical relations everywhere; and the purpose of the new scientific movement was, as its founder Francis Bacon proclaimed, "to search out the causes of things"' (p. 3). The effect of the growing availability, from the twelfth century onwards, of Latin translations of Aristotle and Galen should not be overestimated: Charles Homer Haskins says: 'In the main . . . they took the results of Greek and Arabic science rather than its methods. Medicine became the study of Galen and Hippocrates scholastically interpreted; physics the logical interpretation of Aristotle's treatises; geography the study of books, not travel or even maps. Aristotle became in the course of time a hindrance rather than a help, stereotyping knowledge rather than furnishing a method for its extension, and imposing theories of the universe which science had to abandon as a preliminary to further progress' (*The Renaissance of the Twelfth Century* (Cambridge, Mass., 1927), pp. 331–2).

[2] See B. E. Perry's article 'Physiologus' in *Paulys Real-Enclyclopädie der classischer Altertumswissenschaft*, 58 vols. (Stuttgart, 1894–1980), Halbband 39, cols. 1074–129, col. 1100.

[3] *Geschichte des Physiologus* (Strassburg, 1889), p. 41, p. 42, n. 1, and p. 45.

[4] 'The Bestiary', *History*, NS xvi (1931), 1–11, p. 3.

[5] 'Der Physiologos: eine religionsgeschichtlich-naturwissenschaftliche Untersuchung', *Philologus*, Supplementband xxii (1930), 1–116, pp. 10–11 and p. 13. In Wellman's opinion, Origen cannot have used the *Physiologus*: see p. 6.

Pauly-Wissowa rejects Wellmann's date on the grounds that the way in which the dogmas of the Trinity, the Incarnation, and the Hypostatic Union appear does not necessarily reflect fourth-century developments[1] and proposes the second century, adding that any conclusion 'im großen ganzen auf einer subjektiven Grundlage ruhen muß';[2] Wellmann's suggestion of Caesarea is unacceptable to Pauly-Wissowa because Wellmann fails to demonstrate beyond doubt that Origen cannot have used the *Physiologus* and that apparent references are due to the later Latin translator of Origen's works or represent other sources.[3] Assuming that the text was indeed written in the second century, Pauly-Wissowa suggests Alexandria.[4] A recent writer on the subject, P. T. Eden, accepts Pauly-Wissowa's date but is cautious on the subject of provenance: 'somewhere within the cultural orbit of Alexandria, and in the Roman province of Egypt or Syria'.[5]

The *Physiologus*, then, is not a handbook of natural history: in its original form it described the properties of animals, birds, and stones, both real, such as the lion, the ant, and the eagle, and mythical, like the charadrius, the myrmecoleon or 'ant-lion', and the sirens, and provided allegorical interpretations of the characteristics enumerated. Unlike Aristotle's *Historia animalium*, the descriptions of the natural habits of the real creatures and stones in the *Physiologus* are not based on direct scientific investigation but on the authority of the Physiologus, 'the natural historian', from whom the work takes its title. As a result of this, statements that are true in the scientific sense are rare in the *Physiologus*: the description of the eagle flying towards the sun and subsequently plunging into a fountain to renew its youth, familiar from the reference in Ps. 102: 5 (A.V. Ps. 103: 5), is typical of the treatise as a whole. It is there only so that a moral (the necessity of spiritual renewal through baptism) can be drawn; that eagles do not scorch themselves in order to undo the effects of old age is not an objection that would have occurred to those for whom the *Physiologus* was written, because natural history in the way Aristotle understood it no longer existed.

Who it is that the anonymous author refers to as 'the Physiologus' we do not know. Some scholars assume that 'the Physiologus' is responsible for the author's immediate source, but there is in fact no indication that the appellation refers to a specific person or book.[6]

---

[1] Pauly-Wissowa, cols. 1101–4. [2] Ibid., col. 1103. [3] Ibid., cols. 1104–5.
[4] Ibid., col. 1104. [5] *Theobaldi 'Physiologus'*, p. 3.
[6] For a full discussion of the problem of sources, see Wellmann, op. cit., and Pauly-Wissowa, cols. 1105–11.

Later traditions certainly do not associate 'the Physiologus' with a *title* known to the anonymous author: late antiquity favoured Solomon, whereas the Middle Ages took 'the Physiologus' to be Aristotle,[1] but the mediaeval identification is unlikely to have been based on anything more than Aristotle's reputation as a natural historian[2] and the need for a named *auctoritas*. It is clear, however, that the form of the chapters goes back to Judaeo-Christian biblical exegesis as developed by the Hellenic Jewish scholar Philo and taken over by Origen and his school. In the original Greek text, a typical item would start with a quotation from the Bible relating to the animal, bird, or stone described (but not all the creatures and stones in the *Physiologus* occur in the Bible), followed by 'the Physiologus has said concerning . . .', introducing the *physis* or description of natural habits. Then came the allegorical explanation, in which each of the characteristics mentioned was given a moral significance, and the allegorical explanation was concluded with 'And so the Physiologus has spoken well concerning . . .'.[3]

In the course of time, the Greek text underwent alterations, resulting in four different redactions. Four different textual groupings can be distinguished within the earliest redaction, two of which form the basis of the Latin versions. One Latin text goes back to the earliest division of the first redaction and is represented by a single manuscript, Bern 318, of the ninth century.[4] This translation is generally known as *versio x*. It does not appear to have had any influence on other Latin or vernacular versions. All other versions, whether Latin or vernacular (though not the oriental versions), go back directly or indirectly to *versio y*, which is the translation made from the branch of the first redaction known as *Π*. *Versio y* itself has not been preserved, however, and can only be reconstructed from its surviving descendants, *versiones a* and *b*: *a* does not derive from *b* or *b* from *a*, but *a* and *b* go back to a lost common source *y. a*, the longer of the two texts,

---

[1] See Lauchert, op. cit., pp. 43–4, and Pauly-Wissowa, cols. 1076–7.

[2] The *Historia animalium* was not translated into Latin until the early thirteenth century, first by Michael Scot from an intermediary Arabic version, and later in the century by William van Moerbeke at the request of St Thomas Aquinas, who used it in his *Summa* (see A. L. Peck, ed. cit., pp. xl–xlii).

[3] The standard edition of the Greek *Physiologus* is *Physiologi graeci variarum aetatum recensiones codicibus fere omnibus tunc primum excussis collatisque in lucem protulit Franciscus Sbordone* (Milan, 1936); an edition is included in Lauchert, op. cit., pp. 229–79. Translations are my own.

[4] Pauly-Wissowa, cols. 1111–15 and col. 1120, and *Physiologus graecus*, ed. Sbordone, pp. xxix–lxv.

is extant in a limited number of manuscripts only and had no influence on later versions of the *Physiologus*, while the shorter text, *b*, lies behind all the later Latin and vernacular versions.[1] These later Latin works include the so-called *Dicta Chrysostomi*, *De bestiis et aliis rebus* attributed to Hugh of St Victor, and the verse *Physiologus* whose author is named as Theobald.[1]

Unlike Theobald's verse *Physiologus*, the *Dicta Chrysostomi* and *De bestiis et aliis rebus* are not party of the *Physiologus* tradition proper. In the twelfth century an important change took place in the *Physiologus*. Until then the order in which the chapters appeared had been fixed; they are not grouped according to any classification, but the lion comes first because he is King of the Beasts: 'We will begin by discussing the lion, surely the king of the living beasts.'[2] (The Latin *versiones a* and *b* omit this introductory sentence.) But in the twelfth century the material is regrouped according to Isidore's classification in Book XII of his *Etymologiae*. Also, additions were made from the *Etymologiae* and from Solinus's *Collectanea rerum memorabilium* (known as *Polyhistor* in its sixth-century revision), which is largely based on Pliny's *Naturalis historia*, and the number of chapters was increased substantially. Because of these differences, it is customary to refer to these texts as bestiaries rather than as versions of the *Physiologus*.[3] From the twelfth century onwards, bestiary manuscripts began to be furnished with illuminations, and moralizations were mostly dropped. It is to these de luxe manuscripts, most of which were produced in England during the twelfth and thirteenth centuries, that the bestiary owed its great popularity in mediaeval England.[4]

But the *Physiologus*, as it still was at the time, was also known in Anglo-Saxon England, although it may not have been available in its entirety—at least, no manuscript of the *Physiologus* survives which is

[1] See Pauly-Wissowa, cols. 1119–22; Francis J. Carmody, *'Physiologus Latinus Versio Y'*, *University of California Publications in Classical Philology*, xii (1933–44), 95–134, pp. 95–8; Francesco Sbordone, 'La tradizione manoscritta del *Physiologus* latino', *Athenaeum*, NS xxvii (1949), 246–80, pp. 246–59; P. T. Eden, ed. cit., pp. 2–4. The most recent contribution is Orlandi, op. cit. I have followed the usage of Pauly-Wissowa and Eden; Carmody complicates matters needlessly by referring to *versio a*, the longer text, as *y*.

[2] *Physiologus graecus*, ed. F. Sbordone, p. 1. F. N. M. Diekstra, 'The *Physiologus*, the Bestiaries and Medieval Animal Lore', *Neophilologus*, lxix (1985), 142–55, suggests that 'some animals are arranged to form oppositional or complementary pairs' (p. 145): he gives the panther and the whale as an example of the former, the unicorn and the beaver of the latter.

[3] *The Bestiary*, ed. M. R. James (Roxburgh Club clxxvi, Oxford, 1928), p. 7; Eden, ed. cit., p. 3.

[4] M. R. James, 'The Bestiary', *History*, NS xvi (1931), 1–11, p. 3.

demonstrably of pre-Conquest English provenance. Nevertheless, the Exeter Book contains pieces in Old English on the Panther, the Whale, and the Partridge.[1] It is not clear whether these three pieces constitute a single poem, complete in itself (except that we have not got all of the Partridge), or whether they are fragments of a larger cycle: hence they cannot be used to prove that the whole of the *Physiologus* was known to the Anglo-Saxons. Nothing is known about the *liber bestiarum* which is the final item on Æthelwold's booklist.[2] Two Anglo-Latin authors can be shown to have had access to the *Physiologus* in some form. Aldhelm used the *Physiologus* in his *Riddles*.[3] Animals that occur in the *Physiologus* figure in a number of them, but there is only one riddle, LXXII, 'Mustela', which has a detail that does not derive from Isidore, Solinus, or Pliny:[4] *Quin magis ex aure praegnantur viscera fetu* (line 6). Isidore specifically mentions this as an error (*Falso autem opinantur qui dicunt mustelam ore concipere, aure effundere partum*[5]), but the *Physiologus* has (*versio b*), *Physiologus dicit quoniam mustela semen masculi per os accipit et sic in utero habet; tempore uero pariendi per aures generat.*[6] This does not prove direct knowledge of the *Physio-*

---

[1] For editions, see *The Old English Physiologus*, ed. Ann Squires (Durham Medieval Texts v, Durham, 1988), *The Old English Elene, Phoenix, and Physiologus*, ed. A. S. Cook (New Haven, 1919), and *The Anglo-Saxon Poetic Records*, vol. III: *The Exeter Book*, ed. G. P. Krapp and E. K. Dobbie (Columbia, 1936); see also Francesco Cordasco, 'The Old English *Physiologus*: its Problems', *Modern Language Quarterly*, x (1949), 351–5. A more recent writer on the subject, Lothar Frank, 'Die Physiologus-Litteratur des englischen Mittelalters und die Tradition' (D. Phil. thesis, Tübingen, 1971), argues that the Old English *Physiologus* is complete in itself, consisting of three chapters that follow one another in the original Latin—not, however, in *versio x*—as they do in the Greek (p. 43) and that they include one representative each of land (panther), sea (whale), and air (partridge) (pp. 45–6). The correspondence in the order of the sections would support the conjecture that the bird in the Old English *Physiologus* is indeed the partridge (see also Frank's pp. 37–42), but his second point cannot be proved.

[2] The list is printed by M. R. James, *List of Manuscripts Formerly in Peterborough Abbey Library, Supplement to the Bibliographical Society's Transactions*, 5 (1926), pp. 19–20, and by A. J. Robertson, *Anglo-Saxon Charters*, 2nd edn. (Cambridge, 1956), p. 72; also by Michael Lapidge, 'Surviving Booklists from Anglo-Saxon England', *Learning and Literature in Anglo-Saxon England: Studies Presented to Peter Clemoes on the Occasion of his Sixty-Fifth Birthday*, ed. Michael Lapidge and Helmut Gneuss (Cambridge, 1985), 33–89, at pp. 52–5.

[3] *pace* J. D. A. Ogilvy, *Books Known to the English, 597–1066* (Cambridge, 1967), p. 222. Professor Ogilvy mentions 'Latin notes on the *natura* of the lion, unicorn and panther' (p. 100) in Corpus Christi College, Cambridge MS 448, which I have not seen.

[4] *Aldhelmi Opera*, ed. R. Ehwald, *Monumenta Germaniae Historica* (Auctores Antiquissimi 15. i, Berlin, 1913), pp. 97–149; the riddle about the weasel is on p. 135. See also Ehwald's note ad loc.

[5] *Etymologiarum sive originum libri XX*, ed. W. M. Lindsay, 2 vols. (Oxford, 1911), XII. III. 3.

[6] *Physiologus latinus: Editions Préliminaires versio B*, ed. F. J. Carmody (Paris, 1939), ch. XXVI (pp. 46–7). *Versio a*, which Carmody calls *y*, has *semen masculi in os accipit, et, preg-*

logus, but it is at least probable that Aldhelm used it here. It was also used by the anonymous Anglo-Saxon author of the *Liber monstrorum* in the chapter on the *autolops*.[1]

In the later Middle Ages, the *Bestiary*, as it had by then become, was widely known and very popular. M. R. James asserts that

the Bestiary may be reckoned as one of the leading picture-books of the twelfth and thirteenth centuries in this country. It ranks in this respect with the Psalter and the Apocalypse.[2]

In his study of the Latin prose versions current in England, James divides the surviving manuscripts of the *Bestiary*, as opposed to the *Physiologus*, into four families. The First Family contains fourteen manuscripts, four of which are certainly foreign.[3] Another manuscript of this Family, which was unknown to James, is the bestiary in the library of Alnwick Castle. Its provenance is not known, but it was in Dorset *c.* 1500.[4] The Second Family consists of twenty-one copies, all of them English.[5] To these should be added the bestiary in Aberdeen University Library, which is probably English.[6] Examining the drawings of the birds in *Bestiary* manuscripts, the zoologist W. B. Yapp has recently been able to distinguish further groupings within the Second Family.[7] The Third Family comprises five manuscripts, one of which, Bodleian Library e Musaeo 136, James does not list and which may have been written in the Low Countries.[8] The two manuscripts in this Family of which the origins are known are both English.[9] The Fourth Family consists of a single manuscript which dates from the fifteenth century. Its provenance is not mentioned, but James must have decided that it was English, because he arrives at a total of thirty-four

nans facta, auribus pariet (ed. Carmody, *University of California Publications in Classical Philology* (1933–44), ch. XXXIV (p. 127)). *Versio x*, for which see *Physiologus Bernensis:* Voll-Faksimile-Ausgabe des Codex Borgarianus 318 des Burgerbibliothek Bern, ed: Christoph von Steiger and Otto Homburger (Basel, 1964), has not got the chapter on the weasel and hence cannot have been used by Aldhelm. It is possible that *versio x*, which had no influence on later versions, Latin or vernacular (see above, p. lxxii), was not known in Anglo-Saxon England; Frank's conjecture about the Old English *Physiologus* (see above, p. lxxiv, n. 2), if it is correct, would lend some slight support to this.

[1] II. 24: see *Liber monstrorum*, ed. Franco Porsia (Bari, 1976), p. 69.
[2] *The Bestiary* (Roxburghe Club clxxvi, Oxford, 1928), p. 1.   [3] *The Bestiary*, p. 11.
[4] *A Thirteenth Century Bestiary in the Library of Alnwick Castle*, ed. Eric George Millar (Roxburgh Club ccvii, Oxford, 1958), p. 3.   [5] *The Bestiary*, p. 14.
[6] M. R. James, 'The Bestiary in the University Library', *Aberdeen University Library Bulletin*, vi (1928), 529–31.
[7] 'A New Look at English Bestiaries', *MÆ*, liv (1985), 1–19.
[8] Frances McCulloch, *Medieval Latin and French Bestiaries* (Chapel Hill, 1960), p. 39.
[9] *The Bestiary*, pp. 23–4.

manuscripts that are 'certainly English'.[1] The Aberdeen and Alnwick bestiaries can probably be added, bringing the number to thirty-six. McCulloch mentions yet another bestiary, Leningrad State Library MS Qu. V. I, which is reckoned to be English in origin and belongs to the First Family.[2] This large number of manuscripts produced in England, thirty-seven in all, is ample proof of the popularity of the *Bestiary* in its Latin prose form. But it was popular in other versions, too.[3]

The most widely known among these was the Anglo-Norman *Bestiary* of Guillaume le Clerc (also called 'le Normand'), which survives in twenty-three manuscripts dating from the thirteenth to the fifteenth centuries, copied both in England and in France. Most of these manuscripts are illuminated.[4] The *Bestiary* of Philippe de Thaün, which is dedicated to Queen Adela, Henry I's second wife, is extant in three manuscripts, two of which were copied in England,[5] and its dedication shows that the King and Queen were interested in animals. In fact, Henry I kept exotic animals in his private zoo at Woodstock, and Alexander H. Krappe thinks that 'it was with this hobby of his master in view, if not at the latter's express orders, that [Philippe de Thaün] composed his *Bestiaire*'.[6] These vernacular manuscripts are none of them de luxe manuscripts.[7] The sixty-four surviving manuscripts of the Latin verse *Physiologus* of Theobaldus, which, as its title indicates, is not a bestiary but a version of the *Physiologus* and which is the source of the Middle English *Physiologus*,[8] have no pictures. This suggests that the *Physiologus* and the *Bestiary* were not popular for their pictures only, but the reason for the plain appearance of the extant manuscripts of Theobald's *Physiologus* is that it was a school text.[9] P. T. Eden does

[1] *The Bestiary*, p. 2.

[2] McCulloch, p. 41. I have not taken Professor McCulloch's further divisions into account here as being too detailed for my purpose.

[3] Another important group of illuminated manuscripts in Latin prose is the manuscripts of the *Dicta Chrysostomi*, a text that originated in France before the ninth century. This version was probably not well known in England: see McCulloch, op. cit., p. 41, and see above, p. lxxiii.   [4] McCulloch, op. cit., p. 57.

[5] McCulloch, op. cit., pp. 48–9; see also John Morson, 'The English Cistercians and the Bestiary', *Bulletin of the John Rylands Library*, xxxix (1956), 146–70, p. 147, and *Le Bestiaire de Philippe de Thaün*, ed. Emmanuel Walberg (Lund and Paris, 1900), pp. i–ix (the dedication to the Queen is printed on pp. vii–viii, from Merton College, Oxford, MS 249).

[6] 'The Historical Background of Philippe de Thaün's *Bestiaire*', *Modern Language Notes*, lix (1944), 325–7, p. 327.   [7] McCulloch, op. cit., p. 46.

[8] See below, part 5, 'The Middle English *Physiologus* and its Sources' (pp. lxxix–xci).

[9] On Theobald's *Physiologus* as a school text which was used throughout Europe, see Nikolaus Henkel, *Studien zum Physiologus im Mittelalter* (Tübingen, 1976), pp. 36–41 and 53–8.

not discuss the origins of the many manuscripts of Theobald's poem, but it is clear that the text was known and used all over the Continent and in England.[1]

The explicitly didactic nature of the *Bestiary*, when it still had its moralizations, made it popular with preachers, too. Beatrice White says that 'from the tenth and eleventh centuries onwards the attention of preachers was constantly directed to the *Bestiary* as a quarry for sermon material' and that 'most monasteries and ministers possessed copies for consultation'.[2] This last statement is hard to prove, although the number of surviving manuscripts of the various versions suggest that this may well have been so. Bestiary material is certainly common in sermons: John Morson shows the extent to which English Cistercians borrowed from the *Bestiary*,[3] and G. R. Owst gives numerous examples of the use of the *Bestiary* in vernacular sermons,[4] which indicates that bestiary lore was thought an attractive means to incite a congregation to virtue. A well-known secular source, however, forms an even better demonstration of the *Bestiary*'s wide appeal: preserving the typical phrasing of the original (*Physiologus dicit*), Chaucer, in the *Nun's Priest's Tale*, wittily compares Chauntecleer's crowing to the singing of the mermaids:

> and Chauntecleer so free
> Soong murier than the mermayde in the see;
> For Phisiologus seith sikerly
> How that they syngen wel and myrily (VII. 3269–72).[5]

Having replaced the prose *Physiologus*, the *Bestiary* continued its life after the Middle Ages, although its appeal was no longer universal. Early printed editions are infrequent,[6] and writers of emblem books rarely made use of the *Bestiary*. The 'inventor' of the emblem, the Italian humanist Alciatus (Andrea Alciati), whose *Emblemata* were first

---

[1] See Eden, op. cit., pp. 7–13 and 77–80, for lists of manuscripts, and see above, p. lxxvi, n. 9.   [2] 'Medieval Animal Lore', *Anglia*, lxxii (1954), 21–30, p. 26.

[3] 'The English Cistercians and the Bestiary', pp. 153–67.

[4] *Literature and Pulpit in Medieval England*, 2nd edn. (Oxford, 1961), pp. 195–204.

[5] Robinson's note, which refers only to Theobald's verse *Physiologus*, is misleading, because Theobald is just one of the versions current in Chaucer's day. Also, the witty allusion 'Phisiologus seith', which is of course to the prose versions, is lost if the reference is only to Theobald. The allusion was first identified by Kenneth Sisam in his edition of the *Nun's Priest's Tale* (Oxford, 1927), p. 51; the new *Riverside Chaucer*, ed. Larry D. Benson (Oxford, 1988), mentions it in its (still patchy) note to lines 3271–2.

[6] The only version that was printed is Theobald's *Physiologus*: see Henkel, op. cit., p. 38. The twelve printed editions that are known are listed in Arnold C. Klebs, *Incunabula scientifica et medica* (Hildesheim, 1963), item 956.

published in 1531, was too proud of his classical learning ever to think of using the *Bestiary* as his source: he went straight back to Pliny—at least, none of his emblems can be traced back exclusively to the *Bestiary*.[1] But the combination of text and picture is reminiscent of the mediaeval illuminated bestiaries, and later emblem writers do in fact occasionally use the *Bestiary* as a source. Commenting on the similarity in method of the *Bestiary* and the emblem books, Albrecht Schöne mentions the emblem collection of Joachim Camerarius, printed in Amsterdam in 1588, who used the *Bestiary*. Nevertheless, on the whole the emblem books do not derive their material from the *Bestiary*: rather, where there are similarities and agreements, the emblem collections and the *Bestiary* go back to the same sources.[2]

Although the *Bestiary* was probably no longer generally read in its entirety, much of the fictitious matter it contained was still current in the seventeenth century and, what is more, appears to have been accepted as fact: witness, for instance, Edward Topsell's *The History of Four-Footed Beasts and Serpents*, originally published in 1607. It is based on the works of Conradus Gesner, but its 'Epistle Dedicatory' shows that it is close to the *Bestiary* in spirit:

Doth the Lord compare the Diuell to a Lyon; euill Iudges to Beares; false prophets to Wolues; secret and crafty persecutors to Foxes; open enemies in hostility to wilde Boares; Heretickes and false preachers to Scorpions; good men to the Fowles of Heauen, and Martyrs to Sheep, and yet we haue no knowledge of the nature of Lyons, Wolues, Beares, Foxes, Wilde-Bores, or Scorpions. Surely when *Solomon* saith to the sluggard go to the Pismire, he willeth him to learne the nature of the Pismire, and then according thereto reforme his manners: And so all the world are bid to learne the natures of all Beasts.[3]

Also, even though Topsell never cites the *Bestiary* as his authority—perhaps because he did not use it directly—he gives one 'fact' which is to be found only in the *Bestiary*, namely the trap in the form of a tree that has been partly sawn through which will cause the weary elephant to fall if it leans against it (p. 160).[4] References to bestiary material in the literature of Elizabethan and Jacobean England are too numerous to list here: they can be found in P. Ansell Robin's *Animal Lore in*

---

[1] On Alciatus, see F. W. G. Leeman, 'Alciatus' Emblemata' (D. Phil. thesis, Groningen, 1984), which has an extensive bibliography.

[2] *Emblematik und Drama im Zeitalter des Barock* (Munich, 1964), p. 44.

[3] Printed in London by William Iaggard, in 2 vols., the second volume being devoted exclusively to serpents. The quotation is from the 'Epistle Dedicatory', the pages of which are not numbered.

[4] Lines 268–80 in the Middle English *Physiologus*.

English Literature.[1] All these erroneous notions must have been widespread enough among the educated for Sir Thomas Browne to devote a whole Book of his *Pseudodoxia Epidemica*, Book III, 'Of divers popular and received Tenets concerning Animals, which examined, prove either false or dubious', to refuting them.[2] 'Crocodiles' tears' and 'licking into shape' (as a bear does its cubs, which are born shapeless) are still used in English today, and 'the pelican in her piety' is familiar from heraldry, but by Sir Thomas Browne's day the tide has already begun to turn: zoology was once more becoming a science, and nature was no longer regarded as a metaphor.

5. THE MIDDLE ENGLISH *PHYSIOLOGUS* AND ITS SOURCES

Although our text has been known as 'the Middle English *Bestiary*' for well over a century, this title is misleading and should be corrected to 'the Middle English *Physiologus*'.[3] The ME *Physiologus* is for the most part a translation of a Latin work by Theobald, which shows no attempt at classification according to Isidore of the creatures described and which invariably allegorizes the characteristics given, making the text a version of the *Physiologus* and not a bestiary. Theobald's identity is unknown,[4] and nothing can be said about the date of his poem beyond that the earliest manuscript, British Library MS 3093, belongs to the late eleventh or early twelfth century.[5] The poem deals with only thirteen creatures, and no more than two of those, the Sirens and the Onocentaurs, do not exist (although the author may well have assumed that Onocentaurs did because they are mentioned in the Old Testament, Isa. 13: 22 and 34: 14 in the Vulgate). One chapter, that on the Spider, does not derive from the *Physiologus* tradition proper, but from Isidore and the *Dicta Chrysostomi*.[6] The ME translator omits the chapter on the Onocentaurs, adding a section on the Dove, taken from Alexander Neckam's *De naturis rerum*, ch. XLVI,[7] to conclude his poem. The ME *Physiologus* is mostly close to

---

[1] (London, 1932).   [2] Ed. Robin Robbins, 2 vols. (Oxford, 1981), I, 160–290.

[3] On the distinction between the *Physiologus* and the *Bestiary* see above, part 4, 'Beasts and Bestiaries' (pp. lxviii–lxxix), p. lxxiii.

[4] See Eden's edition, pp. 5–7.   [5] Eden, pp. 5 and 9.

[6] See Eden, p. 5, and his note on p. 52.

[7] So Bernhard ten Brink, *History of English Literature*, tr. Horace M. Kennedy (London, 1911), I, 196.

the Latin, but it is by no means a literal translation. A detailed comparison, chapter by chapter, will establish how the ME poet worked and whether he used other sources besides Theobald and Alexander Neckam.[1]

Theobald's *Physiologus* begins with a prologue. This appears in all surviving manuscripts, but it is not used by the ME poet in his translation. In the Prologue, Theobald explains what he sets out to do:

Tres leo naturas et tres habet inde figuras,
Quas ego, Christe, tibi ter seno carmine scripsi.
Altera divini monstrant animalia libri,
De quibus apposui, que rursus mystica novi,
Temptans, diversis si possem scribere metris;
Et numero nostrum complent simul addita soldum
(I. Prologus. 1–6).

Theobald did indeed consult more than one source (lines 3–4), but his *divini libri* were versions of the *Physiologus* and Isidore's *Etymologiae*,[2] not theological commentaries. His different metres (line 5) and the ME translator's attempt at rendering Theobald's variety in his own language have been discussed earlier.[3] Theobald's chapters are not in any discernible order, nor are they in an order that matches that of one of the sources, except that, as in all versions of the *Physiologus* and forms of the *Bestiary*, the first chapter is that on the Lion.[4] The ME *Physiologus* also starts with the Lion, and generally the translator keeps the order of his original, but he transposes the chapters on the Fox and the Stag (chapter V and VI respectively in all the extant manuscripts). Lauchert suggests that the ME poet may have done this deliberately in order to have a number of symbols of the Devil in one group: in the source, this supposed group is split by the Stag.[5] But Lauchert's hypothesis is unnecessarily ingenious, for why should the translator not have changed the order of all the sections if his aim was to arrange creatures by what they symbolized? The ME poet may now have the Fox, the Spider, the Whale, and the Sirens together, but the Serpent still interrupts a series of sections which do not contain symbols of the

---

[1] References to Neckam are taken from *Alexandri Neckam de naturis rerum libri duo*, ed. Thomas Wright (Rolls Series 34, London, 1863), pp. 1–354.

[2] Eden notes, '"holy" because Theobaldus would not have doubted the ascription of the "Dicta" . . . to *Saint* John Chrysostom' (p. 25, n. 3—Eden's italics).

[3] See above part 3, 'Versification' (pp. lii–lxviii).

[4] See above, p. lxxiii.

[5] *Geschichte der Physiologus*, pp. 124–5.

Devil (Lion, Eagle, Ant, Stag), coming as it does after the Eagle, and the group of types of the Devil is followed by another four chapters which should logically go with the Lion, the Eagle, the Ant and the Stag. It is more likely that the ME poet was content to preserve Theobald's order as he found it and that his transposition of the Stag and the Fox is accidental.

The ME *natura* of the Lion, to use the heading given in the manuscript (which ultimately goes back to Greek *physis*[1]), is a faithful but somewhat prolix rendering of the original, thirteen alliterative long lines corresponding to nine Latin hexameters. Although the ME poet does not use tags here, his verse lacks conciseness in comparison with that of Theobald: for instance, *Cauda cuncta linit, que pes vestigia figit, / Quatinus inde suum non possit querere lustrum* (I. 4–5) becomes

> Alle hise fet steppes after him he filleð,
> Draӡeð dust wið his stert ðer he [dun] steppeð,
> Oðer dust oðer deu ðat he ne cunne is finden;
> Driueð dun to his den, ðar he him berӡen wille (4–8).

The ME *significacio* is not a translation at all. The Latin moralization takes the form of an apostrophe to Christ, in which the three characteristics described are given their allegorical explanations, but without direct reference to the *natura*: the Latin *significacio* is, as it were, a poem in its own right. By contrast, the ME equivalent is a relentless, point-for-point, allegorization of the *natura*, and it owes little to the Latin. In lines 14–19 the hill, the lion, the hunter, and the lion's descent from the hill into his den, are all neatly explained: *Welle heӡ is tat hil, ðat is heuenriche, / Vre louerd is te leun, ðe liueð ðerabuuen* (14–15), and so forth. Similarly, lines 20–4, which correspond to I. 15–16, have no verbal connexion with the original *significacio*. In the allegorization of the third characteristic, one phrase, *pervigil ut pastor* (I. 18), is picked up from Theobald and expanded into

> Wakeð, so his wille is, so hirde for his folde.
> He is hirde, we ben sep, silden he us wille,
> If we heren to his word ðat we ne gon nowor wille (24–6).

The chapter on the Eagle shows major differences between source and translation. The ME poet's use of short rhymed lines, rhyming aabb etc. in the *natura*, abab etc. in the *significacio*, has led to greater verbosity, sixty-six short rhyming lines equalling twelve elegiac couplets (i.e. twenty-four lines) in Theobald. Stopgaps such as *boðe be*

---

[1] See above, p. lxxii.

niȝt & bi dai (37; amplifying *ai*) and *fare he norð er fare he suð* (88) are employed to make up the rhymes. Authorial intrusion (27–8) and address to the listeners (35, 63) are not paralleled in the Latin. Some of the differences can only be described as padding on the ME poet's part (e.g. 31–4), but others are more interesting. A number are minor and merely indicate that the poet is not following his source closely in this section: the Eagle's eyes misting over as an effect of old age (II. 7–8) is not mentioned in the ME *Physiologus*; the moulting of the Eagle (46) is not in Theobald; *cadit nido* [*sic*] (10) is not in the ME; the ME *Physiologus* omits the reference to original sin (*ab origine matris*, II. 15), and the final couplet, *Jam novus est panem super omnia mella suavem / (Panis id est Christus, fit sine morte cibus)* (II. 23–4) is rendered *Tilen him so ðe sowles fode / Đurȝ grace off ure Driȝtin* (92–3), leaving out the bread and the honey. In the remaining cases, however, the differences are substantial and involve deliberate changes by the translator. At II. 11–14 Theobald makes a mistake by saying (Eden's paraphrase) '(1) that the eagle *breaks* his backward-curving beak against a rock, and can then eat unimpeded; (2) that it keeps its upper beak intact, and manages to eat by scraping it sideways against the food'.[1] The two are, of course, incompatible; the translator perceived the inconsistency and wisely left out the second alternative (56–61). The ME *significacio* shows that the poet does not always retain Theobald's allegorical explanations. The ME poet explains the Eagle's recovery of his youth explicitly as man's renewal through baptism and devotes nearly the entire *significacio* to this (62–82), where Theobald has only one line, *Fit in Christo ter mersus gurgite vivo* (II. 19; *ter* has no literal equivalent in II. 1–14—the Eagle is said to plunge just once—and must refer to baptism in the name of the Father, the Son, and the Holy Ghost).[2] The ME poet interprets the crookedness of the Eagle's beak, which sun and fountain have not cured (51–5), as the newly baptized infant's ignorance of the rudiments of the faith (84–93). This appears to be the translator's own invention—at least, it is not Theobald, who has *Os terit obliquum per verba precantia Christum / (Quod Christus petra sit, firmat apostolus id)* (II. 21–2), and it is not in any other version of the *Physiologus*, or in Latin works which the ME author may have known, the

---

[1] The paraphrase is Eden's: p. 29, n. 5.

[2] But cf. *versio a, et descendit in fontem, et tingit per se ter, et renouabitur et nouus efficitur* (*Physiologus versio y* [my *versio a*], ed. Carmody, p. 118); *ter* is not explicitly connected with the Trinity here but it is in *versio b*: *Nisi ergo: baptizatus fueris in nomine patris et filii et spiritus sancti* [Matt. 28: 19] (*Physiologus latinus: éditions préliminaires versio B*, ed. Carmody, p. 19).

Dicta Chrysostomi, Pseudo-Hugh of St Victor's *De bestiis et aliis rebus* and Alexander Neckam's *De naturis rerum*.[1] In addition to these differences, Lothar Frank, in his discussion of the ME *Physiologus*, draws attention to line 80, *Ðat is te sunne sikerlike*, which does not derive from Theobald and in which God is equated with the sun.[2]

For the Serpent, the poet uses alliterative lines, sixty of which translate fifty-six Latin lines in sapphic stanzas. This suggests that the translator has not expanded his source or padded out his own verse; however, the ME is not particularly close to the Latin here. The poet has made a considerable number of changes, and the *significacio* is certainly not a literal translation. Minor differences are: the Serpent fasts for ten days in the ME *Physiologus* (97), whereas no period is mentioned in Theobald; line 104, in which the Serpent is said to spit out all the poison *ðat in his brest is bred fro his birde-time* (105) has no equivalent in Theobald; lines III. 11–12, *In aquis ergo minus hunc timebo / Absque veneno*, are omitted in the ME, as are lines III. 47–8, in which the virtuous man putting the Devil to flight is compared to the sun chasing away the night. The more substantial differences are all in the *significacio*. The first part, lines 118–36, is a free and much expanded rendering of a single stanza in Theobald, III. 25–8. The association of the Serpent with the Devil, *Elded art fro eche blis, so ðis wirm o werld is* (124; cf. 94, *An wirm is o werlde, wel man it knoweð*), is not in the original. Similarly, the emphasis on humility (128–34) is the translator's, not Theobald's. Although the reader/listener is addressed, as in the Latin, there are no verbal parallels. Lines III. 37–40 of Theobald, a stanza which is not part of the allegorical explanation, is left out entirely. Lines 149–52 are not in the Latin; Theobald's equation of clothes with sin (III. 45) is not in the ME. Finally, the ME poet does not exhort his audience to imitate the Serpent, unlike Theobald (III. 51–4), thus avoiding the twofold interpretation of the Serpent as the Devil and the prudent man which would otherwise be the result.

Natura and *significacio* are not separated in Theobald's chapter on the Ant: each characteristic is immediately followed by its allegorical

---

[1] The exact date of the *Dicta Chrysostomi* is unknown, but it is from before the ninth century (see Manitius, *Geschichte der lateinischen Literatur des Mittelalters*, III, 731); the only complete edition is still 'Physiologus nach einer Handschrift des XI. Jahrhunderts', ed. G. Heider, *Archiv für Kunde Österreichischer Geschichts-Quellen* 5 (1850), 541–82. *De bestiis et aliis rebus* cannot be dated with any precision, but it could well have been known to the ME poet (see Manitius, III, 227–8). Neckam was, of course, used for the section on the Dove, but not for that on the Eagle.

[2] *Die Physiologus-Literatur des englischen Mittelalter*, p. 72.

meaning. This is not taken over by the Middle English poet, who re-organizes and adds to the Latin, restoring the familiar pattern of *natura* followed by *significacio*. The ME cannot really be called a trans-lation here: rather, elements in the original are picked up and expanded. For instance, four lines in the source, IV. 1–2 and 5–6, are rendered by fourteen lines in the ME poem, 153–66. There are no verbal correspondences, and the Ant's cave (162–3) is not mentioned in Theobald. Similarly, lines 165–71 correspond to lines IV. 9 and 11–14 of the source, but not closely, and the Ant's preference for wheat (165, 180) is not in the original: Theobald merely states that the Ant shuns barley (9). The same happens in the *significacio*, except that the ME poet briefly appears to copy the pattern of his source when, in lines 180 ff., he restates the relevant characteristics and then gives the moralizations:

Ðe mire suneð ðe barlic ðanne ȝe fint te wete—
Ðe olde laȝe we oȝen to sunen, ðe newe we hauen moten.
Ðe corn ðat ȝe to caue bereð, all ȝe it bit otwinne—
Ðe olde laȝe us lereð to don god & forbedeð us sinne, etc.

The ME poet interprets the allegory differently at several points: IV. 3–4, in which the supposed Jewish distrust of allegorical explana-tion is mentioned,[1] has no equivalent in the ME but may have occa-sioned the error *ebriche* for *eröliche* at 184. The explanation of the Ant dividing the grain as *binas lex habet una vias, / Que terrena sonat simul et celestia monstrat* (IV. 14–15) is not in the ME; instead, the ME has *Ðe olde laȝe we oȝen to sunen, ðe newe we hauen moten* (181) and *Ðe laȝe us lereð to don god & forbedeð us sinne* (183).

The next animal to be described in the ME *Physiologus*, though not in Theobald,[2] is the Stag. The translator follows his source in giving the first characteristic and the moralization immediately after it and then the second *natura* and its *significacio*. Differences between original and translation are few and mostly limited to padding on the part of the ME poet (thirty lines of elegiac couplets in Theobald produce seventy-four lines of ME rhymed couplets): the result is that the ME *Physiologus* is more explicit and insistent in tone than the Latin *Physiologus* here. Typical additions include *in wude er in ðornes* (207—a stopgap) and *& ȝingi [ð] him ðus, ðis wilde der, / So ȝe hauen nu lered her* (208–9), hortatory statements like *Ðe hertes hauen anoðer kinde /*

---

[1] See Eden, p. 41, n. 1.
[2] On the order of the chapters, see above, pp. lxxx–lxxxi.

Ðat us oʒ alle to ben minde (230–1), *Ðe hertes costes we oʒen to munen* (249), and, in the last line, *Ðerof haue we mikel ned, ðat we ðarwið ne dillen* (260). The list of sins begotten by the Serpent's venom, which is limited to *luxuria* and *avaritia* in Theobald (VI. 11–12), is expanded in the ME:

> Ðerður3 haueð mankin
> Boðen nið & win,
> [G]olsipe & 3iscing,
> 3iuernesse & wissing,
> Pride & ouerwene,
> Swilc atter imene (212–17).

Substantial differences are limited to 244–5, where the near-drowning of the exhausted animal has no parallel in the source or in other existing versions, and the judicious omission of VI. 17–18, where Theobald says that the Stag's horns are a burden though they appear to be an ornament.[1] Finally, the last line, *Sic lex est Christi nostri complenda magistri / Cujus, qui faciet, pascua repperiet* (VI. 29–30), which echo the *pascua* for which the deer are searching (VI. 20), are not in the ME.

The next chapter in the ME *Physiologus* is that on the Fox, and here again the ME translation is considerably longer than the original, fifty-two lines of ME, twenty of which alliterating and thirty-two in four-beat couplets, rendering twenty-two Latin lines in elegiac couplets. One result of this is that the explanation of the allegory is clearer and less compressed in the ME *Physiologus*, but in places the ME poet expands his source without ostensible reason: in the *natura*, *Haut amat agricola, quod rapit altilia* (V. 2) becomes

> Husebondes hire haten for hire harm-dedes:
> Ðe coc & te capun 3e feccheð ofte in ðe tun,
> & te gandre & te gos, bi ðe necke & bi ðe nos.
> Haleð is to hire hole: forði man hire hatieð,
> Hatien & hulen boðe men & fules (263–7),

and *dentibus* (V. 10) is padded out to *Tetoggeð & tetireð hem mid hire teð sarpe; / Fret hire fille & goð ðan ðer 3e wille* (379–80). In the *significacio*, *Nos et dissimulat, quod mala non faciat* (V. 14) is rendered:

> Ðe deuel dereð dernelike:
> He lat he ne wile us no3t biswike.
> He lat he ne wile us [d]on non loð
> & bringeð us in a sinne & ter he us sloð (285–8),

---

[1] Note that the Latin source is corrupt here: see Eden's note, p. 51, n. 3.

and the ME poet adds a warning against gluttony (289–92) which is not in any other version. Other small differences are: the image of swallowing up in *Quem quasi deglutit, cum secum ad Tartara ducit* (V. 17) is absent from the ME, which has *& for his sinfule werk / Ledeð man to helle merk* (299–300); Theobald's complaint against the evils of his age in V. 19–20 is not echoed by the ME poet (V. 19 corresponds to 303–4). The manuscript of the *Physiologus* divides the allegorical explanation into two parts, each preceded by the word *significacio*, in order to emphasize the twofold significance of the allegory: *Twifold forbisne in ðis der / To frame we muȝen finden her* (281–2, corresponding to V. 11, *Inde tenet duplam, quam prodest nosse, figuram*). The first part explains the Fox as the Devil (283–300), the second part as the deceitful man (301–12). Whether this division in the manuscript originated with the author or with a scribe we have no way of finding out, but it certainly clarifies the *significacio*. There are no major differences between source and translation, except that the ME leaves out the cryptic *Mortuus est vere, qui mortem fecit habere* (V. 13).[1]

The chapter on the Spider is one of those that are furthest removed from Theobald; in fact, the ME *Physiologus* is not really a translation of the Latin here. The apostrophe to the fly (VII. 4–6) and the passage on the fragility of the Spider's web, which is allegorized as the punishment for sin (VII. 16–18), are not in the ME. The Spider's biting his prey to death and drinking its blood (326–7), which is explained as the evil man's treatment of others (332–4) may have been inspired by *comedit* in

> Hos sequitur homo vermiculos,
> Decipiendo suos socios,
> Quos comedit faciens miseros (VII. 11–13).

The ME poem cannot be demonstrated to owe anything to Latin texts such as *De bestiis et aliis rebus*, the *Dicta Chrysostomi*, and Neckam's *De naturis rerum*, all of which, unlike the Greek and Latin *Physiologus*, mention the Spider.

With the Whale, the ME poet returns to translation, and he generally remains close to the Latin here. The *natura* is one of the more successful parts of the poem: it is vivid and, on the whole, agreeably free

---

[1] See Eden's explanation, p. 47, n. 2. He notes, 'he is *truly* dead (*mortuus est vere*, 13) to those who are aware that he is alive and, to defeat him, have achieved spiritual perfection'. Eden cites *versio b*, *spiritalibus tamen et perfectis in fide vere mortuus est et ad nihilum redactus est.*

from padding. For instance, *Ad se pisciculos ut trahat exiguos / . . . Piscis pisciculos claudit, conglutit et illos* (VIII. 8, 11) becomes

> Wan he it felen, he aren faȝen:
> He cumen & houen in his muð,
> Of his swike he arn uncuð.
> Ðis cete ðanne hise chaueles lukeð,
> Ðise fisses alle in sukeð (346–50).

VIII. 18–22 is rendered in a similarly lively way:

> Sipes on festen
> & alle up gangen
> Of ston mid stel in ðe tunder
> [B]el to brennen one ðis wunder,
> Warmen hem wel & heten & drinken.
> Ðe fir he feleð & doð hem sinken,
> For sone he diueð dun to grunde,
> He drepeð hem alle wiðuten wunde (369–76).

This last line is a considerable improvement on Theobald's *sicque carina perit* (VIII. 23); the same goes for the ME poet's description of the equinoctial gales, *Ðanne sumer & winter winnen* (357), which translates *cum vadit vel venit estas* (VIII. 13). The allusion to the story of Jonah in the whale, *Non sic, non sic jam sorbuit ille Jonam* (VIII. 12), and the comparison of the Whale's breath to flowers, *Unde velut florum se flatus reddit odorum* (VIII. 7; the ME merely has *ðe swetteste ðing ðat is o londe*, 344), are omitted. There are no substantial discrepancies between original and translation in the *significacio*. The ME has no mention of wizards as the creation of the Devil (VIII. 24) and the translator appears to have misunderstood the Latin at 379–80, where he renders *Mentes cunctorum, qui sunt ubicunque virorum, / Esurit atque sitit, quosque potest, perimit* (VIII. 25–6)

> He doð men hungren & hauen ðrist
> & mani oðer sinful list.

The chapter on the Siren is not a translation of Theobald, although, in the ME *natura*, *selcuðes* (391) may echo *monstra* (IX. 1) and *manie stefnes* (398) *vocibus . . . multis* (IX. 2). Unlike Theobald's Sirens, the ME Siren is a mermaid (*mereman*, 392, and *mere*, 398, 405, are the ME words equivalent to *sirena* in the manuscript heading), half woman, half fish:

> Fro ðe noule niðerward ne is ȝe no man like
> Oc fis to ful iwis mid finnes waxen (394–5).

The sirens of classical antiquity were, of course, half women, half birds, like Theobald's (IX. 7–8), but this may have been a tradition with which the ME translator was not familiar outside Theobald. The sirens are birds in the Latin prose *Physiologus* and in the *Dicta Chrysostomi* but not in *De bestiis et aliis rebus*, which, strangely, cites 'physiologus'—perhaps the *Physiologus* tradition (cf. *Physiologus dicit* in the Latin prose versions) rather than a specific text—as its authority:

Syrenae animalia sunt ipsis acquientibus mortifera quae ut physiologus describit, superne usque ad umbilicum figuram muliebrum habent, inferna vero pars usque ad pedes piscis habet figuram.[1]

In the second part of the chapter (col. 78C), Pseudo-Hugh of St Victor quotes Isidore's description of the sirens *verbatim*, but tacitly substitutes *pisces* for *volucres* and *squamas et caudam piscinam* for *alas et ungulas*. The ME poet may have used *De bestiis et aliis rebus* here—Alexander Neckam does not mention sirens—but Edmund Faral has pointed out that the fish tail starts appearing in the late seventh or eighth century.[2] The *significacio*, a warning against hypocrites, owes nothing to existing sources and is in all probability the poet's own, although it may have been inspired by the allegorical explanation of the Onocentaurs in Theobald (ch. X), who represent people

> in more biformes,
> Unum dicentes, aliud tibi mox facientes,
> Qui foris ut fantur, sed intus non operantur

(X. 3–5; the Sirens are not allegorized separately, but X. 1, *Est honocentauris itidem natura biformis*, suggests that the explanation—at least up to line 6—is meant to apply to the Sirens as well).

In the section on the Elephant, the translator is generally faithful to his original but with some notable exceptions. The *natura* is one of the livelier parts of the *Physiologus*: as with the *natura* of the Whale, a lot happens in it, and the ME poet is clearly at his best when describing action: compare, for instance, Theobald XI. 18–24 and 473–92 of the ME translation. The ME *natura* differs from the Latin at a number of points. At XI. 4, *Aversi coeunt, cum sibi conveniunt*, *aversi* is taken to mean *behinden* (427) instead of 'in private'. The Latin is ambiguous here: *aversi* can mean 'from behind' (see the *Oxford Latin Dictionary* s.v.

---

[1] *PL* 177, cols. 9–164, col. 78.
[2] 'La queue de poisson des sirènes', *Romania*, lxxiv (1953), 433–506; see also McCulloch, *Medieval French and Latin Bestiaries*, p. 176.

āuersus and Eden, p. 65, n. 1), although that is not what Pliny, the original source here, intended when he wrote *pudore numquam nisi in abdito coeunt* (VIII. 5. 12–13). But Pliny is equally unambiguous elsewhere:

coitus aversis elephantis, camelis, tigribus, lyncibus, rhinoceroti, leoni, dasypodi, cuniculis, quibus aversis genitalia (X. 63. 173),

which is presumably the source of this curious misconception. Neckham and the *Dicta Chrysostomi* do not mention the subject; in *De bestiis et aliis rebus* the context suggests the meaning 'in private' (*aversi* is contrasted with the elephants' general way of life, *gregatim*, col. 74). However, the misapprehension must have lived on until Sir Thomas Browne's day, for he corrects it in his *Pseudodoxia Epidemica* (I. 164). *nec faciunt geminum* (XI. 6) is omitted; the small tree trunk, *ligno arboris exiguo* (XI. 12), becomes *a tre. . . / Đat is strong & stedefast is* (451–2); the final characteristic of the Elephant, *Deque pilis hujus si fit sub domate fumus, / Serpentes cedunt, queque venena gerunt* (XI. 25–6), which has nothing to do with the preceding material and for which no allegorical explanation is provided by Theobald, is left out by the ME translator. The most striking difference between translation and source in the *natura* is the addition

> Oc he arn so kolde of kinde
> Đat no golsipe is hem minde,
> Til he noten of a gres,
> Đe name is mandragores (429–32).

Pliny, Isidore, and Solinus do not refer to the mandrake root in connexion with the elephant, and neither does Neckam; if a specific source for this passage exists, it must be *De bestiis et aliis rebus*, ch. XXV, or the *Dicta Chrysostomi*, ch. VIII. The workings of the mandrake root are of course familiar from Gen. 30: 14–16; the Vulgate calls it *mandragoras*. Theobald and the ME *Physiologus* differ considerably in the *significacio*: *in comedendo reum* (XI. 32, referring to the Devil) is not in the ME, perhaps because the phrase has no literal equivalent in XI. 1–26 (the hunter, who could be interpreted as the Devil in the allegory, is not destroyed: he is not even mentioned after XI. 14). XI. 33–6 is not translated in the ME *Physiologus*: the ME poet may have noticed that *odor* (XI. 33), referring to the sweetness of the Elephant's breath (mentioned in *De bestiis et aliis rebus*, ch. XXV) is not used in the Latin *natura*.

The chapter on the Turtle Dove is only loosely based on Theobald. Although there are no substantial differences between the ME

Physiologus and Theobald's *Physiologus* here, a number of lines in the ME have no equivalent in the Latin: lines 513, 516, and, in the *significacio*, 523, 531–2 (the references to heaven and hell are not in Theobald). A curious, but minor, difference appears at 517, *Be hire make ʒe sit o niʒt, o dai ʒe goð & fleʒeð*, where the Latin has *Nocte dieque juncta manebit, / Absque marito nemo videbit* (XII. 2ᵇ–3ᵃ): the translator seems to have misread his source here.

The section on the Panther is closer to the original again, thirty ME lines in four-beat couplets translating twenty-three Latin hexameters. Stopgaps to make up rhymes are frequent: 552, 558, 564. The ME *natura* does not differ greatly from the Latin source: however, the description of the Panther's spots as *Wit & trendled als a wel, / & itt bicumeð him swiðe wel* (537–8) and the dragons cowering in their *pit / Als so he weren of dede offriʒt* (561–2) are the translator's own. Departures from the original in the *significacio* includes *So euen-sterre ouer erðe fen* (566), which has no equivalent in the Latin; *quia quot vult, tot tibi sumit* (XIII. 15) is not translated; the sweet smell of the Panther's breath is not allegorized in the source, but it is explained as the Gospel in the ME *Physiologus* (577–8); the emphasis on obeying God's precepts in order to defend ourselves against the Devil's onslaughts (581–4) is not in Theobald (XIII. 20–3).

Theobald ends with a modest *subscriptio*, *Carmine finito sit laus et gloria Christo / Cui, si non alii, placeant hec metra Tebaldi*, which is not in all the manuscripts. It is not in the ME *Physiologus* either: the ME poet does not have a formal conclusion and adds a chapter on the Dove, which is taken from Alexander Neckam's *De naturis rerum*, I. LVI. The ME poet gives *seuene costes* (587); Neckam lists eight, but not all the *naturae* given in the ME are in Neckam. In Neckam each characteristic is immediately followed by its moralization, and this pattern is copied by the ME poet.[1] He does not preserve the order of his original. The translator's first *natura*, *ʒe ne haueð in hire non galle* (589) is Neckam's third, *Felle carere dicitur*. His moralization is slightly different: *sic et amaritudinis fraterni odii ignara est ecclesiae caritas*. The ME poet's second and fourth characteristics are not in Neckam; since they cannot, as far as I have been able to ascertain, be traced to any other

---

[1] In Hall's opinion (p. 624), *De bestiis et aliis rebus* is closer to the ME *Physiologus* than Alexander Neckam. This is not so, because *De bestiis et aliis rebus*, I. 11 (*PL* 177, col. 142), merely lists a large number of qualities (sixteen, *pace* Hall) without moralizations; there are no close verbal correspondences with the ME *Physiologus*. As in Neckam, a characteristic in this section of the poem is followed immediately by its allegorical explanation.

source, they are probably his own. The third feature is based on Neckam's second, *Non vescitur cadavere, sed purissimum granum eligit.* The ME poet's fifth is Neckam's first, *Columba siquidem gemitum habet pro cantu*, but the allegorization is different: *sanctae ecclesiae vel etiam cujuscunque fidelis animae typum gerens.* The sixth *natura* is Neckam's fifth, *Super aquarum fluenta residet, ut accipitris effugiat insidias.* Neckam's moralization, *Sic et fidelis anima Sacra Scriptura quasi speculo utitur, ut tuta sit a circuitu hostis antiqui*, clarifies the otherwise cryptic ME *significacio*, *& we in boke wið deueles nome* (600).[1] The final ME *natura* and *significacio* are based on Neckam's seventh,

Sicut etiam columba in foraminibus petrae secure latitat sic et anima piis meditationibus vacans in vulneribus Jesu Christi meditatur et quiescit,

the main clause failing to achieve the dignified simplicity of

In Cristes milce ure hope is best (602).

Even bearing in mind that a verse translation can never be accurate, the ME poet did not set out to produce a slavish rendering of his source. He consults other sources but rarely and bases his *Physiologus* primarily on Theobald's *Physiologus*, but he did not set out to produce a line-by-line translation of his source. Sometimes the ME poet's verse is livelier, as in the *naturae* of the Whale and the Elephant, sometimes duller, when, lacking the restraining influence of Theobald's strict Latin metre, he pads and uses tags to make up rhymes. He is at his most interesting when he approaches Theobald intelligently, departing from Theobald's allegorical explanations and exercising his own judgement when he tidies up inconsistencies in his source, as he does in the *significaciones* of the Eagle and the Elephant. Some sections, such as those on the Spider and the Siren, are based only remotely on Theobald. Often the poet improved on his source, and the result is that the ME *Physiologus* is not altogether without charm; an unfortunate effect of the many changes the translator has made is that it is not possible to trace the particular manuscript—should it survive—or family of manuscripts which the ME poet used for his version of Theobald's *Physiologus*.

[1] See the Commentary ad loc.

6. EDITORIAL PROCEDURE

Since the *Physiologus* survives in a single manuscript which is at several removes from the author's copy, an edition must be a conservative one, the editor's aim being to reproduce the manuscript text as faithfully as possible rather than to attempt to restore the author's original. For this reason emendations have been made only where the manuscript is obviously in error.

The text has been transcribed from the manuscript, British Library MS Arundel 292. The spelling is that of the manuscript, except that *p* is transcribed as *w*. Abbreviations, but not the tironian note (which is here reproduced as '&'), have been silently expanded.

In the manuscript the poem is written out as prose, individual lines or, in the case of alliterative long lines and septenaries, half-lines being separated by a *punctus*. This is the sole mark of punctuation in the manuscript. It has not been reproduced here: punctuation is editorial in order to render the poem more accessible to the modern reader. The *litterae notabiliores*, which in the manuscript serve to indicate major divisions, have been preserved in the edited text. Word division and capitalization are editorial.

Letters that are not in the manuscript are enclosed in square brackets; where a word has been emended the reading of the manuscript is given in the footnotes. Whenever this involves no more than the omission of a letter or letters found in the manuscript an asterisk precedes the word. Letters written on an erasure are enclosed in round brackets; whenever possible, the letters which the scribe first wrote are given in the footnotes. To this end the manuscript has been examined under ultraviolet light. Letters added in the margin or above the line are enclosed in ` ´. The apparatus further records the position of the headings on the manuscript page, the place of scribal additions (in the margin or above the line) and valuable emendations proposed by earlier editors. When I have accepted previous editors' emendations, I have acknowledged this in the apparatus. The following *sigla* are used for earlier editions cited, whether of the whole poem or of parts of it (for full references see the Bibliography):

BS	Bennett & Smithers	M	Mätzner
DW	Dickins & Wilson	Mo¹	Morris, *Miscellany*
E	Emerson	Mo²	Morris, *Specimens*
H	Hall	WH	Wright & Halliwell.

BIBLIOGRAPHY

MANUSCRIPT

British Library MS Arundel 292, ff. 4ʳ–10ᵛ

EDITIONS OF THE ENTIRE TEXT OR MAJOR PARTS OF IT

Altdeutsche Blätter, ed. T. Wright (Leipzig, 1836–40), II. 99–120 (not consulted for textual purposes).

Altenglische Sprachproben, ed. E. Mätzner (Berlin, 1867), I. 55–75.

Early Middle English Texts, ed. Bruce Dickins and R. M. Wilson (London, 1951), pp. 58–61.

Early Middle English Verse and Prose, ed. J. A. W. Bennett and G. V. Smithers, 2nd edn. (Oxford, 1968), pp. 165–73.

A Middle English Reader, ed. O. F. Emerson, 2nd edn. (New York and London, 1915), pp. 14–20.

An Old English Miscellany, ed. R. Morris (EETS, os 49, London, 1872), pp. 1–25.

Reliquiae Antiquae, ed. T. Wright and J. O. Halliwell (London, 1841), II. 208–27.

Selections from Early Middle English, ed. Joseph Hall (Oxford, 1920), pp. 176–96.

Specimens of Early English, ed. R. Morris, 2nd edn. (Oxford, 1887), pp. 133–40.

ON THE MIDDLE ENGLISH *PHYSIOLOGUS*

A. J. Bliss, 'Three Middle English Studies', *EGS*, ii (1948–9), 40–54.

Cyril Brett, 'Notes on Old and Middle English', *MLR*, xxii (1927), 217–64.

Norman Davis, 'Notes on the Middle English *Bestiary*', *MÆ*, xix (1950), 56–9.

J. P. Gumbert and P. M. Vermeer, 'An Unusual Yogh in the *Bestiary* Manuscript—A Palaeographical Note', *MÆ*, xl (1971), 56–7.

Einer S:son Hallbeck, 'The Language of the Middle English Bestiary' (D. Phil. thesis, Lund, Christianstad, 1905).

H. C. Matthes, '*Bestiary* 345 f.', *Anglia*, lxxiv (1956), 445–8.

G. V. Smithers, 'A Middle English Idiom and its Antecedents', *EGS*, i (1947–8), 101–13.

—— 'Ten Cruces in Middle English Texts', *EGS*, iii (1949–50), 65–81.

BEASTS, BESTIARIES, AND THE *PHYSIOLOGUS*

Aristotle, *Historia animalium*, ed. and tr. A. L. Peck, 3 vols. (London and Cambridge, Mass., 1965–).

Le Bestiaire de Philippe de Thaün, ed. Emmanuel Walberg (Lund and Paris, 1900).

The Bestiary, ed. M. R. James (Roxburgh Club clxxvi, Oxford, 1928).

Francesco Cordasco, 'The Old English *Physiologus*: its Problems', *MLQ*, x (1949), 351–5.

C. C. Coulter, 'The Great Fish in Ancient and Medieval Story', *Transactions and Publications of the American Philological Association*, lvii (1926), 32–50.

Grover Cronin, Jr., 'The Bestiary and the Mediaeval Mind—Some Complexities', *MLQ*, ii (1941), 191–8.

De bestiis et aliis rebus, *PL* 177.

F. N. M. Diekstra, 'The *Physiologus*, the Bestiaries and Medieval Animal Lore', *Neophilologus*, lxix (1985), 142–55.

Lothar Frank, 'Die Physiologus-Literatur des englischen Mittelalters und die Tradition' (D. Phil. thesis, Tübingen, 1971).

G. Heider, 'Physiologus nach einer Handschrift des XI. Jahrhunderts', *Archiv für Kunde Österreichischer Geschichts-Quellen*, v (1850), 541–82.

Arnold Clayton Henderson, 'Medieval Beasts and Modern Cages: The Making of Meaning in Fables and Bestiaries', *PMLA*, xcvii (1982), 40–9.

Nikolaus Henkel, *Studien zum Physiologus im Mittelalter* (Tübingen, 1976).

Isidore of Seville, *Etymologiarum sive originum libri XX*, ed. W. M. Lindsay, 2 vols (Oxford, 1911).

M. R. James, 'The Bestiary', *History*, NS xvi (1931), 1–11.

Francis Klingender, *Animals in Art and Thought to the End of the Middle Ages* (London, 1971).

Alexander H. Krappe, 'The Historical Background of Philippe de Thaun's *Bestiaire*', *MLN*, lix (1944), 325–7.

Friedrich Lauchert, *Geschichte des Physiologus* (Strassburg, 1889).

Liber monstrorum, ed. Franco Porsia (Bari, 1976).

Frances McCulloch, *Medieval Latin and French Bestiaries* (Chapel Hill, 1960).

John Morson, 'The English Cistercians and the Bestiary', *Bulletin of the John Rylands Library*, xxxix (1956), 146–70.

Alexander Neckam, *De naturis rerum libri duo*, ed. Thomas Wright (Rolls Series 34, London, 1863).

The Old English Elene, Phoenix and Physiologus, ed. A. S. Cook (New Haven, 1919).

The Old English Physiologus, ed. Ann Squires (Durham Medieval Texts v, Durham, 1988).

Giovanni Orlandi, 'La tradizione del Physiologus e i prodomi del bestiario latino', *Settimane di studio del Centro italiano di studi sull'alto medioevo*, xxxi (1985), 1057–106.

B. E. Perry, 'Physiologus', *Paulys Real-Encyclopädie der classischer Altertumswissenschaft*, Halbband 39, cols 1074–129.

Physiologi graeci variarum aetatum recensiones codicibus fere omnibus tunc primum excussis collatisque in lucem protulit Franciscus Sbordone (Milan, 1936).

Physiologus latinus: Editions préliminaires versio B, ed. F. J. Carmody (Paris, 1939).

Physiologus latinus versio Y ed. F. J. Carmody (University of California Publications in Classical Philology xii, Los Angeles 1933–44), 95–134.

C. Plini Secundi Naturalis historiae libri XXXVII, ed. C. Mayhoff, 5 vols (Leipzig, 1892–1909).

P. Ansell Robin, *Animal Lore in English Literature* (London, 1932).

Francesco Sbordone, 'La Tradizione manoscritta del *Physiologus* latino', *Athenaeum*, NS xxvii (1949), 246–80.

C. Iulii Solini Collectanea rerum memorabilium, ed. Th. Mommsen (Berlin, 1905).

Theobaldi 'Physiologus', ed. P. T. Eden (Mittellateinische Texte und Studien vi, Leyden and Cologne, 1972).

A Thirteenth Century Bestiary in the Library of Alnwick Castle, ed. Eric George Millar (Roxburghe Club ccvii, Oxford, 1958).

Lynn Thorndike, *A History of Magic and Experimental Science During the First Thirteen Centuries of our Era*, 2 vols (London, 1923).

Edward Topsell, *The Historie of Four-Footed Beasts and Serpents*, 2 vols (London, 1607).

Kenneth Varty, *Reynard the Fox: A Study of the Fox in Medieval Art* (Leicester, 1967).

Max Wellmann, 'Der Physiologos: eine religionsgeschichtlich-naturwissenschaftliche Untersuchung', *Philologus*, Supplementband xxii (1931), 1–116.

Beatrice White, 'Medieval Animal Lore', *Anglia*, lxxii (1954), 21–30.

W. B. Yapp, 'A New Look at English Bestiaries', *MÆ*, liv (1985), 1–19.

Note: At the time of going to press, Wilma George and W. B. Yapp, *Natural History in the Medieval Bestiary* (London, expected publication date 1989) and a *Beasts and Birds of the Middle Ages: The Bestiary and its Legacy*, ed. W. B. Clark and M. T. McMunn (Philadelphia, 1989) had not yet appeared.

THE *PHYSIOLOGUS*

Ð e leun stant on hille; & he man hunten here
Oðer ður3 his nese smel smake ðat he ne33e,
Bi wilc weie so he wile to dele niðer wenden,
Alle hise fet steppes after him he filleð,
Dra3eð dust wið his stert ðer he [dun] steppeð, 5
Oðer dust oðer deu ðat he ne cunne is finden;
Driueð dun to his den, ðar he him ber3en wille.

*ij*ᵃ

An oðer kinde he haueð: wanne he is ikindled,
Stille lið ðe leun, ne stireð he nout of slepe
Til ðe sunne haueð sinen ðries him abuten; 10
Ðanne reiseð his fader him mit te rem ðat he makeð.

*iij*ᵃ

Ðe ðridde la3e haueð ðe leun: ðanne he lieð to slepen,
Sal he neure luken ðe lides of hise e3en.

Significacio prime nature

W elle he3 is tat hil, ðat is heuenriche;
Vre Louerd is te leun, ðe liueð ðerabuuen. 15
Wu! Ðo him likede to li3ten her on erðe,
Mi3te neure diuel witen, ðo3 he be derne hunte,
Hu he dun come, ne wu he dennede him in ðat defte meiden,
Marie bi name, ðe him bar to manne frame.

`*ij*ᵃ *et ij*ᵃ´

Ðo ure Dri3ten ded was & doluen, also his wille was, 20
In a ston stille he lai til it kam ðe [ð]ridde dai.
His fader him filstnede swo ðat he ros fro dede ðo
Vs to lif holden.
Wakeð, so his wille is, so hirde for his folde.

*Natura leonis i*ᵃ] *in body of text, end of first line after* hunten   5 dun] *so Mo*², *E, H*
*ij*ᵃ] *in body of text, end of line, after* ber3en wille   *iij*ᵃ] *in body of text, end of line, after*
makeð   *significacio*] *in body of text, end of line, after* e3en   *prime nature*] *in body of
text, end of line, after* Vre   *ij*ᵃ *et ij*ᵃ] *in outer margin*   21 ðridde] *so WH, M, Mo*²,
E; MS dridde

He is hirde, we ben sep, silden he us wille,   25
If we heren to his word ðat we ne gon nowor wille.

Natura aquile

K iðen I wille ðe ernes kinde,
 Also Ic it o boke rede:
Wu he neweð his ȝuðhede,
Hu he cumeð ut of elde   30
Siðen hise limes arn unwelde,
Siðen his bec is alto wrong,
Siðen his | fliȝt is al unstrong,   f. 4ᵛ
& his eȝen dimme.
Hereð wu he neweð him: 35
A welle he sekeð ðat springeð ai,
Boðe bi niȝt & bi dai;
Ðerouer he fleȝeð & up he teð
Til ðat he ðe heuene seð,
Ðurȝ skies sexe & seuene,   40
Til he cumeð to heuene.
So riȝt so he cunne
He houeð in ðe sunne.
Ðe sunne swi[ð]eð al his fliȝt
& oc it makeð his eȝen briȝt;   45
Hise feðres fallen for ðe hete
& he dun mide to ðe wete
Falleð in ðat welle grund,
Ðer he wur[ð]eð heil & sund
& cumeð ut al newe,   50
Ne were his bec untrewe.
His bec is ȝet biforn wrong,
Ðoȝ hise limes senden strong.
Ne maiȝ he tilen him non fode
Himself to none gode.   55
Ðanne goð he to a ston
& he billeð ðeron;
Billeð til his bec biforn
Haueð ðe wrengðe forloren.

Natura aquile] *in body of text, at end of line, after* **nowor wille**   44 swiðeð] *so E; MS*
swideð   49 wurðeð] *so E; MS* wurdeð

Siðen wið his riȝte bile 60
Takeð mete ðat he wile.

Significacio

Al is man, so is tis ern—
 Wulde ȝe nu *listen—
Old in hise sinnes dern
Or he bicumeð Cristen. 65
& tus he neweð h(im, ðis man,
Ðanne he) nimeð to kirke;
Or he it biðenken can,
Hise eȝen weren mirke.
Forsaket ðore Satanas 70
& ilk sinful dede;
(Takeð him to Iesu Crist,
For he) sal ben his mede.
Leueð on ure Loue[r]d Crist
& lereð prestes lore. 75
Of hise eȝen wereð ðe mist,
Wiles he dreccheð ðore.
H(is hope is al to Gode ward
& of his luue) he lereð,
Ðat is te sunne sikerlike: 80
Ðus his siȝte he beteð.
Naked falleð in ðe funt-fat
& cumeð ut al newe,
Buten a litel—wat is tat?
His muð is ȝet untrewe. 85
His muð is ȝet wel unkuð
Wið pater noster and crede.
Fare he norð er fare he suð,
Leren he sal his nede:
Bidden bone to Gode 90
& tus his muð riȝten,
Tilen him so ðe sowles fode
(Ðurȝ grace off ure Driȝtin. f. 5ʳ

Significacio] in body of text, end of line, after listlen   63 listen] *so* M, Mo¹, Mo², E, H,
BS; MS listlen   66 him] *corrected out of* hu   74 Louerd] *so* WH, M, Mo¹, Mo²,
E, BS; MS loued   78 His] i *corrected out of* a   79 lereð] E le[t]eð

Natura serpentis j^a

An wirm is o werlde, wel man it knoweð:
Neddre is te name; ðus he him neweð:　　　　　　95
Ðanne he is forbroken & forbroiden & in his elde al forwurden,
Fasteð til his fel him slakeð, ten daies fulle,
Ðat he is lene & mainles & iuele mai gangen.
He crepeð cripelande forð; his craft he ðus kiðeð:
Sekeð a ston ðat a ðirl is on,　　　　　　　　　100
Narwe buten he nedeð him, nimeð vnneðes ðurȝ,
For his fel he ðer leteð, his fles forð crepeð.
Walkeð to ðe water ward, wile ðanne drinken,
Oc he speweð or al ðe uenim
Ðat in his brest is bred fro his birde-time.　　　105
Drinkeð siðen inoȝ & tus he him neweð.

`ij`^a´

Ðanne ðe neddre is of his hid naked & bare of his brest-atter,
If he naked man se, ne wile he him noȝt (n)eȝȝen,
Oc he fleð fro him, als he fro fir sulde.
If he cloðed man se, cof he waxeð,　　　　　　110
For up he riȝteð him, redi to deren;
To deren er to ded maken, if he it muȝe forðen.
Wat if ðe man war wurðe & weren him cunne,
Fiȝteð wið ðis wirm & f[a]reð on him fiȝtande?
Ðis neddre, siðen he nede sal,　　　　　　　　115
Makeð seld of his bodi & sildeð his heued:
Litel him is of hise limes, bute he lif holde.

[*Significacio*]

Knov, Cristene man, wat tu Crist hiȝtest
Atte kirke-dure, ðar ðu cristned were:
Ðu hiȝtes to leuen on him & hise laȝes luuien,　　120
To helden wit herte ðe bodes of holi k[i]rke.
If ðu hauest is broken, al ðu forbre[d]es
Forwur[ð]es & forȝelues eche lif to wolden.

Natura serpentis j^a] *in body of text, end of line, after* Driȝtin
broiden] *E* forbroken　　　forwurden] *E* forbroiden
114 fareð] *so Mo¹, E, H; MS* freð　　　*Significacio*] *so WH, H
Mo¹, H; MS* krke　　　122 forbredes] *MS* forbreðes
forwurdes

96 forbroken & for-
ij^a] *in outer margin*
121 kirke] *so WH,*
123 forwurðes] *so E; MS*

Elded art fro eche blis, so ðis wirm o werld is.
Newe ðe for[ð]i, so ðe neddre doð: it is te ned.   125
Feste ðe of stedefastnesse & ful of ðewes
& helpe ðe poure | men ðe gangen abuten.   f. 5ᵛ
Ne deme ðe noȝ[t] wur[ð]i ðat tu dure loken
Up to ðe heuene ward,
Oc walke wið ðe erðe, mildelike among men;   130
No mod ðu ne cune, mod ne mannes vncost,
Oc swic of sineȝinge
& bote bid tu ðe ai, boðe bi niȝt & bi dai,
Ðat tu milce mote hauen of ðine misdedes.
Ðis lif bitokneð ðe sti ðat te neddre gangeð bi   135
& [Cr]is[t] is ðe [ð]irl of ðe ston ðat tu salt ðurȝ gon.
Let ðin filðe fro ðe, so ðe wirm his fel doð;
Go ðu ðan to Godes hus ðe godspel to heren:
Ðat is soule drink, sinnes quenching.
Oc or sei ðu in scrifte to ðe prest sinnes tine,   140
Feȝ ðe ðus of ði brest-fil[ð]e & feste ðe forðward
Fast at tin herte ðat tu firmest hiȝtes:
Ðus art tu ȝing & newe; (forðward) be ðu trewe.
Nedeð ðe ðe deuel noȝt, for he ne mai ðe deren noȝt,
Oc he fleð fro ðe, so neddre fro [ð]e nakede.   145
On ðe cloðede ðe neddre is cof & te deuel cliuer on sinnes.
Ai ðe sinfule bisetten he wile
& wið al mankin he haueð nið & win.
Wat if he leue haue of ure Heuen-Louerd
For to deren us, so he ure eldere or dede?   150
Do we ðe bodi in ðe bale & berȝen ðe soule,
Ðat is ure heued ȝeue(lic: helde we it wurðlic.)

Natura formice

Ðe mire is maȝti: mikel ȝe swinkeð,
In sumer & in softe weder, so we `ofte´ sen hauen.
In ðe heruest hardilike gangeð   155
& renneð rapelike & resteð hire seldum
& fecheð hire fode ðer ȝe it mai finden.

125 forði] *so E; MS* fordi   128 noȝt] *so Mo¹, E, H; MS* noȝ   wurði] *so E; MS* wurdi   136 Crist] *so H; MS* tis   ðirl] *MS* dirl, *cross-bar of first letter erased*   141 Feȝ] *H reads* Seȝ   brest-filðe] *MS* brest-filde   145 ðe] *so E; MS* de   *Natura formice*] *in body of text, end of line, after* wurðlic   154 ofte] *in inner margin*

Gaddreð ilkines sed, boðen of wude & of wed,
Of corn & of gres, ðat ire to hauen es.
Haleð to hire ʼholeʼ ðat siðen hire helpeð: 160
Ðar ʒe wile ben winter | aʒen. f. 6ʳ
Caue ʒe haueð to crepen in, ðat winter hire ne derie,
Mete in hire hule *ðat ʒe muʒe biliuen.
Ðus ʒe tileð ðarwiles ʒe time haueð, so it her telleð.
Oc finde ʒe ðe wete, corn ðat hire qwemeð, 165
Al ʒe forleteð ðis oðer se[d] ðat Ic er seide.
Ne bit ʒe nowt ðe barlic beren abuten,
Oc suneð it & sakeð forð, so it same were.
ʒet is wunder of ðis wirm more ðanne man weneð:
Ðe corn ðat ʒe to caue bereð, al ʒet bit otwinne, 170
Ðat it ne forwurðe, ne waxe hire fro, er ʒe it eten wille.

Significacio

Ðe mire muneð us mete to tilen,
Long liuenoðe ðis little wile ðe we on ðis werld wunen,
For ðanne we of wenden, ðanne is ure winter.
We sulen hunger hauen & harde sures, buten we ben war here: 175
Do we forði, so doð ðis der, ðanne be we derue
On ðat dai ðat dom sal ben, ðat it ne us harde rewe.
Seke we ure liues fod, ðat we ben siker ð[o]re,
So ðis wirm in winter is ðan ʒe ne tileð nummore.
Ðe mire suneð ðe barlic ðanne ʒe fint te wete— 180
Ðe olde laʒe we oʒen to sunen, ðe newe we hauen moten.
(Ðe corn) ðat ʒe to caue bereð, all ʒe it bit otwinne—
Ðe laʒe us lereð to don god & forbedeð us sinne,
It be[t] us e[röl]iche bodes & bekne[ð] euelike,
It fet te licham & te gost, oc nowt o ʒeuelike. 185
Vre Louerd Crist it leue us ðat his laʒe us fede,
Nu & o Domesdei & tanne (we ha)uen nede.

159 ire] *Mo²*, *BS* hire   160 hole] *below the line*   163 ðat] *so BS; MS* ðat ðat
164 tileð] *followed by erased punctus*   166 sed] *MS* seð   178 ðore] *so H; MS*
ðere; *WH, M, Mo¹, Mo² read* dere; *Mo²* [ð]ere   184 bet] *so Mo¹, Mo², H, BS; MS* ben
eröliche] *so M, Mo¹, Mo², H, BS; MS* ebriche   bekneð] *so BS; MS* bekned
186 leue] *M, H, BS* lene   ðat] *followed at end of line by erased* his

Natura cervi

Đe hert haueð kindes two
& forbisnes oc (also):
Đus it is on boke set   190
Đat man clepeð 'Fisiologet'.

He draȝeð ðe neddre of [ð]e ston
Đurȝ his nese up onon,
Of ðe stoc er of ðe ston,
For it wile ðerunder gon   195
& sweleð it wel swiðe:
Đerof him brinneð siðen.
Of ðat attrie ðing
Wiðinnen he | haueð brenning.   f. 6ᵛ
He lepeð ðanne wið mikel list: 200
Of swet water he haueð ðrist.

He drinkeð water gredilike
Til he is ful wel sikerlike:
Ne haueð ðat uenim non miȝt
To deren him siðen non wiȝt.   205
Oc he werpeð (er) hise hornes
In wude er in ðornes
& ȝingi[ð] him ðus, ðis wilde der,
So ȝe hauen nu lered her.

Significacio prima

Alle we atter draȝen off ure eldere,   210
Đe broken Driȝtinnes word ðurȝ ðe neddre.
Đerðurȝ haueð mankin
Boðen nið & win,
[G]ols(i)pe & ȝiscing,
Ȝiuernesse & wissing,   215
Pride & ouerwene,
Swilc atter imene.
Ofte we brennen in mod
& wurðen so we weren wod;
Đanne we ðus brennen,   220
Bihoueð us to rennen

Natura cervi] *in body of text, end of line, after* also   192 ðe] MS de
208 ȝingið] MS ȝingid   Significacio prima] *in body of text, end of line, after* her
213 win] *followed by erased letter*   214 golsipe] *so* Mo¹, H; MS kolsipe
216 euerilc] *so* Mo¹, Mo², H

To Cristes quike welle,
Ðat we ne gon to helle;
Drinken his wissing:
It quenchet ilc siniȝing; 225
Forwerpen pride eueril[c] del,
So hert doð hise hornes;
Ȝin[g]en us tus to Gode ward
& ȝemen us siðen forðwar[d].

`Natura ijᵃ´

Ðe hertes hauen anoðer kinde 230
Ðat us oȝ alle to ben minde:
Alle he arn off one mode,
For, if he fer fecchen fode
& he ouer water ten,
Wile non at nede oðer flen, 235
Oc on swimmeð biforn
& alle ðe oðre foleȝen.
Weðer so he swimmeð er he wadeð,
Is non at nede ðat oðer lateð
Oc leiȝeð his [ch]in-bon 240
On oðres lendbon.
Ȝef him ðat biforn teð bilimpes for to tirȝen,
Alle ðe oðre cumen mide & helpen him for to herien,
Beren him of ðat water-grund
Up to ðe lond al heil & sund 245
& forðen here nede.
Ðis wune he hauen hem bitwen
Ðoȝ he an hundred togiddre ben.

`Significario ijᵃ´

Ðe hertes costes we oȝen to munen:
Ne oȝ ur non oðer to (sunen) 250
Oc eurilc luuen oðer,
Also he were his bro[ð]er;
Wurðen stedefast his | wine, f. 7ʳ
Liȝten him of his birdene;

---

228 ȝingen] *MS* ȝinȝen   229 forðward] *MS* forðwarð   *Natura ijᵃ*] *in inner margin*   240 chin-bon] *MS* skinbon   243 herien] *M* her[t]en; *Moʹ* her[t]ien   *Significacio ijᵃ*] *in outer margin*   252 broðer] *MS* broder

Helpen him at his nede; 255
God ʒiueð ðerfore mede:
We sulen hauen heuenriche
ʒef we *betwixen us ben briche.
Ðus is ure Louerdes laʒe luuelike to fillen;
Herof haue we mikel ned, ðat we ðarwið ne dillen. 260

Natura wulpis

A wilde der is ðat is ful of fele wiles:
Fox is hire to name for hire qweðsipe.
Husebondes hire haten for hire harm-dedes:
(Ðe coc) & te capun ʒe feccheð ofte in ðe tun,
& te gandre & te gos, bi ðe necke & bi ðe nos. 265
(Haleð is to) hire hole: forði man hire hatieð,
Hatien & hulen boðe men & fules.
Listneð nu a wunder ðat tis der doð for hunger:
Goð o felde to a furʒ & falleð ðarinne,
In eried lond er in (erð)-chine, for to bilirten fuʒeles. 270
Ne stereð ʒe noʒt of ðe stede a god stund deies
Oc dareð, so ʒe ded were, ne draʒeð ʒe non onde.
Ðe rauen is swiðe redi, weneð ðat ʒe rotieð,
& oðre fules hire fallen bi for to winnen fode.
(Derflike) wiðuten dred he wenen ðat ʒe ded beð. 275
He wullen on ðis (foxes) fel & ʒe it wel feleð:
Liʒtlike ʒe lepeð up & letteð hem sone,
ʒelt hem here billing raðe wið illing,
Tetoggeð & tetireð hem mid hire teð sarpe;
Fret hire fille & goð ðan ðer ʒe wille. 280

Significacio

T wifold forbisne in ðis der
To frame we muʒen finden her:
Warsipe & wisedom
Wið deuel & wið iuel man.
Ðe deuel dereð dernelike: 285
He lat he ne wile us noʒt biswike,
He lat he ne wile us [d]on non loð

---

258 betwixen] *MS* ben twixen; *M, Mo¹, H, BS* b[i]twixen   *Natura wulpis*] *in body*
of text, end of line, after dillen   267 hulen] *H, DW* huten   *Significacio*] *in red, in*
body of text, end of line, after wille   287 don] *so DW; MS* ðon

& bringeð us in a sinne & ter he us sloð.
He bit us don ure bukes wille,
Eten & drinken wið uns(k)il,   290
& in ure skemting
He doð raðe a foxing. |
He billeð one ðe foxes fel   f. 7ᵛ
Wo so telleð idel spel,
& he tireð on his ket   295
Wo so him wið sinne fet;
& deuel ȝeld swilk billing
Wið same & wið sending
& for his sinfule werk
Ledeð man to helle merk.   300

`Significacio´

Ðe deuel is tus ðe [fox] ilik,
Mið iuele breides & wið swik,
& m[e]n, also ðe foxes name,
Arn wurði to hauen same.
For wo `so´ seieð oðer god   305
& ðenkeð iuel on his mod
Fox he is & fend iwis—
Ðe boc ne leȝeð noȝt of ðis.
So was Herodes fox & flerd
Ðo Crist kam into ðis middel-erd: 310
He seide he wulde him leuen on
& ðoȝte he (wulde) him fordon.

Natura [*a*]*ranee*

Seftes sop ure Seppande, sene `is´ on werlde,
Leiðe & lo[dl]ike, ðus we it leuen,
Man`i´kines ðing, alle manne to wissing.   315
Ðe sp(innere) on hire [web] swi[ðe] ȝe (weveð),
Festeð atte hus-rof hire fo [ð]redes,
O rof er on ouese, so hire is on elde,

Significacio] *in outer margin, in red*   301 fox] *so Mo´, H, DW*   303 men] man;
DW man[i]   304 to hauen] *H, DW* hauen to   305 so] *in outer margin*
Natura aranee] *in body of text, end of line, after* fordon   aranee] *so Mo´, H; MS* iranee
314 lodlike] *so Mo´; MS* loldike   315 manikines] *first* i *above line*   316 web]
H [webbe]   swiðe] *MS* swid; *H* swid[e]   317 ðredes] *MS* dredes

Wer(peð) ðus hire web & weueð on hire wise.
Ðanne ȝe it haueð al idiȝt, ðeðen ȝe driueð,   320
Hitt hire in hire hole, oc ai ȝe it biholdeð
Til ðat ðer fleȝes faren & fallen ðerinne,
Wiðeren in ðat web & wilen ut wenden.
Ðanne renneð ȝe rapelike, for ȝe is ai redi:
Nimeð anon to ðe net & nimeð hem ðere.   325
Bitterlike ȝe hem bit & here bane wurðeð,
Drepeð & drinkeð here blod, doð ȝe hire non oðer god,
Bute fret hire fille & dareð siðen stille.

Signif(icacio)

Ðis wirm bitokneð ðe man ðat oðer b(i)`s´(wikeð),
On stede er on stalle, stille er lude,   330
In mot er in market, er oni oðer wise.
He h(i)m bit ðan he h(i)m bale selleð
& he drinkeð (his) blod wanne he h(i)m dreueð
& ðo fr`e´teð h[i]m al ðan he him iuel werkeð.

Natura cetegrandie

Cethegrande is a fis,   335
Ðe moste ðat (in water) is.
Ðat tu | wuldes seien ȝet   f. 8ʳ
Ȝef ðu it soȝe wan it flet,
Ðat it were a neilond
Ðat sete `one´ ðe se-sond.   340
Ðis fis ðat is vnride,
Ðanne him hungreð, he gapeð wide.
Vt of his ðrote it smit an onde,
Ðe swetteste ðing ðat is o londe.
Ðerfore oðre fisses to him draȝen.   345
Wan he it felen, he aren faȝen.
He cumen & houen in his muð;
Of his swike he arn uncuð.
Ðis cete ðanne hise chaueles lukeð,

319 weueð] ð *crossed in red*   Significacio] *in body of text, end of line, after* stille
332 him¹, him²] *both corrected out of* hem   333 him] *corrected out of* hem
334 freteð] *first* e *above line, in red, same hand*   him] *so M, H; MS* hem
Natura cetegrandie] *in body of text, end of line, after* werkeð   340 one] *substituted in outer
margin for letter erased from text following* sete; one *in margin preceded by erased* o
349 ðanne] ð *crossed in red*

Ðise fisses alle in sukeð.   350
Ðe smale he wile ðus biswiken;
Ðe grete mai[ȝ] he noȝt bigripen.
Ðis fis wuneð wið ðe se-grund
& liueð ðer eure heil & sund
Til it cumeð ðe time   355
Ðat storm stireð al ðe se,
Ðanne sumer & winter winnen:
Ne mai it wunen ðerinne,
So droui is te sees grund,
Ne mai he wunen ðer ðat stund   360
Oc stireð up & houeð stille
Wiles ða[t] weder is so ille.
Ðe sipes ðat arn on se fordr(iuen),
Loð hem is ded & lef to liuen;
Biloken hem & sen ðis fis: 365
A neilond he wenen it is.
Ðerof he aren swiðe faȝen
& mid he(re m)iȝt ðarto he draȝen.
Sipes on festen
& alle up gangen   370
Of ston mid stel in ðe tunder
[B]el to brennen one ðis wunder,
Warmen hem wel & heten & drinken.
Ðe fir he feleð & doð hem sinken,
For sone he (diueð dun to grunde: 375
He drepeð hem alle wiðuten wunde).

`*Significacio*´

Ðis deuel is mikel wið wil & maȝt,
So wicches hauen in here craft.
He doð men hungren & hauen ðrist
& mani oðer sinful list.   380
Tolleð men to him wið his onde:
(Wo so) him foleȝeð, he findeð sonde.
Ðo arn ðe little, in leue laȝe;
Ðe mikle ne maiȝ he to him draȝen—
Ðe mikle, I mene ðe stedefast,   385

352 maiȝ] *MS* maig   362 ðat] *so H; MS* ðar   372 bel] *MS* wel   *Sig-*
nificacio] *in outer margin*   383 Ðo] *followed in outer margin by erased* ðe

In riȝte leue mid fles & gast.
Wo so listneð deueles lore,
On lengðe it sal him rewen sore:
Wo so festeð hope on him,
He sal him folȝen to `helle dim´. | 390

Natura sirene f. 8ᵛ

I n ðe se senden selcuðes manie.
Ðe mereman is a meiden ilike:
On brest & on bodi oc (al ðus ȝe is bunden):
Fro ðe noule niðerward ne is ȝe (no man like)
Oc fis to ful iwis mið finnes waxen. 395
Ðis wunder wuneð in wankel stede ðer ðe water sinkeð.
Sipes ȝe sinkeð & scaðe ðus werkeð.
Mirie ȝe singeð, ðis mere, & haueð manie stefnes,
Manie & sille, oc it (ben wel ille.
Sipmen here) steringe forȝeten for hire stefninge, 400
Slumeren & slepen & to late waken:
Ðe sipes sinken mitte suk, ne cumen he nummor up.
Oc wise men & warre aȝen cunen chare,
Ofte arn atbrosten mid he[re] *best ouel.
He hauen told of ðis mere, ðat ðus uniemete, 405
Half man & half fis, sum ðing tokneð bi ðis.

`*Significacio*´

F ele men hauen ðe tokning
Of ðis forbisnede ðing:
Wiðuten weren [sepes] fel;
Wiðinnen arn he wulues al. 410
He speken godcundhede
& wikke is here dede.
Here dede is al vncuð
Wið ðat spekeð here muð.
Twifold arn on mode: 415
He sweren bi ðe rode,
Bi ðe sunne & bi ðe mone

& he ðe leȝen sone.
Mid here saȝe & mid here song
He ðe swiken ðerimong: 420
Ðin aȝte wið swiking,
Ði soule wið lesing.

Natura elephantis

Elpes arn in Inde riche,
 On bodi borlic, berȝes ili[ch]e.
He togaddre gon o wolde,   425
So sep ðat cumen ut of folde
& behinden he hem sampnen
Ðanne he sulen oðre strenen.
Oc he arn so kolde of kinde
Ðat no golsipe is hem minde   430
Til he noten of a gres,
Ðe name is mandragores.
Siðen he biȝeten on
& two ȝer he ðermide gon.
Ðoȝ he ðre hundred ȝer   435
On werlde more ˋwuneden her´, |
Biȝeten he neuermor non,   f. 9ʳ
So cold is hem siðen blod & bon.
Ðanne ȝe sal here kindles beren,
In water ȝe sal stonden,   440
In water to mid-side,
Ðat wanne hire harde tide
Ðat ȝe ne falle niðer noȝt—
Ðat is most in hire ðoȝt,
For he ne hauen no lið   445
Ðat he muȝen risen wið.
Hu he resteð him, ðis der,
Ðanne he walkeð wide,
Herkne wu it telleð her:
For he is al unride,   450
(A tre he sekeð) to ful iȝewis
Ðat is strong & stedefast is

Natura] *in body of text, end of line, after* lesing   *elephantis*] *in body of text, end of line, after*
berȝes   424 iliche] *MS* ilike   436 wuneden her] *in lower margin, below* on
werlde more, *preceded by paragraphus*

& leneð him trostl[i]ke ðerbi
Ðanne he is of walke weri.
Ðe hunte haueð biholden ðis,   455
Ðe him wille swiken,
Wor his beste wune is
To don hise willen.
Saʒeð ðis tre & underset
O ðe wise ðat he mai bet   460
& hileð it wel, ðat he it nes war
Ðanne he makeð ðerto char.
Himseluen sit, [a]lon bihalt
Weðer his gin him out *biwalt.
Ðanne cumeð ðis elp unride   465
& leneð him up on his side,
Slepeð bi ðe tre in ðe sadue
& fallen bo[ð]en so togaddre.
ʒef ðer is no man, ðanne he falleð,
He remeð & helpe calleð,   470
Remeð reufulike on his wise,
Hopeð he sal ðurʒ helpe `ri´sen.
Ðanne cumeð ðer on gang[en],
Hopeð he sal him don u[p] standen;
Fikeð & fondeð al his miʒt: 475
Ne mai he it forðen no wiʒt.
Ne canne ðan non oðer
`Oc´ (remeð) mid his broðer.
Manie & mikle cume ðer sa[ken],
Wenen him on stalle maken,   480
Oc for ðe helpe of hem alle
Ne mai he cumen so on stalle.
Ðanne remen he alle a rem
So hornes blast oðer belles drem.
For here mikle reming   485
Rennande cumeð a ʒungling:
Raðe to him luteð,

453 trostlike] *so* H; MS trostlke   457 beste] *immediately followed by erased* w
463 alon] MS olon   464 biwalt] *so* M, H; MS biwarlt   468 boðen] MS boden
472 risen] ri *substituted in inner margin for* si *in body of text*   473 gangen] MS
gangande   474 up] *so* H; MS ut   478 oc] *substituted in inner margin for* o *in body
of text*   479 saken] MS sacande, se *substituted in inner margin for* sa *(by different hand;*
cf. 472, 478?)

His snute him under puteð
& mitte helpe of hem alle
Ðis elp he reisen on stalle   490
& tus | atbreste[ð] ðis huntes breid   f. 9ᵛ
O ðe wise ðat Ic haue ʒu seid.

Significacio

Ðus fel Adam ður ʒ a tre,
Vre (fir)ste fader, ðat fele we.
Moyses wulde him reisen,   495
Miʒte it no wiʒt forðen.
After (him prophetes) alle,
Miʒte her[e] non him maken on stalle,
On stalle, I seie, ðer he er stod,
To hauen heuenriche god.   500
He suggeden & sorʒeden & weren in ðoʒt
Wu he miʒten him helpen o[ʒ]t.
Ðo remeden he alle o[re] steuene,
Alle heʒe up to ðe heuene.
For here care & here calling   505
Hem cam to Crist, heuen-king.
He ðe is ai in heuene mikel
Wurð her man & tus was litel:
[Ð]rowing ðolede in ure manhede
& tus Adam `he´ underʒede,   510
Reisede him up & `al´ mankin,
Ðat was fallen to helle dim.

Natura turturis

In boke is ðe turtres lif writen o rime,
Wu laʒelike ʒe holdeð luue al hire lif-time:
Ʒef ʒe ones make haueð, fro him ne wile ʒe siðen—   515
Muneð, wimmen, hire lif, Ic it wile ʒu reden!
Bi hire make ʒe sit o niʒt, o dei ʒe goð & fleʒeð;
Wo so seit he sundren ovt, I seie ðat he leʒeð.
Oc if hire make were ded & ʒe widue wore,

491 atbresteð] MS atbrested   Significacio] in body of text, end of line, after fader
497 him] corrected out of prophetes (erased)   498 here] MS her   502 oʒt] MS
ovt   503 ore] MS onder   509 ðrowing] MS drowing   510 he] in inner
margin, written above imperfectly erased him (by different hand?)   511 al] in inner margin
Natura turturis] in body of text, end of line, after dim

Ðanne fleʒeð ʒe one & fareð, non oðer wile ʒe more,   520
Buten one goð & one sit & hire olde luue abit:
In herte haueð him niʒt & dai, so he were o liue ai.

Significacio

List ilk le[f]ful man herto & herof ofte reche:
Vre sowle atte kirke-dure ches hire Crist to meche.
He is ure soule spuse, luue we him wið miʒte   525
& wende we neure fro him ward, be dai ne be niʒte. ˎ
Ðoʒ he be fro ure siʒte faren, be we him alle trewe:
Non oðer louerd ne leue we, ne non | luue newe.   f. 10ʳ
Leue we ðat he liueð ai upon heuenriche
& ðeðen he sal cumen eft & ben us alle briche   530
For (to demen) alle men, oc nout o ʒeueli[ch]e:
Hise loðe men sulen to helle faren, hise leue to his riche.

Natura pantere

Panter is an wilde der,
Is non fairere on werlde her:
He is blac so bro of qual   535
Mið wite spottes sapen al,
Wit & trendled als a wel,
& `itt´ bicumeð him swiðe wel.
Wor so he wuneð, ðis panter,
He fedeð him al mid oðer der.   540
Of ðo ðe he wile he nimeð ðe cul
& fet him wel til he is ful.
In his hole siðen stille
Ðre daʒes he slepen wille;
Ðan after ðe ðridde dai   545
He riseð & remeð lude so he mai.
Ut of his ðrote cumeð a smel
Mið his rem forð oueral,
Ðat ouercumeð haliwei(e)
Wið swetnesse, Ic ʒu seie,   550
& al ðat eure smelleð swete,

Be it drie, be it wete,
For ðe swetnesse off his onde,
Wor so he walkeð o londe,
Wor so he walkeð er wor so he wuneð,   555
Ilk der ðe him hereð to him cumeð
& fole(ʒ)eð him upone ðe wold
For ðe swetnesse ðe Ic ʒu haue told.
Ðe dragunes one ne stiren no[ʒ]t
Wiles ðe panter remeð oʒt   560
Oc daren stille in here pit
Als so he weren of dede offriʒt.

Significacio

Crist is tokned ðurʒ ðis der,
Wos kinde we hauen told ʒu her;
For he is faier ouer alle men   565
So euen-sterre o`uer´ erðe fen.
Ful `wel´ he taunede his luue to man
Wan he ðurʒ `holi´ spel him wan
& longe he lai her in an hole—
Wel him [ð]at he it wulde ðolen.   570
Ðre daies slep he al onon
Ðanne he ded was in blod & bon.
Vp he ros & remede in wis
Of helle pine, of heuene blis
& steʒ to heuene vue[ma]st,   575
Ðer wuneð wið | Fader (& Holi Gast.   f. 10ᵛ
Am)onges men a swete [s]mel
He let her of his holi spel,
Worðurʒ we muʒen folʒen him
Into his godcundnesse fin;   580
& ðat wirm, ure wiðerwine,
Wor so of Godes word is dine,
Ne dar he stiren, ne no man deren
Ðerwile he laʒe & luue beren.

556 to him] *preceded in MS by struck out* to him   557 foleʒeð] o *corrected out of* n
559 noʒt] *MS* nout   Significacio] *in body of text, end of line, after* offriʒt
566 ouer] uer *in outer margin*   567 wel] *in outer margin*   holi] *in outer margin*
570 ðat] *MS* dat   575 uvemast] *MS* vuenest; *M, Mo', H* vue[m]est
577 smel] *so M, Mo', H; MS* mel

Natura columbe & significacio

Ð e culuer haueð costes gode: 585
Alle wes oȝen to hauen in mode.
Seuene costes in hire kinde:
Alle it oȝen to ben us minde.
Ȝe ne haueð in hire non galle—
Simple & softe be we alle.   590
Ȝe ne liueð noȝt bi laȝt—
Ilc robbinge do we of hac.
Ðe wirm ȝe leteð & liueð bi ðe sed—
Of Cristes lore we haue ned.
Wið oðre briddes ȝe doð as moder—   595
So oȝ ur (ilk) to don wið oðer.
Woning & groning is lic hire song—
Bimene we us: we hauen don wrong.
In water ȝe is wis of heuekes come—
& we in boke wið deules nome.   600
In hole of ston ȝe makeð hire nest—
In Cristes milce ure hope is best.

Natura columbe & significacio] *in body of text, end of line, after* beren   596 ilk] *preceded*
by erased letter; l *corrected out of* b

COMMENTARY

LION

1 The ME *Physiologus* omits the Prologue which appears in all surviving manuscripts of the Latin original: see above, Introduction, part 5, 'The Middle English *Physiologus* and its Sources' (pp. lxxix–xci), p. lxxx.

2 *nese smel*: 'sense of smell' (so Hall); this appears to be the only occurence of the phrase: see *MED* s.v. *nese* n., sense 1(b). *MED*'s nearest parallel, first noticed by Mätzner, is from *Ancrene Riwle* (Nero), 45/32, *Smel of neose is þe ueorðe of þe vif wittes.*

2 *smake*: 'perceive by scent': in early ME the verb is rare in transitive use, as Hall observes: the earliest examples *OED* gives s.v. *smack v.*[1] are both from *Ayenbite of Inwit*, *Huo þet hedde wel ytasted and ysmacked þe ilke zuetnesse þet god yefþ to his urendes* and *Huanne þe man onderuangþ þise yeofþe he . . . smackeþ and uelþ þe zuetnesse of god* (but note that in both instances the verb appears coupled with another verb).

5 *ðer he [dun] steppeð*: in the manuscript this half-line does not have the required number of beats (only one instead of two). Morris (*Specimens*), followed by Emerson and Hall, inserts *dun* with the object of restoring the alliteration as well as rectifying the metre. Also, *dun* improves the sense. However, the line could be taken to alliterate on *st* (*stert-steppeð*), in which case the missing beat could begin with any sound. If the possible alliteration on *st* is taken into account, insertion of *dun* would create 'double' alliteration, *ab/ab*, which is rare in this text: see above, Introduction, part 3, 'Versification' (pp. lii–lxviii), p. lx. Yet it seems best, on balance, to accept Morris's suggestion and not leave the line metrically deficient, since [*dun*] is not in fact against the metrical rules for the *Physiologus*.

6 *deu*: F. Holthausen, in a review of Morris's *Miscellany* (*Archiv*, lxxxviii (1892), 365–6), suggests emending *deu* to *fen*, arguing that *dust oðer [fen]*, which he translates 'trockene und [*sic*] feuchte Erde', gives better sense and that his emendation restores the rhyme with *den* (7). In fact, his suggestion is not a substantial improvement on the manuscript reading as far as sense is concerned, and, although internal rhyme is permitted in the alliterative sections (see above, Introduction, part 3, pp. lx–lxi), the first half-line of one line does not rhyme with the first half-line of the next.

6 *he*: i.e. the hunter.

7 The two half-lines are not linked by alliteration. This is common in the *Physiologus* and hence does not constitute a reason for emending the text: see above, Introduction, part 3, pp. lviii–lix.

10 Translates *dum sol se tertio gyrat* (I. 6).

10 Holthausen suggests *Til ðe sunne haueð ðries· sinen him abuten*, but this is wrong: lines in the alliterative sections can be linked by internal rhyme (*sinen*: *abuten*) or have no linking device at all: see above, Introduction, part 3, pp. lvii–lxi, esp. p. lx. Most of Holthausen's emendations are, in fact, based on ignorance of early ME prosody; the same goes for most of Hall's emendations *metri causa*.

11 *reiseð his fader him*: Hall transposes, *his fader him reiseð*, which is unnecessary: the adverb *ðanne* causes inversion of subject and verb, as in OE (cf. line 56).

16 *wu*: Hall suggests 'how (anticipating "hu", l. [18]) when it pleased him'. This is possible but gives a syntactically awkward sentence. Besides, the lines Hall quotes in support of his suggestion, lines 447–9, do not provide an exact parallel, because the sentence in lines 447–9 can be analysed neatly as a main clause (449) with an object clause (447–8) depending on it, while Hall's interpretation of *wu* would produce an impossibly awkward sentence. Also, exclamatory *wu* (cf. OE *hu* as an exclamation) gives better sense.

12–13 The third *natura* is ultimately based on Cant. 5. 2, *Ego dormio, sed cor meum vigilat*. The Latin prose *Physiologus*, ch. I, also quotes Gen. 49: 9, *Catulus leonis Iuda... quis suscitabit eum?* Christ is, of course, specifically identified with the Lion of the tribe of Juda in Apoc. 5: 5.

17 *ðoȝ... hunte*: this clause is ambiguous. Mätzner, in his edition, takes *hunte* as a noun, *be* as a verb, and *derne* as an adjective, translating *derne hunte* 'a crafty, subtle hunter'. I prefer to take *hunte* as a verb and *derne* as a noun, because it gives slightly better sense: so *MED* s.v. *derne*, adj., sense 6(b).

18 Hall assumes that there is a half-line missing after *Hu... come* and takes *ne ... meiden* as two half-lines. But there is no break in the sense, and there is no *punctus* dividing two half-lines in the manuscript at this point (although Hall does print one in his diplomatic edition): hence *Hu ... meiden* is one line, albeit a somewhat long one, alliterating on *d*. (On the punctuation of the manuscript, see above, Introduction, part 1, 'The Manuscript' (pp. ix–xv), p. xi.)

21 *[ð]ridde*: the only difference between *d* and *ð* in this hand is a cross-bar, and as a result the scribe frequently writes *d* for *ð* because he omits the cross-bar accidentally. Elsewhere the text has *ðridde*—21, 545—and *OED* s.v. *third* cites no examples of the spelling *dridde*. Other cases of *d* for *ð* are: *swideð* (44), *wurdeð* (49), *forwurdes* (123), *fordi* (125), *wurdi* (128), *brest-filde* (141), *de* (145, 192), *bekned* (184), *ȝingid* (208), *swid* (316: for *swi*[*ðe*]), *dredes* (317), *atbrested* (491), *drowing* (509), *dat* (570). The reverse occurs in *ðon* (287) and *seð* (166).

23 *Vs... holden*: Hall states that there is a half-line missing before this one, but the sense runs on normally from the previous line. His assertion that this supposed missing half-line should correspond to *mortis vindex* in the source

(I. 16) is impossible to substantiate since the poet is not translating literally here.

26 *ðat*: this is ambiguous: *ðat* can be taken either as a relative (the relative is usually *ðat* with inanimate antecedents: see above, Introduction, part 2, §II. D. 3, p. xxvi), or as a conjunction, 'so that'.

EAGLE

The section is based on Ps. 102: 5, *renovabitur ut aquilae iuventus tua.*

27 Holthausen, loc. cit., p. 367, suggests that a line such as line 231, *Ðat us oʒ alle to ben minde*, or line 588, *Alle it oʒen to ben us minde*, should be supplied to make up the rhyming couplet, but since there is no break in the sense this is unnecessary. The source has *Esse ferunt aquilam super omne volatile primam, / Que se sic renovat quando senecta gravat* (II. 1–2), which is of no help.

32 *Also wrong*: several previous editors, Wright and Halliwell, Morris (*Specimens* and *Miscellany*), Mätzner, and Emerson, print *al to-wrong*, but *alto wrong* is the way the words are divided in the manuscript, and *OED* does not record an adjective *towrong*. For *also* see *OED* s.v. *all*, adv., senses C. 14–15.

40 Bennett and Smithers, correcting Hall, are no doubt right when they point out that *skies* means 'clouds', translating *nubes* (II. 17), and that *sexe & seuene* is 'probably a mere tag'. They note that it is 'probably a variation on "cinque et six", the highest throw at dice, from which it derives the association of chance'. They compare *Troilus and Criseyde* IV. 622, *But manly sette the world on six and seuene*, 'the first instance of the phrase recorded in *O.E.D.*'.

51 Translate, 'If his beak were not crooked' (Hall).

56–61 In addition to this, Theobald has *vel mordens, ut solet, escam / Atterit obliquum* (II. 13–14: i.e. scraping its beak sideways against the food), which, as Eden points out, is incompatible with the Eagle's first solution to the problem of its twisted beak: see Eden's note and see above, Introduction, part 5, 'The Middle English *Physiologus* and its Sources', p. lxxxii.

63 *listen*: the manuscript form *listlen* is not recorded in *OED* or *MED* except as a scribal error: see *MED* s.v. *listenⁱ*. Besides, it makes a bad rhyme.

64 *dern*: *MED* s.v. *derne*, adj.³, sense 3, quotes lines 62 and 64–5 and states that *dern* means 'stealthy, insidious, crafty; dishonest, deceptive; immoral, evil', but as these lines refer to the unbaptized infant the meaning is rather 'innate (but not apparent)': so Norman Davis, glossary to Bennett and Smithers. *sinnes dern* translates *peccatis que sunt ab origine matris* (II. 15).

68 *can*: Norman Davis regards this as 'an early example of the northern auxiliary of past tense, possibly altered from *gan* in a late recension not much earlier than the date of the manuscript' ('Notes on the Middle English Bestiary', *MÆ*, xix (1950), 56–9, p. 57).

70, 72 *Satanas*: *Crist*: the absence of rhyme might suggest textual corruption, but these four lines make sense as they stand and the source does not indicate that anything has been lost. Hall proposes *ðore satanas forsakeð* and *to ihesu crist him self bitakeð*, but these conjectures are metrically impossible, because in the *significacio* of the Eagle the four-beat lines which do not end in a word in final *-e* have the fourth beat on the last syllable (with the exception of the irregular lines 86 and 90, on which see above, Introduction, part 3, p. lxv).

76 *wereð*: Bennett and Smithers note: '*O.E.D.*, following Morris, derives from OE *werian*, "to defend", and translates "From his eyes he keeps off the mist". But *Phys.* has: *Tunc caligo consumitur igne propinquo*. Thus we may translate "The mist wears off his eyes" or ?"the mist of his eyes fades away".' This is an attractive suggestion, but *OED* s.v. *wear*, v.¹, records nothing to support it.

78–81 These four lines lack rhyme, but since there is no break in the sense, it is unlikely that anything should have been lost. *lereð*: *beteð* is perhaps acceptable as an instance of assonance (see above, Introduction, part 3, p. lxiv); Hall rightly rejects Emerson's *le[t]eð* on the grounds that *leten of* requires an adverb of degree: see *MED* s.v. *leten*, sense 15.

80 *ðat*: i.e. God.

80 *sunne*: this is not in the source (see above, Introduction, part 5, p. lxxxiii), but it appears in the Latin prose *Physiologus*, *versiones a* and *b*: *a* has *et euolans in altitudinem solis iustitie, qui est Christus Ihesus* (ch. VIII), and *b* has *et sustuleris oculos cordis tui ad dominum, qui est sol iustitiae* (ch. VIII). The phrase goes back to Malachias 4. 2, *Et orietur vobis timentibus nomen meum Sol iustitiae, et sanitas in pennis eius*. The ME *Physiologus* seems closest to *b* here.

84. I take *litel* to be a noun 'little thing', and *wat* to be an interrogative, 'what' (so Mätzner and Morris), but Hall, followed by Bennett and Smithers, regards *litel* as an adjective, *wat* as a noun, and *tat* as a conjunction, translating 'but a small something (= a slight imperfection) is that his mouth is still crooked'. However, *what* is not recorded as a noun in ME (see *OED* s.v. *what* E. 1–3: all the examples are post 1650 and are marked 'substantival nonce-uses'). Also, lines are mostly end-stopped in the *Physiologus*. Accordingly, *buten* is a preposition meaning 'except'. (*Winner and Waster*, 225, *Liue upon littel-whattes*, appears to me to be another, earlier, example of 'substantive nonce-use'; it carries the alliteration. I think we can assume, with *OED*, that *what* is not normally used as a noun in ME.)

89 *nede*: 'what is lacking, what is necessary' (so Norman Davis, glossary to Bennett and Smithers) or, perhaps, 'wants, needs' (so *MED* s.v. *nede*, n.¹, sense 1(a)). *nede* does not appear to be an adverbial genitive: no construction analogous to *his thankes* (see *OED* s.v. *thank*, n., sense 2b) is recorded by *MED* (s.v. *nede*, n.¹) or *OED* (s.v. *need*, n.).

SERPENT

96 *forbroken...forwurden*: Emerson suggests *forbroken & in his elde al forwurden*, but the line is not hypermetrical: as it stands in the manuscript, it is a satisfactory line, alliterating on *f*, of the pattern *ax/xa*.

96 *forbroiden*: in OE the past participle *brogden*; the form -*broiden* is due to 'levelling of the palatal *g* of the pres. into the p.p.' and subsequent vocalization of palatal *g* (see *The Owl and the Nightingale*, ed. E. G. Stanley, note to lines 1381–4).

103–106 In the prose *Physiologus, versio a* (the Serpent is not in *versio b*), this is a separate characteristic, prefaced by *Secunda eius natura est*. As in Theobald, the Serpent's spitting out its venom before drinking water is independent of the sloughing off of its skin and is not part of its renewal: contrast the ME text, line 106. The venom is allegorized as *terrestres malasque concupiscentias* (*versio a*, ch. XIII), which need to be spat out before hearing God's word in church: Theobald followed *a* here (III. 33–6). In *De doctrina christiana*, II. 16, Augustine says that nature can help us understand Scripture: the Serpent's habit of protecting its head explains Matt. 10: 16, *Estote...prudentes sicut serpentes*; the Serpent's squeezing through a narrow hole to renew its youth is a demonstration of Matt. 7: 13–14, *Intrate per angustam portam...Quam angusta porta et arcta via est quae ducit ad vitam, et pauci sunt qui inveniunt eam.*

104 This line translates *vomit ante virus* (III. 10). It is excessively short, but there is no break in the sense and neither is there anything in the source to suggest that something has been lost.

107–117 Natura secunda: what appears as one *natura* here and in Theobald (III. 13–20, where the clothed man subsequently pursues the Serpent) is in fact two separate characteristics in the prose *Physiologus, versio a*: following *Tertia eius natura est*, we get the naked man and the clothed man—clothing standing for mortal sins, of which we must divest ourselves—and the *Physiologus* then continues *Quarta quoque natura serpentis: quando uenerit homo et uoluerit eum occidere* etc. (ch. XIII).

107 Hall assumes that *ðanne ðe neddre is of his hid naked* is one line and that *& bare of his brest-atter* is 'an abridged line', which he proposes to restore to *in bodi & in brest· bare of his atter*. Holthausen suggests *and fre and bare of his brest-atter* (loc. cit., p. 366), but both these changes are no more than speculation. The ME is only a loose paraphrase of the Latin here, so the source is of no help. Holthausen (p. 366) says that *ðanne...naked* is a complete line, but the first half-line would want a beat then, and the manuscript has no *punctus* after *is*. On balance, it seems best to take *ðanne...brest-atter* as one line, which lacks alliteration, the beats falling on *neddre, naked, bare,* and *brest*.

112 *to ded maken*: this phrase appears to occur only here: it is not listed in *MED* s.v. *deth* n., sense 3a(b), but would seem to be analogous to *don to deth* and *putten to deth*, which *MED* does list and glosses 'condemn or put (sb.) to death, kill'. Hall suggests omitting *to*, but the phrase *ded maken* is not recorded before 1400 (see *MED* s.v. *ded* adj., sense 2a(c)).

114 *f[a]reð*: the manuscript reading *freð* is nonsense. We can be reasonably sure that the scribe left out *a*. *fareð on*, 'attacks', makes perfect sense in the context: see *MED* s.v. *faren*, sense 4.

114 *fiȝteð, fiȝtande*: one of these may be the result of textual corruption, but since the poet elsewhere uses words derived from the same stem within a single line (e.g. line 116, *seld*, *seldeð*), there is insufficient ground for emendation.

115 Hall suggests that *he seð ðat* was lost after *siðen*, but *nede* is unlikely to be an infinitive, as the normal infinitive ending in this text is -(*e*)*n*, not -*e* (see above, Introduction, part 2, 'Language', §II. E. 4 (p. xxix)). Holthausen takes *nede* to be a subjunctive and supplies *him weren* after *sal*; this is reasonable, though no more than a conjecture (*nerien him* would have the added merit of providing the alliteration, but *MED* s.v. *nerian* has only one example of its use, which is dated 1175). The least unsatisfactory solution, because it would not evolve conjectural emendation, is to take *nede* as an adverb ('This serpent, since he needs must, makes a shield' etc.) and accept this line as another short line, like line 104.

123 *forȝelues*: if the manuscript reading is correct, this is a *hapax legomenon*. Hall suggests *forwelkes*, which he translates 'dost wither', but *MED* lists only a past participle *forwelked* and the two occurrences given, from Lydgate and the *Romance of the Rose*, are considerably later than our text. A better solution might be *forwelwes* (*MED* compares OE *unforwealwod*, 'unwithered, unspoilt'). The earliest instance listed, s.v. *forwelwen*, is from *Ancrene Wisse*. It is quite possible that the manuscript reading is correct, however, and that the word is connected with OE *gealu*, -*o*, adj. *MED* and *OED* do not question the manuscript reading here.

123 *eche . . . wolden*: Hall translates 'so far as the attainment of eternal life is concerned': *wolden* means 'attain, win' (see *OED* s.v. *wield*, v., sense 2).

124 *elded*: from OA *eldan*, 'grow old'; Mätzner glosses 'grown old, shut out by old age'. Hall glosses 'severed by age' and adds that this is 'the writer's interpretation of silicernus' (Theobald, III. 22). Since the line makes sense, it seems best to accept it as it stands and not to adopt Holthausen's conjecture, *Newe ðe (it is te ned), / so ðe neddre doð, forði*, which is highly speculative and syntactically awkward.

125 This line does not scan. In the manuscript, *so ðe neddre doð* is preceded and followed by a *punctus*: presumably the purpose of the punctuation here is syntactic rather than metrical. Since the line makes sense, it seems best to accept it as it stands.

126 Comparing the source, *Sit cibus parcus, minuantur artus, / Unde non mandis, miseros juvabis* (III. 25–6), Hall suggests that *stedefastnesse* must be a mistake for a word denoting 'fasting', and that the second half of the line may have been a translation of *muniantur artes*, a misreading of Theobald's *minuantur artus* (it would have to be a 'misreading' on the part of the ME poet, for no such manuscript variant is recorded by Eden). Hall emends to *Feste þe* [*sic*] *of fastenes· & filste þe* [*sic*] *of þewes* [*sic*], 'that is fortify thyself by fastings and help thyself by virtues'. All this is ingenious, but too speculative to be acceptable.

129 This line has only two beats, but as the sense runs on naturally to the next line it is best not to attempt to supply a second half-line: cf. line 132.

132. Another two-beat line: see note to line 129, above.

135 The prose *Physiologus*, *versio a*, quotes Matt. 7: 14, *Angusta enim est porta, et cum tribulatione uia, que ducit ad uitam, et pauci sunt qui intreunt per eam* (ch. XIII): cf. *narwe* in the *natura* (101).

135 *Đis lif*: direct object of *bitokneð* (so Hall): lines 135–6 translate *Signat hunc callem lapidis foramen* (III. 29).

136 [*Cr*]*is*[*t*]: the manuscript reading *tis* is impossible, for what would *tis* refer to? Since the source has *Signat et petram Christus* (III. 30), Hall's conjecture [*Cr*]*is*[*t*] should be adopted.

141. *ðe*²: probably an article and not a reflexive pronoun: *MED* lists no examples of reflexive use s.v. *fasten*, v. (1), sense 8.

141. *forðward*: Hall emends to *foreward*, but this is unnecessary: see *MED* s.v. *forth-ward*, n.

142 *fast*: adverb, 'firmly', rather than verb. The verb which *MED* lists as *fasten*, v. (1), appears in its Old Norse form, with *e* in its stem, in this text: see the Glossary s.v. *festeð*.

142 *firmest*: Hall rightly takes this word to mean 'first of all, at the very beginning' (cf. *MED* s.v. *firmest*, adv., sense 1): the reference is to the renewal of baptismal vows (118–19). *MED*'s 'formerly' (it is listed as an example of sense 2) is less satisfactory.

144. *nedeð*: Mätzner suggests *neggeð* (i.e. *neȝȝeð*), but *nedeð*, 'troubles, oppresses', makes perfect sense: see *MED* s.v. *neden*, v. (1), sense 1(c).

144. *noȝt*²: Hall omits the second *noȝt*, but there are no reasons, syntactic or metrical, for doing so: in fact, an emphatic negative, *ne . . . noȝt*, is better in the context.

146 *cliuer*: this is the first occurrence of this word listed in *OED* s.v. *clever*. The next occurrence is dated 1580–95. *OED* quotes Sir Thomas Browne, who mentions *clever* as a word 'of no general reception in England, but of common use in Norfolk, or peculiar to the East Angle counties' (1682). Browne was not a native of Norfolk: he was born in London in 1605, but he moved to Norwich in 1637 and lived there until his death in 1682 (see the *Dictionary of National Biography*).

152 *helde*: Hall suggests *silde*, but *helde* makes good sense as an imperative plural, not, as Hall thought, a preterite subjunctive (cf. the infinitive *helden*, also with *e*, in line 121).

ANT

This section is based ultimately on Prov. 6: 6–8, *Vade ad formicam, o piger, et considera vias eius, et disce sapientiam. Quae, cum non habeat ducem nec praeceptorem nec principem, parat in aestate cibum sibi, et congregat in messe quod comedat.* Theobald and, following him, the ME *Physiologus*, omit the first *natura* given in the prose *Physiologus*, which is that the ants walk in a line, each one carrying grain in its mouth without being attacked by ants who are not carrying food: this is a mark of their wisdom, which we should imitate (*versio a*, ch. XIV, and *versio b*, ch. XI). Theobald has only *Quando suo solitum portat in ore cibum* (IV. 2), which as the preceding line, *Exemplum nobis prebat formica laboris*, makes clear is an example of the ant's toil, not its wisdom.

155 This is a short line, but since a *punctus* follows *heruest* and the initial letter of *hardilike* is rubricated a *caesura* is meant to come after *heruest* and *in* takes the first beat.

159 *ðat...es*: Bennett and Smithers take *hauen* to be a verb and translate 'that is to be had for her'. This seems forced; it is better to take *hauen* as a noun, 'property, possessions', from OE *hæfn* (see *MED* s.v. *haven*, n. (2)) and translate 'that she has as her property' or, following Hall, 'which constitutes her wealth'.

159 *ire*: Bennett and Smithers emend to [*h*]*ire*, but this is unnecessary: the form without *h*- is well attested (see *MED* s.v. *hir(e)*, pron. (2)). Latin *formica* is probably responsible for the feminine pronouns.

161 *ðar*: Bennett and Smithers take *ðar* as a conjunction, which is not impossible; however, as the syntax of the *Physiologus* is predominantly paratactic, it is perhaps better to interpret it as a demonstrative adverb. The sentence has no parallel in the source.

163 *ðat...biliuen*: *biliuen* is the way the word is written in the manuscript; Bennett and Smithers print *bi liuen*. Hall suggests that *biliuen* is the correct division and that the first *ðat* replaced *mide*. The first *ðat*, which precedes the *punctus*, is probably an error, but it is hard to see why it should have displaced *mide*: it is far more likely that the scribe repeated *ðat* by mistake and did not notice the first *ðat* when he put a *punctus* before the second *ðat*. If Hall thought that the first *ðat* was a mistake for *mide*, he probably did not take into account that *ðat* here could be a conjunction, meaning 'in order that' or 'so that': translate 'in order that she may remain alive'.

164 *her*: i.e. in Theobald.

165–8 The versions of the prose *Physiologus* (*versio a*, ch. XIV, and *versio b*, ch. XI) quote Job 31: 40 here, which in the *Vetus latina* has *Pro tritico prouidi mihi hordeum* (the Vulgate has *Pro frumento oriatur mihi tribulus, et pro hordeo spina*) and both versions observe that barley is fit only for cattle (*Hordea autem esca est pecorum*: *a*) or brute beasts (*Hordeum enim brutorum animalium cibus est*: *b*). In all likelihood it was from the *Physiologus* that the image found its way into mediaeval homilies: Beryl Smalley quotes from a sermon by Jacques de Vitry, who knew Theobald's *Physiologus* (he mentions it as a school text in one of his sermons: see Henkel, op. cit., p. 55, n. 137): there are two kinds of sermon; one is like barley, the other like wheat: 'Quid per frumentum nisi doctrina sive predicatio clericis proposita? Quid per ordeum nisi predicatio laicis proposita? Que quamvis grossior longe tamen fertilior et utilior quam predicatio clericis facta' (*The Study of the Bible in the Middle Ages*, 3rd edn., Oxford, 1983, p. 254, n. 2).

166 *se*[*d*]: the cross-bar was presumably added to the *d* accidentally, producing *ð*, perhaps through attraction to the following *ðat*. *ð* for *d* occurs also at 287, *ðon*. The reverse, *d* for *ð*, is far more common: see above, note to line 22.

167 *bit*: Mätzner's 'eats' does not fit the context. Hall, proposing OE *bidan*, translates, 'she cannot endure the carrying of barley about', but see rather G. V. Smithers, 'A Middle English Idiom and its Antecedents', *EGS*, i (1947–8), 101–13: Professor Smithers says that *bit* is from *bidden* (OE *biddan*) and means 'wishes to'. Bennett and Smithers translate 'she has no wish to go on carrying barley'. *MED* s.v. *biddan* does not list this sense, but Professor Smithers' suggestion is no doubt correct.

171 *hire fro*: Professor Davis (glossary Bennett and Smithers) translates 'so that she loses it'.

174 Suggested by *tempore judicii, quod similis est hiemi* (IV. 18).

175 Hall regards *We . . . sures* as a complete line and substitutes a missing half-line after *buten . . . here, er we henne wende*, but this is unnecessary. *we . . . sures* would be a short line, and it is possible to see the *punctus* after *hauen* as syntactic, not metrical (see Introduction, part 1, p. xi and p. xi n. 1), and take the whole of 175 as one line, though a long and hence not entirely satisfactory one.

176 *derue*: *MED* quotes lines 172 and 175–6 s.v. *derf*, sense 2, but the meanings it gives, 'strong, sturdy, powerful; great', are unsatisfactory. Professor Davis glosses 'confident', which fits the context better but is not given s.v. *djafr* in *An Icelandic-English Dictionary*, ed. Richard Cleasby and Gudbrand Vigfusson, 2nd edn. (Oxford, 1957), which gives 'strong'. 'Strong' or perhaps 'bold' would make satisfactory sense. Holthausen suggests *trewe* to rhyme with *rewe* in the next line; Hall suggests emending to *glewe*, 'wise, prudent'. However, it is not certain that all the septenaries in lines 176–87 of the *significacio* were meant to rhyme in pairs: see Introduction, part 3, p. lxvii above. The least unsatisfactory solution is to keep the manuscript reading and translate 'strong'.

178 *ure liues fod*: 'our provisions'; Hall's *here* for *ure* is unnecessary.

178 *ð[o]re*: the manuscript form *ðere* spoils the rhyme; *ð[o]re*, which is a possible minority form in this text (see the Glossary s.v. *ðer*, adv. demons.), restores it. *ðore* appears to be an East Midlands form in early ME: see above, Introduction, part 2, §IV, p. xxxvi. The emendation was proposed by Holt-hausen and accepted by Hall.

184 *be[t]*: the manuscript reading *ben* must be an error for *bet*: a verb in the singular is clearly required (cf. *bekne[ð]*—MS *bekned*—in the same line), because *it* is singular, referring back to *laʒe* (183). Morris's emendation *be[t]*, 'offers', makes sense and it fulfils this requirement. The scribe may have made this mistake because the text sometimes uses the singular *it* with the plural verb *ben*, as in lines 399 and 588 (see above, Introduction, part 2, §II. D. 1, p. xxv).

184 *e[rðl]iche*: the manuscript's *ebriche*, 'Hebrew', does not make sense here. Mätzner's suggestion, *e[rðl]iche*, is supported by the source: *Hoc est, quod binas lex habet una vias, / Que terrena sonat simul et celestia monstrat, / Nunc mentem pascit et modo corpus alit* (IV. 14–16). Bennett and Smithers suppose that *ebriche* 'may be due to a reminiscence of the Latin [*res spiriuales, Quas*] *Judaeus non amat*', but this attractive speculation presupposes that the scribe responsible for the mistake knew Theobald's poem.

186 *leue*: so Morris. Mätzner, Hall and Bennett and Smithers read *lene*, which gives equally good sense; in my opinion, the manuscript reads *leue*, but *n* and *u* are often hard to distinguish in this hand.

STAG

188 *forbisnes*: translates *figuras* (VI. 1).

196 *sweleð*: emendation to *swel[ʒ]eð*, as Hall proposes, is unnecessary: *OED* lists *sweleð* as a possible form s.v. *swallow*, v., but forms with *ʒ* are more common.

197 *him*: reflexive: 'himself'.

210–11 Hall asserts that these lines were 'no doubt originally couplets', but irregularities are too frequent in the sections in couplets for this to be certain: see above, Introduction, part 3, p. lxiv.

214 *[g]olsipe*: *golnesse* is frequent in ME (see *MED* s.v.), but *golsipe*, 'lechery', appears to be a *hapax legomenon* in ME—though not of course in OE—the only instances listed in *MED* s.v. being from the *Physiologus*. The manuscript form *kolsipe* must be an error: the OE etymon is *gālscipe*, and the word appears at line 430 as *golsipe*. *golnesse*, which is from the same stem, always has *g*- in ME.

217 *imene*: 'together', but the scribe appears to have left a little space between *i* and *m*. Mätzner reads *I mene*, 'I mean', which fits the context less well; Morris prints *i-mene*, Hall, who gives a diplomatic transcript, *i mene*.

225–6 These lines lack rhyme, but lack of rhyme occurs elsewhere in the poem, as in lines 70–2, which, like these lines, make sense, so it seems best to reject Holthausen's *Forwerpen pride hornes / In wude er in ðornes* as unfounded.

228 *ȝin[g]en*: the difference between *ȝ* and *g* in this scribe's hand is no more than a hook (see above, Introduction, part 1, p. x), but confusion is nevertheless rare: see above, p. xliv, n. 8.

229 *forðwar[d]*: the form in the manuscript, *forðwarð*, is not attested by *MED* or *OED*, and the emendation restores the rhyme.

230–48 *Natura secunda*: this *natura*, which is in Theobald, does not derive from the main *Physiologus* tradition proper, but it is in Pliny, VIII. 32 (50) and Solinus, 19. 12. Both Pliny and Solinus add the detail that the deer go by scent to find dry land, but both assume that the animals cross seas. Since this detail is not in Isidore, who has them cross *immensa flumina vel maria* (XII. I. 19), Isidore is probably Theobald's source (as he would be likely to anyway); Theobald's deer do no more than cross *fluvios*.

240 *[ch]inbon*: the manuscript reading *skinbon* does not fit the context, which suggests 'chin': *Portant suspensum gradientes ordine mentum, / Alter in alterius clunibus impositus* (VI. 21–2). The archetype may have had *sinbon*, which is a possible reflex of OE *cin-bān*: *MED* lists the form *shin* s.v. *chin*. The form is rare, however, so the more common *chinbon* is preferable.

242–3 *tirȝen*: *herien*: the two words are close enough in sound to make an acceptable rhyme (see above, Introduction, part 3, p. lxiv), and hence Hall's emendation *teren* (OE *tēorian*) is unnecessary.

242–6 In the source, the stag at the head of the column merely moves to the rear when he is tired: *Sed qui precedit, fessus ad ima redit* (VI. 24). The translator must have misunderstood the Latin (so Bennett and Smithers): *ima* can of course also mean 'bottom', but plainly does not here.

243 *herien*: the sense of the OE etymon *hergian*, 'harry, plunder', is not close to the meaning 'drag' required by the context. 'Drag' is recorded in ME (see *MED* s.v. *herien* v. (2), sense 3(b)), but the earliest example is not until Chaucer. The choice, then, is either to emend or to accept the manuscript reading as antedating the first instance given by *MED*. I would favour the latter; however, Norman Davis, loc. cit., pp. 57–8, proposes *ferien*, 'carry', and dismisses the manuscript reading as 'clearly mak[ing] no sense'. He justifies *ferien* as follows, 'Its meaning is taken up by the next line—*beren him of ðat water grund*—and in some thirteenth-century hands *f* written close to a following letter, and with the curve at the top abnormally short, might resemble *h*.' Mätzner prints *herten*, 'encourage', which spoils the rhyme; Morris suggests *hertien*, which has the advantage of preserving the rhyme and which is accepted by Hall.

246 This line stands on its own; a line may have dropped out here (Hall conjectures *& cumen to here stede*, 'answering to "atque viam peragunt"'), but there does not appear to be a break in the sense.

253 *wine*: a dative (so Norman Davis, glossary to Bennett and Smithers), dependent on *stedefast*, which is an adjective (adverbs are normally marked with an ending in this text: see above, Introduction, part 2, §II. C. (p. xxiv)).

254 *birdene*: forms with *d* occur from the early twelfth century onwards (see *OED* s.v. *burden*, *burthen*, n.), so it is unnecessary to regard this as another example of d for ð (for which, see above, note to line 21).

258 *betwixen*: the manuscript's *ben twixen* is a mechanical error, due to attraction to the subject pronoun *we*. Although the manuscript's usual form is *bi-*, not *be-* (see the Glossary for examples), *be-* is to be preferred here as involving less alteration and giving a better indication of how the corruption arose.

259 *to fillen*: translate: 'to be observed'. Cf. Rom. 13: 20, *Plenitudo legis est dilectio.*

FOX

263 *hire*: following the Latin source—*vulpes* is of course feminine—the Fox is referred to by feminine pronouns throughout, although OE *fox* is masculine (so Dickins and Wilson).

267 *hulen*: Hall terms this reading 'hardly possible'; Dickins and Wilson claim that the verb 'is known only in the sense "to remove the hull, skin"' and emend to *hu[t]en*, 'revile'. But *hulen* is not the verb derived from the OE noun *hulu*: it is from a different stem, cognate with MDu *hulen* and AN *ouler*. Its earliest occurrence listed in *MED* s.v. *houlen* is dated 1332, but the meaning given, 'pursue or chase away by shouting', fits the context perfectly. Mätzner's *hunten* and Holthausen's *hurlen* do not fit the context.

268–80 Statement based on observation is rare in the *Physiologus* and the *Bestiary*, but the account of the Fox feigning death may be an exception. In his *Reynard the Fox: A Study of the Fox in Medieval Art* (Leicester, 1967), Kenneth Varty includes four stills from a Russian film made in the Caucasus in 1961, which show a fox pretending to be dead in order to attract birds and then seizing a crow (p. 91 and illustrations 147–50). The Fox's trick appears in some branches of the Reynart cycle: see Varty, pp. 91–2.

276 *wullen*: Mätzner emends to *billen* on the grounds that *wullen* does not fit the context. He is mistaken: *wullen* means 'wish to land', the verb of motion having been omitted, as common.

275 *derflike*: *MED* s.v. *derfli*, adv., quotes lines 274–5 under sense 1(a), 'boldly, fearlessly; sternly; vehemently'. But 1(b), 'without hesitation or delay, promptly', fits the context better; *dred* would mean 'doubt' in that case rather than 'fear' (despite *MED* s.v. *dred(e)*, n., sense 1(a)).

292 *foxing*: this appears to be a *hapax legomenon*: see *MED* s.v. *foxing*, which does not record any other occurrences. It is probably a word made up by the poet.

297 *billing*: the only other instances of this word listed in *MED* s.v. *billing* are much later (*c.* 1440). They are both from the *Promptorium parvulorum*, which is a Norfolk text, like the *Physiologus*.

297 *ȝeld*: Mätzner notes, 'für *gelt* = *geldeð* steht *geld*'; Hall glosses 'requites' and compares *ȝelt* (278), which shows that he, like Mätzner, regards *ȝeld* as an indicative. Whereas *ȝelt* is obviously a syncopated third person sg. pres. ind., *ȝeld* is more likely to be a subjunctive, since the text has no examples of an endingless third person pres. sg. ind. (see above, Introduction, part 2, §II. E. 1), although it must be admitted that the text has no other examples of an endingless subjunctive (see Introduction, part 2, §II. E. 2). A subjunctive would fit the context: 'May the Devil pay back . . .'.

297 *swilk*: although all earlier editors read *swilk* without comment, it should be noted that in this case it is hard to distinguish badly written *i* followed by badly written *l* (curving back) from the two-compartment *a* characteristic of this type of hand, so the manuscript could read *swak*, 'weak' (cf. Middle Low German *swak*). However, ME *swak* is rare, occurring only in *Genesis and Exodus*: see Arngart, p. 43 and *OED* s.v. *swac*. Also, *swilk* fits the context better.

301 [*fox*]: it is clear from the context that *fox* has been omitted; also, the insertion of *fox* improves the scansion of the line. The source supports this emendation: *Demon ab insidiis vulpecule est similis* (V. 18).

303 *m[e]n*: the manuscript reading *man* is ungrammatical (lack of concord) and must be an error. The source has *Et cum fraude viri sunt vulpis nomine digni, / Quales hoc omnes tempore sunt homines* (V. 19–20), the first part of which is close enough to our text to justify the emendation to *m[e]n*. *men* is closer to the Latin than the suggestion *man[i]* made by Dickins and Wilson; see also H. C. Matthes, '*Bestiary* 345f', *Anglia*, lxxiv (1956), 445–8. However, although lines 301–4 make sense as emended, they are far removed from the Latin, probably because the ME poet misunderstood his original: in Theobald, it is *deceitful men* who are worthy of the name of fox—and that is all of us. The ME poet ignores the 'evils of the age' theme and uses *vulpis nomine* both in its literal (*ðe foxes name*) and in its transferred sense (*same*, 'disgrace'), which is absurd.

304 *to hauen*: Hall's transposition to *hauen to* (followed by Dickins and Wilson) is unnecessary, because the line makes sense as it stands: 'deserve to experience disgrace', Besides, the idiom listed by *MED* s.v. *shame* n., sense 3(b), meaning 'endure tribulations or torment; also, be disgraced' (the required sense) is *hauen shame*: Hall's *hauen to same* is not attested.

SPIDER

Theobald's source for this section is not the prose *Physiologus*, which does not have a chapter on the Spider, but the *Dicta Chrysostomi*. With the exception of lines 316–17, the ME *Physiologus* is not close to Theobald in this section: see above, Introduction, part 5, p. lxxxvi.

314 *lo*[*dl*]*ike*: the scribe transposed two letters: the manuscript reading *loldike* is not recorded and does not make sense. Forms with *d*, such as *lodlike*, are well attested, so *d* is not necessarily an error for *ð* here (see *MED* s.v. *lothli*, adj.).

316 [*web*]: the context requires a noun following *hire*; *web*, besides fitting the context semantically, also provides the alliteration (although lines without alliteration are common in the alliterative sections of the *Physiologus*: see above, Introduction, part 3, p. lviii). The form *web* appears in line 319, and the *Physiologus* does not always add an ending to a noun in the prepositional case (see above, Introduction, part 2, §II. A. 1 (p. xxii)), so [*web*] is perhaps to be preferred to Hall's [*webbe*]. The suggestion was first made by Holthausen.

316 *swi*[*ðe*]: the manuscript form *swid* has *d* for *ð*; the form *swið* does not occur for the reflex of OE *swiðe* in this text (see the Glossary s.v. *swiðe*), hence the suggestion *swi*[*ðe*]. The source offers some slight support, although *assiduus* is an adjective (but it is not very far removed from *swiðe*, 'quickly', in meaning): *Vermis araneus exiguus / Plurima fila net assiduus, / Texere que studet artificus* (VII. 1–3). The suggestion is Holthausen's; Mätzner proposes *swinc*, but his line, *De spinnere on hire swinc ʒe weveð*, is too short.

317 *fo*: an adjective, from OE *fāh*, meaning 'hostile': so A. J. Bliss, 'Three Middle English Studies', *EGS*, ii (1948–9), 40–54, p. 53. *fo dredes* is how the words appear in the manuscript; Mätzner and Hall wrongly assume a *hapax legomenon fod-redes*, 'plans, means of securing food' (Hall's gloss).

318 *elde*: 'hill', from OE (cf. WS *hylde*). Translate: 'as if she were on a hill' (literally, 'it is for her as if on a hill'), i.e. the Spider moves about on the roof and the eaves as if on a hill. Hall suggests [*f*]*elde* and explains the half-line, 'she moves on a ceiling as if she were on the ground', but the text mentions sloping, not flat, surfaces, and, moreover, Hall's solution involves an unnecessary emendation. Mätzner emends *hire* to *ʒe* and glosses 'when she is old', which does not make sense in the context.

329–34 Like Theobald's moralization, the ME *significacio* sees the Spider as the deceitful man, but Theobald returns to the *Dicta Chrystostomi* (a text of the relevant section of which can be found in Eden's note, p. 52) when he connects the fragile web of the Spider with the futility and short-lived nature of human evil:

COMMENTARY 37

Ille tamen mala queque facit,
Cum moritur, quasi tela cadit,
Quamodo dictus araneus it (VII. 16–18).

(The *Dicta Chrysostomi* admonish man to perform good works because otherwise his life will be as transitory as the Spider's web.) The ME *Physiologus*
concentrates on the murderous character of the Spider—biting its victims to
death and drinking their blood—and not on the fragility of its web.

332 *bale selleð*: *selleð* is rare with an abstract object, but cf. *Ic ȝeafe heom mine
milse; & sylle heom forȝefenesse* (*12th Cent. Hom.* 132), quoted by *OED* s.v. *sell*, v.,
sense 21 (also quoted Hall).

333 *dreueð*: *MED* cites lines 329 and 333 s.v. *dreven*, v. (1), from OE *dræfan*,
sense (b), 'to attack'. However, sense (c), 'to trouble (sb), annoy, vex', seems
more appropriate, and the verb could equally well be *dreven*, v. (2), from OE
drēfan, *dræfan*, *gedrefan*.

334 *h[i]m*: the syntax requires a singular, not a plural. The scribe corrected the
other errors of *him* for *hem* (333 and two in 332) but must have missed this one.

WHALE

335 –76 Natura: the ME *Physiologus* follows Theobald, who, reversing the
order of the prose *Physiologus* (*versio a*, ch. XXX, and *versio b*, ch. XXIV), takes
the Whale eating small fish first and the Whale drowning sailors second. On
the legend, see C. C. Coulter, 'The Great Fish in Ancient and Medieval
Story', *Transactions and Publications of the American Philological Association*, lvii
(1926), 32–50.

338 *flet*: *MED* s.v. *fleten* gives 'swim' for this (sense 1(b)), but the context (see
lines 339–40) requires the gloss 'float' (sense 1(a)).

343 *it . . . onde*: for this use of *it*, see Mustanoja, *Middle English Syntax*, p. 132:
here it 'occurs in a pleonastic function carried out by *there* in Pres. E.'.

335 –7 Translate *Si sit tempestas, cum vadit vel venit estas / Et pelagus fundum tur-
bidat omne suum* (VIII. 13–14): the reference is to the equinoctial gales.

362 *ða[t]*: the manuscript form *ðar* is a scribal error: the context requires a
demonstrative.

363 *sipes*: the meaning 'ships' is impossible: this is *OED*'s sense 7, 'a ship's
company or crew'. The earliest occurrence, which this would antedate, is
R. Brunne, *Chron.*, *Do dight & mak ȝow bone, þe schip are Sarazins alle.*

368 *mid here miȝt*: this expression usually includes the adjective *al*: see *MED*
s.v. *might*, sense 3(f), where the only other example without *al* is from the
Physiologus as well (line 525; but cf. 475).

369 –70 If *festen: gangen* can be said to make an acceptable rhyme (inflectional
rhyme appears to be permitted: see above, Introduction, part 3, p. lxiv), these

lines form a couplet of two-beat lines. Unless the poet varied his metre here to draw attention to a high point in his narrative (for examples of this see above, Introduction, part 3, pp. lxiii–lxiv), this is unsatisfactory, but neither the context nor the source suggests that anything has been lost. *festen* is followed by a *punctus* in the manuscript, which suggests that the scribe interpreted *sipes . . . gangen* as two lines, but the mark of punctuation could be syntactic rather than metrical: cf. line 374, which has a *punctus* after *feleð*, and line 386, which has one after *leue*.

372 [*b*]*el*: the manuscript reading *wel* is unsatisfactory, for, as Hall observed, *brennen* does not occur in absolute use (in the meaning 'light a fire', which appears to be required in this context): see *MED* s.v. *brennen*. As Professor Davis has pointed out (*MÆ*, xix (1950), p. 59), Hall's own suggestion *wel* [*m*] is impossible, because it does not have the meaning 'blazing fire' which Hall wanted. Professor Davis proposes to read [*b*]*el*, from OE *bǣl*, 'bonfire', 'which gives exactly the meaning required'; furthermore, 'the alliterating phrase which would result, i.e. *bel to brennen*, . . . taken with the parallel opening phrases of the neighbouring lines, *Of ston mid stel* in l. [371] and *warmen hem wel* and *ðe fir he feleð* in ll. [373–4], would bring these four lines into a metrical group. In these four rhyming couplets there is no necessary alliterative link between the beginning and end of a line, so that the *w* of *wunder* is irrelevant. The mis-writing *wel* might well have been occasioned by *wel* in the following line. Finally, the Latin *Accendunt* vigilem *quem navis portitat ignem* [VIII. 19; Professor Davis's italics] may have suggested to the translator the idea of "watch-fire", which could be a stage in the development of the meaning of *bale* towards the later use to mean "signal-fire, beacon".' The argument about a metrical group comprising lines 371–4 is dubious: although alliteration is frequent in the rhyming sections of the poem, it is never more than ornamental and metrical groups do not exist within the sections in rhyming couplets, so what is no more than a pleasing effect created by a conjectural emendation cannot be used to defend this suggestion. Nevertheless, Professor Davis's proposed emendation is a good one and should be adopted.

383 *in leue laȝe*: 'weak in faith': translates Theobald's *modicos fidei* (VIII. 27), a phrase he took over from the prose *Physiologus* (*versio b*, which has *Sic patiuntur omnes qui sunt modicae fidei*, is closer than *versio a*'s *et gluttit pusillos omnes illos pisciculos, hoc est modicos in fide*).

387–90 Translate *In quo confidit quisquis vel spem sibi ponit, / Ad Stiga cum rapitur, quam male decipitur* (VIII. 29–30). The prose *Physiologus*, which deals with the Whale's natural habits in reverse order (see above, note to lines 335–76), concludes by equating the Whale's sweet breath with sexual licence (*versio b. Dubii autem et modicae fidei homines, dum uadunt post uoluptates et luxurias diaboli, decipiuntur; dicente scriptura: Unguentis et uariis odoribus delectantur, et sic confringitur a ruinis anima* [Prou. 27. 9]; *versio a* has *Ioseph effugiit cetum magnum, principis cocorum mulierem, sicut in Genesis scriptum est* etc.—various Old Testament examples of male and female fortitude follow).

SIREN

The ME *Physiologus* omits Theobald's Onocentaurs. As in the prose *Physiologus*, Sirens and Onocentaurs are described in the same chapter (*a*: ch. XV; *b*: ch. XII), because they appear together in Isa. 13: 22 and because they both have, in Theobald's words, a 'double nature' (*natura biformis*, X. 1). They share the same moralization, so perhaps Eden would have done better not to split the Sirens and the Onocentaurs up into two separate sections, the first of which necessarily lacks a *significacio*. He does not mention if and how the manuscripts divide the two.

395 In Theobald, as in the prose *Physiologus* and in classical tradition, the Sirens are half women, half birds: see above, Introduction, part 5, p. lxxxviii.

395 *miõ*: it is possible to read this, and *miõ* in line 548, as *mid* with an accent over the *i*, but the scribe does not generally write accents.

397 *sinkeõ*: this could be *OED* s.v. *sink*, v., sense 4a, 'of water, etc.: To go down; to fall to a lower level; to subside' (earliest example from *Genesis A*), but this meaning appears to be rare. The occurrence of the same form in the next line suggests that *sinkeõ* may be an error here, but cf. a similar case in line 114 (and see the accompanying note).

398 *mere*: *MED* s.v. *mere* n. (4) lists this as a shortened form of *mere-min*: its only other occurrence is in the Titus text of *Ancrene Riwle*, where the word appears as *mare* (Bodley 34 has *meareminnes*). Mätzner compares ON *mara*, which he glosses *nympha*; however, its meaning is rather 'the nightmare, an ogress' (Cleasby-Vigfusson s.v.). It is conceivable that ON *mara* influenced *mere*, but the sense is not really close enough.

400 *stefninge*: *OED* lists *stefninge* as a form of the verbal noun derived from *steven*, 'to make an uproar, shout' (and, used transitively, 'to deafen with noise'), but this sense seems strange when applied to beings that are said to sing sweetly (398). Only one other example from the ME period is given: York Myst. xxxii. 6 *Ʒe stynte of youre steuening so stowte*, which certainly suggests shouting and uproar.

404 *mid . . . ouel*: the manuscript reading, *mid he brest ouel*, does not make sense at all. *ouel* may be OE *afol*, with *a* > *o* (Jordan, §29), 'power'; the fact that it is a rare word (two instances only in *MED* s.v. *avel*, n., both with *a*) may explain why the scribe miswrote it. It is tempting to assume that *brest* is a corruption of *best*, in which case Morris's emendation *he[re]* is a good one. *MED* even provides a parallel: *Wit & Will* B/34, *Bowed him bakward with his best auel.* Unfortunately this reference is dated by *MED* 'c. 1400', which is a century later than the date of our manuscript. However, the two occurrences of the word in OE which Bosworth-Toller records s.v. *afol*, both *Eallum mid afole*, glossed 'with all his power', may provide some slight support. Hall, on the other hand, takes *ouel* to be a corruption of *iuel*. G. V. Smithers, 'Ten Cruces in Middle English Texts', *EGS*, iii (1949–50), 65–81, states that the corruption of *ouel* is 'palaeographically not possible' (p. 81) and suggests that *ouel* is in fact from MDu *ovel, oevel*, 'unpleasant, involving misfortune'. He retains the manuscript reading *brest* and assumes it is ON *brestr*, 'breast'; he points to two instances in Laȝamon where its native cognate *burst* is collocated with a verb 'escape' similar in form to *atbrosten* (1347: *Brutus at bræc al buten burstan*; 1610: *þe king Goffar iseih his burst· unæðe him seolf atbreac*). This is an attractive suggestion, but it should be rejected on the grounds that *ouel* = MDu *ovel* cannot be paralleled elsewhere (as Professor Smithers admits; his assertion that *ouese*, line 318, may be another word of MDu origin, MDu *ovese*, rather than OE *ofes*, is no more than speculation, and as such provides no support) and that *mid he[re] brest ouel* still fails to make complete sense unless it could be proved that the phrase is an idiom meaning 'by the skin of their teeth' (a literal wound, as in the two lines from Laȝamon, would not fit the context of the *Physiologus* where the sailors are either shipwrecked or they escape).

405 *herd told*: Mätzner omits *herd*, Hall *told*, but there is in fact nothing wrong with this phrase, which means 'heard tell'.

405 *uniemete*: this is an adjective used as a noun, 'grotesque one'.

409 [*sepes*]: the manuscript has *wulues*, which is nonsense. The scribe's eye must have been caught by *wulues* in the next line; the allusion is obviously to Matt. 7: 15.

415 Translates *in more biformes* (X. 3).

419 *song*: 'singing' is odd here, and *song* has no parallel in the source; it probably refers back to the Sirens' song of the *natura*.

421–2 This is not in the source. Theobald ends with *Utpote sunt multi, qui de virtute locuti / Clunibus indulgent: his o quam pulpita fulgent* (X. 6–7). It is not clear whether *pulpita* refers to preaching or to the stage (see Eden's note). It is conceivable that the ME translator left it out because of the possible impropriety of *clunibus*.

ELEPHANT

424 *ili[ch]e*: the manuscript form *ilike* spoils the rhyme: see above, Introduction, part 2, §IV, p. xxxvi).

425–6 Translate *Hi simul incedunt ut oves, cum pascua querunt* (XI. 3).

427 *behinden*: 'from behind' or 'back to back': on this curious misapprehension, see above, Introduction, part 5, pp. lxxxviii–lxxix. Theobald has *aversi*, which in the context means 'in private', but this is not the commonest sense of the Latin word. The ME translator obviously took it in its literal sense; see the *Oxford Latin Dictionary* s.v. *āuersus*.

439 *kindles*: this is a singular, 'young one', and not, *pace MED* s.v. *kindel*, sense
1(a), a plural. The Latin has *Ast unum generans* etc. (XI. 7), and line 433 has
Siðen he biʒeten on. Elephants are said to give birth only once in their lives:

> Ðoʒ he ŏre hundred ʒer
> On werlde more wuneden her,
> Biʒeten he neuermor non
> So cold is hem siðen blod & bon (435–8).

It is clear, then, that the context requires a singular. In fact, *-les* in *kindles*
represents the OE suffix *-els* here, which (so *OED* s.v. *-els*) is used to form
'instrumental sbs. or verbal abstracts', as in OE *rǣdels*, 'riddle', from *rǣdan*.
The ME singular of the word *kindel* is not recorded with *-s* and the word did
not appear in OE (see *OED* s.v.); the *-s* here must be due to analogy with
words like ME *redels*, 'riddle', and *biriels*, 'tomb'.

440–1 Holthausen presumes that the repetition of *in water* is an instance of
dittography and proposes *mid wambe*, comparing Philippe de Thaün's *tresque a
sun ventre*. But since the context makes sense, dittography is unlikely; also, as
there is no evidence that the ME poet knew Philippe's work, the comparison
cannot be made.

442 *wanne . . . tide*: Hall rejects Mätzner's suggestion, 'when mischief betides
her', because in his opinion 'the order of the words is against that interpretation: tide is impersonal and harde is an adverb'. *tide* need not be impersonal, however, whenever it takes the dative: see *OED* s.v. *tide*, v.[1], sense 1b,
which has a possible parallel from *Trin. Coll. Hom.* 29, *Witte wel hwat þu hauest,
walte* [i.e. consider] *hwat þe tide*. But *hire* could be a possessive instead: perhaps this fits the context slightly better. *harde* is probably a noun; the sense
'birth pangs', which Hall considers, is not attested, although *harde* does of
course refer to birth pangs (and cf. Theobald, *Cum parit, in magna, ne cadat, extat
aqua*, XI. 8), but its meaning is something like 'difficult time' (*MED* s.v. *hard*,
n., sense 2(b)).

443–6 This goes back to Theobald, XI. 9–10, but the prose *Physiologus* and the
Dicta Chrysostomi (text quoted by Eden, p. 64, note) give a different explanation
for why the Elephant gives birth standing in water: it is because of her enemy,
the serpent. *Versio b* is clearer than *versio a*: *et si extra aquam peperit, capit draco* [i.e.
serpent] *pecus illud et deuorat. Ideo in aquam altam ingreditur, ut ibi pariat* (*versio b*, ch.
XXXIII). It omits the hunter's trick, which is the second part of the ME *natura*
(447–92), which *versio a* does include (ch. XX); it would seem, then, that in the
course of time the explanation of the Elephant's habit of resting leaning against
a tree became attached to its strange way of giving birth as well.

In the Greek *Physiologus* (ed. Sbordone, ch. 43), however, the three elements
were quite separate: first, it is related how the female gives birth standing in
water. Then the hatred between the elephant and the snake is mentioned; the
third characteristic given is that the elephant has no joints in its legs, a statement that Aristotle, in the *Historia animalium*, had proved to be untrue

(498. a. 8–12). Possibly the odd phrasing of the account of how the female gives birth was responsible for the confusion: 'So when the time has come for her to give birth, she goes to a pool of standing water and walks into it until the water reaches her udders, and so thereafter she gives birth to her young one in the water, and it goes to her thighs and sucks its mother's teat.' One could imagine how the unnecessary mention of the mother elephant's leg could give rise to the fusing of the third, originally separate, characteristic with the first. In this connexion it is interesting to see that Pliny, who antedates the Greek *Physiologus*, merely says that snakes lie in wait for elephants in rivers and kill them there (VIII. 12), but he does not mention the way the *Physiologus* thinks the elephant gives birth. The absence of joints in the legs Pliny associates with the elk (VIII. 15), on the authority of Caesar's *De bello gallico*, and Solinus follows him here (20. 7). The fact that the elephant's fear of the serpent immediately follows the strange description of how the female gives birth, in which it is not revealed why this has to be done in the water, may explain why later versions, such as the Latin *versiones a* and *b*, Isidore (XII. II. 16) and the *Dicta Chrysostomi* merge the two.

451 *iȝewis*: this spelling is not recorded elsewhere in ME; see *MED* s.v. *iwis*.

458 *willen: swiken: willen* probably makes an acceptable rhyme: see above, Introduction, part 3, p. lxiv. Hall's suggestion *wiken* would make a perfect rhyme, but since *hise* refers to the Elephant, not to the hunter, a word meaning 'office, duty, function' (*OED* s.v. *wike*) would be out of place.

460 *bet*: probably not instead of *best* for the sake of the rhyme (Hall): translate 'that he may better'.

462 *he makeð*: i.e. the Elephant.

463 [*a*]*lon*: the manuscript form *olon* must be an error for *alon*: no form *olon* is recorded in *MED* (s.v. *alon(e)*) or *OED* (s.v. *alone*).

464 The manuscript reads *biwarlt*, which spoils the rhyme and is not attested elsewhere. *MED* s.v. *biwelden* accepts Mätzner's emendation to *biwalt*, but is has no further examples of sense 2(b), 'of an enterprise: to work out, succeed'.

473 *gang*[*en*]: the manuscript reading *gangande* spoils the rhyme. *gangande* was substituted for *gangen* (so Hall); the reason is probably that the construction with *gangen* was obsolescent when Arundel 292 was written: Mustanoja, *Middle English Syntax*, states: 'in early ME a plain infinitive of manner is not uncommon with *come*. The idiom becomes rarer towards the end of the period and eventually disappears, the place of the infinitive being taken by the present participle' (p. 536).

479 [*saken*]: the manuscript form *sacande*, which should be emended to *saken*, like *gangande* (for reasons, see above, note to line 473), was corrected from *secande*, 'apparently in a different hand' according to Norman Davis (loc. cit., p. 57, n. 1). But this correction, like the other ones on f. 9ʳ, was done in lead pencil, not in ink, which makes it difficult to assess whether the corrector was the scribe or not, and if not, whether he was contemporary with the scribe. It is perhaps worth noting that the last six lines of f. 9^r lack rubrication (i.e. from line 479, *ðer*, to line 491, *ðus*).

480 *him . . . maken*: *OED* does not give this expression s.v. *stall*, n.^{1}. Its meaning is 'put him on his feet again': cf. *OED*'s sense 1, 'standing-place, place, position'.

502 *o*[*3*]*t*: the manuscript reading *ovt* destroys the rhyme: see above, Introduction, part 2, §IV, p. xxxvi.

503 *o*[*re*] *steuene*: the manuscript's *onder steuene* is nonsense. This line has no parallel in the source; the meaning required is obviously something like 'with a single voice'. Mätzner suggested *mid are steuene. mid* is not necessary for the sense and introduces an extra syllable which disturbs the metre (although the latter is a minor consideration: lines in the sections in short couplets do not have a rigidly fixed number of syllables: see above, Introduction, part 3, p. lxii); *are* is a valuable suggestion, but OE long *a* had become *ō* in the South and in the Midlands by the early thirteenth-century (Jordan, §44), so even the archetype is unlikely to have had *ā*: hence Mätzner *are* should be altered to *ore*. The most probable explanation for this textual corruption is that the dative feminine of the indefinite article was becoming obsolete, and that the form *ore* was garbled as a result, producing the meaningless *onder*. Holthausen's *luder steuene*, changed to *ludere steuene* by Hall, fits the context but involves a greater degree of alteration.

409 [*ð*]*rowing*: the manuscript reading *drowing* is another case of *d* for *ð* (see note to line 21): *ðrowing* is the verbal noun from OE *þrōwian* (see *OED* s.v. *throw* v.^{2}, sense 2, where *throwing* is glossed 'suffering; passion; *esp*. the Passion of Christ).

TURTLE DOVE

The prose *Physiologus*, *versio a*, does not deal with the Turtle Dove's virtue of conjugal fidelity: instead, it explains Cant. 2: 12, *Uox turturis audita in terra nostra*, as the bird's love of solitude (ch. XLI). *Versio b*, on the other hand, takes the same quotation from Scripture and then goes on to say: *Physiologus dicit ualde uirum suum diligere* (ch. XXVIII). The Turtle Dove's fidelity to her dead mate symbolizes the Church's love for Christ: this is also the tradition that Theobald follows.

515 *siðen*: this could be OE *siþþan*, 'then, afterwards', or OE *siþian*, 'go, depart'. The former seems more likely in this context: *siðen* would then be contrasted with *ones. siðen: reden* is acceptable as an example of inflectional rhyme: see above, Introduction, part 3, p. lxiv. Hall proposes emending to *seden*, from OE *scēadan*, which would make a perfect rhyme. The nearest sense

would be sense 1d s.v. *shed*, v., in *OED*, 'part company', but it does not appear
to be used with the preposition *from*, so Hall's suggestion should be rejected.

531–2 *ʒeueli[ch]e. riche*: the manuscript form *ʒeuelike* spoils the rhyme: see
above, Introduction, part 2, §IV, pp. xxxvii–xxxviii.

PANTHER

535 *qual*, 'whale', is the only example in this text of the Norfolk spelling *qu*
for the reflex of OE *hw*: see above, Introduction, part 2, §I. C. 4(ii) (p. xxi).
MED s.v. *bro*, n. (1) derives *bro* from ON *brá*, 'eyelash', and takes *bro of qual* to
mean 'the brow or back of a whale'; this is the only example of *bro* in this
sense, sense (b), which *MED* regards as derived from sense (a), 'the bank (of a
stream); the brink or raised edge (of a ditch or pit)'. *blac* is OE *blæc*, 'black',
not OE *blāc*, 'pale'. Cyril Brett, 'Notes on Old and Middle English', *MLR*,
xxii (1927), 217–64, remarks laconically that 'there is no need for emendation. . . . A whale's brow *is* black' (p. 260).

535–7 Translate *Qui niger ex albo conspargitur orbiculato* (XIII. 2).

541 *cul*: 'choice', from the AN verb *cuillir*: see A. J. Bliss, 'Three Middle
English Studies', *EGS*, ii (1948–9), 40–54, p. 54. This gives better sense than
Mätzner's suggestion, '*cul = cowl* scheint bildlich für *fell* gebraucht zu sein',
or Hall's 'rump' (OF *cul*).

559 *no[ʒ]t*: the manuscript form *nout* destroys the rhyme: see above, Introduction, part 2, §IV, p. xxxvi.

565 *Cf. Ps. 44: 3, Speciosus forma prae filiis hominum*, which is quoted in the prose
Physiologus, *versio b*, in the chapter on the Panther (ch. XXIII).

575 *vue[ma]st*: 'highest'; the manuscript reads *vuenest*, in which *n* is a simple
slip for *m* (wrong number of minims) and the ending *-est* represents OE *-æst*,
without shortening before *-st*. What is needed for the rhyme (: *Gast*) is the
form of the suffix which did undergo shortening, becoming *-ast* in ME. On the
treatment of OE long vowels before the consonant cluster *-st*, see Jordan, §23,
esp. Remark 1; see also *OED* s.v. *uvemast* and see above, p. xxxvi.

580 *fin*: Hall emends to *afin* or *in fin*, 'at our ending', but this is unnecessary:
fin, 'perfect' (OF), fits the context.

DOVE

Theobald's section on the Panther is his last; the ME section on the Dove is
based on Alexander Neckam's *De naturis rerum*, I. LVI: see above, Introduction, part 5, pp. xc–xci. The prose *Physiologus* has a chapter on doves, but it
has nothing in common with Alexander Neckam or the ME *Physiologus*: it
consists of a series of allegorical explanations of the colours of different kinds
of dove.

591 *bi laȝt*: in the manuscript these words are written *bilaȝt*. The only possible meaning for this form, which would have to be a past participle, is 'deluded' (*MED* s.v. *bilacchen*), but 'deluded' does not fit the context. The objection to reading *bi laȝt*, on the other hand, is that the noun *laȝt* does not appear elsewhere. If the sentence from Neckam on which this line would seem to be based, *Non vivit ex raptu, quia non detrahit proximo*, is taken as a parallel, *bi laȝt* may correspond to *ex raptu*. *laȝt* could then be related to the verb *lacchen* (from OE *læccan*, past participle *læht*), 'snatch' or 'seize (sb. or sth.) as prey' (*MED* s.v., sense 2(a)). The meaning of the phrase would be 'by snatching'.

592 This line is problematic. *Pace* Holthausen and Hall, the manuscript has *hac*, not *bac*. None of the earlier suggestions is satisfactory: Holthausen proposes *iþagt* (*sic*), from OE *geþeaht*, 'thoughts', which fits the context but is pure speculation. Mätzner interprets *hac* as the reflex of OE *ēac*, 'also', but this spelling is not recorded (see *MED* s.v. *ek(e)* adv.): Mätzner's nearest approximation is *æke*, from Laȝamon's *Brut*. Hall's attempt to see *bac* as the adverb 'back' simply does not make sense. A possibility that has not, as far as I know, been advanced is that *hac* could be an adverb, 'ruthlessly', derived from the adjective listed by *MED* as *hak*, 'ruthless, unsparing', probably from ON *hākr*: the text has occasional examples of endingless adverbs (see above, Introduction, part 2, §II. C (p. xxiv)). However, *MED* gives only one instance, which is considerably later than the *Physiologus*: Castleford's *Chronicle*, *On þam and þaires þai were so hak þat alle þe britons þai draf or brak*. The adverb is not recorded at all. The second difficulty is *of*. If *hac* is an adverb, 'ruthlessly', *of* could be taken as the adverb 'away' (*MED* s.v. *of*, adv., sense 1(d)), but no examples of *of*, 'away', with *don* are listed. The final problem is the lack of rhyme. Common sense suggests that either *hac* or *laȝt* is a corruption. *hac* cannot, as far as I can see, be emended to rhyme with *laȝt*, but if *la[c]* were to be read for *laȝt*, the result would be a perfect rhyme. *la[c]* could be *MED* s.v. *lak*, n., sense 2(a), 'misdeed, offence, sin', and the assumption would be that a copyist had substituted a word that meant the same but spoilt the rhyme, but this conjecture is highly speculative and should not be included in the text.

597 *lic*: not an adverb (Hall), but an adjective, going with *woning & groning*: translate, 'her singing is like wailing and lamentation'.

598 *bimene we us*. *MED* s.v. *bimenen*, v. (1), places this line under sense 3(a), 'to feel regretful, repent', but the other two examples it gives are dubious. *OED* s.v. *bemoan* puts it under sense 2, 'reflex. to lament or bewail one's lot' and does not list 'to feel regretful, repent' at all. *MED* gives 'to lament, mourn, complain—usually reflex.' as sense 1(a), and this is where the present instance belongs.

599–600 These lines are unintelligible without the Latin original. Neckam has 'Super aquarum fluenta residet, ut accipitris effugiat insidias. Sic et fidelis anima Sacra Scriptura quasi speculo utitur, ut tuta sit a circuitu hostis antiqui.' Presumably what this means is that the Dove uses the surface of the water as a mirror in which it can see the shadow of the approaching hawk; in the same way we should use the Scripture as a mirror to defend ourselves against the Devil.

APPENDIX

ME ITEMS IN THE HAND OF SCRIBE 1, MS ARUNDEL 292, f. 3ʳᵛ

Editorial procedure is the same as for the *Physiologus*: see above, p. xcii. Unlike the lines of the *Physiologus*, the lines of these poems are written out as verse, not prose: the line division of the manuscript has been preserved.

Creed   f. 3ʳ

I leue in Godd almicten Fader,
Ðatt heuene & erðe made to gar,
& in Ihesu Crist his leue Sun,
Vre onelic Louerd ik him mune,
Ðatt of ðe Holi Gost bikennedd was;   5
Pinedd under Ponce Pilate,
On rode nailedd for mannes sake;
Ðer ðolede he deadd wiðuten wold
& biriedd was in [ð]e roche cold.   10
Dun to helle licten he gan;
Ðe ðridde dai off deadd atkam;
To heuene he steȝ in ure manliche;
Ðar sitteð he in hijs Faderes riche.
O Domesdai sal he cumen aȝen   15
To demen dede & liues men.
I leue on ðe Hali Gast,
Al Holi Chirche stedefast,
Men off alle holi kinne,
& forȝiuenesse of mannes sinne,   20
Vprisinge of alle men,
& eche lif I leue. Amen.

The Lord's Prayer

Fader ure ðatt art in heuene blisse,
Ðin heȝe name, itt wurðe bliscedd;
Cumen itt mote ði kingdom;   25
Ðin hali wil, it be al don

10 ðe] de

In heuene & in erðe all so,   f. 3ᵛ
So itt sal ben ful wel, Ic tro;
Ȝif us all one ðis dai
Vre bred of iche dai   30
& forȝiue us ure sinne,
Als we don ure wiðerwinnes;
Leet us noct in fondinge falle,
Ooc fro iuel ðu sild us alle. Amen.

Hail Mary

Marie ful off grace, weel [ð]e be,   35
Godd of heuene be wið ðe.
Oure alle wimmen bliscedd tu be;
So be ðe bern ðatt is boren of ðe.

In manus tuas

Louerd Godd, in hondes tine
I biqueðe soule mine;   40
Ðu me boctest wið ði deadd,
Louerd Godd of soðfastheed.

'Three things that make me fear'

Wanne I ðenke ðinges ðre,
Ne mai Hi neure bliðe ben.
Ðe ton is [ð]at I sal awei;   45
Ðe toðer is I ne wot wilk dei;
Ðe ðridde is mi moste kare:
I ne wot wider I sal faren.

'Meditation on death'

If man him biðocte,
Inderlike & ofte,   50
Wu arde is te fore
Fro bedde te flore,
Fro flore te pitte,
Fro pitte te pine
Ðat neure sal fine,   55
I wene non sinne
Sulde his herte winnen.

35 ðe] de   45 ðat] dat

GLOSSARY

The glossary aims at recording every form of every word that occurs in the text, but when a form appears more than three times only three representative instances are given; when there are more, this is indicated by 'etc.'. When a form of a word occurs twice in the same line, superscript numbers following the line number distinguish the two appearances. When a reading is the result of emendation, an asterisk follows the line number; a dagger refers the reader to the Commentary.

The entries are in alphabetical order, but following manuscript practice *u* and *v* are not distinguished. *y* is to be found under *i*; *ʒ* has a separate place after *g*, and in the same way *ð* follows *t*.

The significance of the ending *-e* is often uncertain, but when this spelling can be taken as an unambiguous indication that a noun is in the prepositional case the form has been marked 'p.c.'.

Etymologies have been given only when they are new or controversial. They are enclosed in square brackets; an asterisk denotes a reconstructed form. Old Norse words are given in the normalized spelling of thirteenth-century Icelandic usual in grammars; in accordance with this practice long vowels are marked with an acute accent.

The following abbreviations are used:

adj.	adjective	n.	noun
adv.	adverb, adverbial	nWS	non-West Saxon
AN	Anglo-Norman	OA	the Anglian dialect of Old
art.	article		English
aux.	auxiliary	obliq.	oblique
cf.	compare (indicating uncertain	OE	Old English
	or indirect relation)	*OED*	*Oxford English Dictionary*
comp.	comparative	OF	Old French
conj.	conjunction	OFris	Old Frisian
dat.	dative	p.c.	prepositional case
def.	definite	pers.	personal
demons.	demonstrative	phr.	phrase
e	early	pl.	plural
fem.	feminine	poss.	possessive
gen.	genitive	pp.	past participle
impers.	impersonal	prec.	preceding (word)
imperat.	imperative	prep.	preposition
ind.	indicative	ppres.	present participle
indef.	indefinite	pres.	present
inf.	infinitive	pret.	preterite
infl.	influenced	pron.	pronoun
int.	interjection	reflex.	reflexive
interr.	interrogative	rel.	relative
l	late	sg.	singular
L	Latin	subj.	subjunctive
masc.	masculine	sup.	superlative
MDu	Middle Dutch	s.v.	sub voce
ME	Middle English	v.	verb
MED	*Middle English Dictionary*	WS	the West Saxon dialect of Old
MLG	Middle Low German		English

a *indef. art.* a, an, 21, 36, 56 etc.; **an**, 8, 94, 248 etc.
abit *pres. ind. 3 sg.* waits for, 521.
abuten *prep.* around, 10 (postponed); from place to place, 127, 167.
Adam *n.* Adam, 493, 510.
after *prep.* after, behind, 4; after, 497, 545.
aȝen *adv.* ~ . . . *chare see* **chare.**
aȝen *prep.* (postponed) against; *winter* ~ to meet the winter, 161.
aȝte *n.* possessions, 421 [OE æht; see *MED* s.v. *aughte* n.].
ai *adv.* always, 36, 133; continually, 147, 321, 324; forever, 507, 522, 529.
al *adj.* all, 104, 148; entire, 356, 514; **alle,** 4, 210, 231 etc.; ~ *his miȝt see* **miȝt.**
al *adv.* entirely, 33, 44, 50 etc.; quite, 450; ~ *ðus see* **ðus.**
al *conj.* ~ . . . *so* just as, 62.
al *n.* all of it, 170; **all,** 182.
alon *adv.* alone, on his own, 463*†.
als *conj. see* **also** *conj.*
also *adv.* in the same way, 189; like, 303; **als,** 537; **as,** 595.
also *conj.* as, 20, 28; as if, 252; **als so,** 562; **als,** 109.
alto *adv.* completely, 32† [OA al(l) *adv.* + OE tō: see *OED* s.v. all, C 14–15].
among *prep.* among, 130.
amonges *prep.* among, 577.
an *see* **a.**
& *conj.* and, 20, 34, 37 etc.; if, 1.
anon *see* **onon.**
anoðer *adj.* another, a second, 230.
aren, arn, art *see* **ben.**
as *see* **also** *adv.*
at *prep.* in, 142; ~ *nede see* **ned.**
atbresteð *pres. ind. 3 sg.* escapes, 491*; **atbrosten** *pp.,* 404.
atte *prep.* + *definite article* at the, 119, 317, 524.
atter *n.* venom, 210, 217.
attrie *adj.* venomous, poisonous, 198.

bale *n.* sufferings of the world, 151; injury, pain, 332.
bane *n.* murderer, 326.
bar *see* **beren.**
bare *adj.* ~ *of* devoid of, lacking, 107.
barlic *n.* barley, 167, 180.
be *prep. see* **bi.**
be *v. see* **ben.**
bec *n.* beak, 32, 51, 52 etc.

behinden *adv.* in the rear, backwards, 427†.
bekneð *pres. ind. 3 sg.* shows, 184.
bel *n.* blazing fire, 372*† [OE bæl].
belles *n. gen. sg.* bell's, 484.
ben *v.* be, 73, 161, 530 etc.; **art** *pres. ind. 2 sg.,* 143; **is** *3 sg.,* 14, 15, 24 etc.; **es,** 159; **arn** *pl.,* 31, 232, 304 etc.; **aren,** 346, 367; **be,** 176; **ben,** 25, 248, 399; **senden,** 53, 391; **was** *pret. ind. sg.,* 20; **weren** *pl.,* 69, 501; **be** *pres. subj. sg.,* 552, **beð,** 275 (twice); **ben** *pl.,* 175, 178; **were** *pret. subj. sg.,* 51, 168, 252 etc.; **wore,** 519; **weren** *pl.,* 219, 562; **be** *imperat. sg.,* 143; *pl.,* 590; *litel him is of see* **litel** *n.*
beren *v.* carry, 167; give birth to, 439; **bereð** *pres. ind. 3 sg.,* 170, 182; **beren** *pl.,* 244; obey and cherish, 584; **bar** *pret.,* 19.
berȝen *v.* save, protect, 151; *v. reflex.* take refuge, 7.
berȝes *n. pl.* mountains, hills, 424.
best *adj. sup.* best-placed, 602; **beste** best, 457; *mid here* ~ *ouel see* **ouel.**
bet *adv. comp.* better, 460†.
bet *pres. ind. 3 sg.* offers, 184*†.
beteð *pres. ind. 3 sg.* remedies, restores, 81.
betwixen *prep.* among, 258*†.
beð *see* **ben.**
bi *adv.* along with it, 274.
bi *prep.* by, 3, 19, 37 (twice) etc.; along, 135 (postponed); beside, 517; by, on, 593; **be** by, during, 526 (twice); *be derne see* **derne.**
bicumeð *pres. ind. 3 sg.* becomes, 65; (+ *obliq.*) becomes, suits, 538.
bidden *v.* ask, 90; **bit** *pres. ind. 3 sg.,* 289; wishes, 167†; **bid** *imperat. sg.,* 133.
biforn *adv.* in front, 52, 58, 236 etc.
bigripen *v.* seize, 352.
biȝeten *pres. ind. pl.* beget, 433, 437.
biholdeð *pres. ind. 3 sg.* beholds, watches, 321; **bihalt,** 463; **biholden** *p.p.* observed, 455.
bihoueð *pres. ind. 3 sg. impers.* (+ *obliq. of person*) it is fitting, 221.
bile *n.* bill, beak, 60.
bilimpes *pres. ind. 3 sg. impers.* (+ *obliq. of person*) it happens, 242.
bilirten *v.* deceive, 270.
biliuen *v.* remain alive, 163† [OE belī-fan].
billeð *pres. ind. 3 sg.* strikes, 57, 58; scratches, 293 [OE bil(l), *n.,* 'sword'].

billing *n.* scratching, 278, 297† [*from prec.*].

biloken *pres. ind. pl. reflex.* look around, 365.

bimene *imperat. pl. reflex.* lament, 598†.

birde-time *n.* time of birth, 105.

birdene *n. p.c.* burden, 254.

bisetten *v.* beset, 147.

biswiken *v.* deceive, 351; **biswike**, 286; **biswikeð** *pres. ind. 3 sg.*, 329.

bit *pres. ind. 3 sg. see* **bidden.**

bit *pres. ind. 3 sg.* bites, 170, 182, 326 etc.

bitokneð *pres. ind. 3 sg.* signifies, symbolizes, 135†, 329.

bitterlike *adv.* fiercely, sharply, 326.

bitwen *prep.* among, 247 (postponed).

biðenken *v.* think about, 68.

biwalt *pres. ind. 3 sg.* succeeds, works out, 464*†.

blac *adj.* black, 535.

blast *n.* blast, 484.

blis *n.* bliss, 124, 574.

blod *n.* blood, 327, 333; ~ & *bon* body, 438, 572.

boc *n.* book, 308; **boke** *p.c.*, 28, 190, 513 etc.

bodes *n. pl.* precepts, 121; teachings, 184.

bodi *n.* body, 116, 151, 393 etc.

boke *see* **boc.**

bon *n. blod & ~ see* **blod.**

bone *n.* request, 90.

borlic *adj.* big, 424 [OE bōrlice, *adv.*].

bote *n.* forgiveness, 133.

boðe *conj.* both, 37, 133, 267; **boðen**, 158, 213.

boðen *adj.* both, 468.

bred *pp.* produced, 105.

breid *n.* trap, 492; **breides** *pl.* tricks, 302.

brennen *v.* kindle, 372; *pres. ind. pl.* burn, 218, 220.

brenning *n.* burning pain, 199.

brest *n.* breast, 105, 393.

brest-atter *n.* venom produced in the breast, 107.

brest-filðe *n. p.c.* impurity in the breast, 141*.

briche *adj.* helpful, 258; (+ *obliq. of person*), 530.

briddes *n. pl.* (small) birds, 595.

briȝt *adj.* clear, keen, 45.

bringeð *pres. ind. 3 sg.* ~ *in* drives to, 288.

brinneð *pres. ind. 3 sg. reflex.* is burnt, burns himself, 197.

bro *n.* back, brow, 535.

broken *pret. ind. pl.* broken, failed to obey, 211; *pp.*, 122.

broðer *n.* brother, 252*, 478.

bukes *n. gen. sg.* belly's, 289.

bunden *pp.* joined, 393.

buten *conj.* but, 101; unless, if ... not, 175; **bute** if only, as long as, 117; except that, but, 328.

buten *prep.* except, 84†.

calleð *pres. ind. 3 sg.* calls for, 470.

calling *n.* calling out, 505.

cam *see* **cumen.**

canne *pres. ind. 3 sg.* can, is able to, 477; **cunen** *pl.*, 403. **cunne** *subj. sg.*, 6, 42, 113; **can** *pret. subj. sg.* (*aux. forming with inf. equivalent of pret.*), 68†; **cune** *imperat. sg.* 131.

capun *n.* capon, 264.

care *n.* distress, misery, 505.

caue *n.* cave, hollow, 162, 170, 182.

cete *n.* whale, 349.

cethegrande *n.* whale, 335.

char *n. makeð* ~ goes, 462 [cf. OA cerran, 'turn'].

chare *v. aȝen* ... ~ return, turn back, 403 (cf. OA cerran, 'turn').

chaueles *n. pl.* jaws, 349.

ches *pret. sg.* chose, 524.

chin-bon *n.* jawbone, chin, 240* [OE cinbān].

clepeð *pres. ind. 3 sg.* calls, 191.

cliuer *adj.* expert in seizing, 146† [cf. cliuer, *n.*, 'claw' *and see OED s.v.* clever].

cloðed *pp.* clothed, 110.

cloðede *n.* clothed man, 146.

coc *n.* cock, 264.

cof *adj.* bold, quick, fierce, 110, 146.

cold *see* **kolde.**

come *n.* approach, 599.

come *pret. subj. sg. see* **cumen.**

corn *n.* corn, grain, 159, 165, 170 etc.

costes *n. pl.* habits, 249, 585, 587.

craft *n.* skill, trick, 99; sorcery, magic art, 378.

crede *n.* creed, 87.

crepen *v.* creep, 162; **crepeð** *pres. ind. 3 sg.* crawls, 99, 102.

cripelande *ppres.* moving lamely, 99 [OE crypel, *n.*].

Crist *n.* Christ, 72, 74, 118 etc.; **Cristes** *gen. sg.*, 222, 594, 602.

Cristen *adj.* Christian, 65; *Cristene*, 118.
Cristes *see* **Crist.**
cristned *pp.* christened, baptized, 119.
cul *n.* choice, 541† [cf. AN cuillir, *v.*].
culuer *n.* dove, 585.
cumen *v.* come, 530; **cumeð** pres. ind. 3 sg., 355, 465, 486 etc.; **cumen** *pl.*, 243, 347, 402 etc.; **kam** *pret. ind. sg.*, 21, 310; **cam**, 506; **come** *pret. subj.*, 18; *cumeð to* reaches, 41; *cumeð ut* emerges, 50, 83; *cumeð ut of* escapes from, frees himself of, 30; *cumeð gangen see* **gangen**; *cume saken see* **saken**; *cumen on stalle see* **stalle.**
cune, cunen, cunne *see* **canne.**

dai *n.* day, 21, 37, 133 etc.; **dei**, 517; **daies** *pl.*, 97, 571; **daȝes**, 544; **deies** *gen. sg.*, 271.
dar *pres. ind. 3 sg.* dares, 583; **dure** *pret. subj. sg.*, 128.
dareð *pres. ind. 3 sg.* lies still, 272; sits still, 328; **daren** *pl.*, 561.
ded *adj.* dead, 20, 272, 275 etc.
ded *n.* death, 364; **dede** *p.c.*, 22, 562; *to ~ maken* kill, 112†.
dede *n.* deed, act, action, 71; behaviour, 412, 413.
dede *pret. ind. sg. see* **don.**
defte *adj.* humble, gentle, 18 [OE dæfte & *defte].
dei, deies *see* **dai.**
del *n. euerilc ~ see* **euerilc.**
dele *n. p.c.* valley, 3.
demen *v.* judge, 531; **deme** *imperat. sg.* consider, 128.
den *n.* den, 7.
dennede *pret. ind. sg. reflex.* sought shelter, 18.
der *n.* animal, creature, 176, 208, 261 etc.; *pl.*, 540.
deren *v.* inflict injury, 111, 112; inflict injury on, 144; harm, 205, 583; **dereð** *pres. ind. 3 sg.*, 285; **derie** *pres. subj. sg.*, 162.
derflike *adv.* without hesitation, promptly, 275†.
dern *adj.* secret; innate (but not apparent), 64†.
derne *n.* darkness *be ~* stealthily, craftily, 17†.
dernelike *adv.* stealthily, 285.
derue *adj.* strong, bold, 176† [ON *derf-, cf. djarfr].

deu *n.* dew, 6†.
deuel *n.* devil, 144, 146, 284 etc.; **diuel**, 17; **deueles** *gen. sg.*, 387; **deueles**, 600.
dillen *v.* be sluggish, 260 [OE *dylle, *adj. related to* dol, 'stupid'].
dun *adj.* dark, 390, 512; **dimme** dim, clouded, 34.
dine *n.* sound, 582.
diuel *see* **deuel.**
diueð *pres. ind. 3 sg.* dives, 375 [OE dȳfan; *for semantic development see OED s.v.* dive, *v.*].
do *see* **don.**
doluen *pp.* buried, 20.
dom *n.* judgement, 177.
Domesdei *n.* Doomsday, Day of Judgement, 187.
don *v.* cause to, make, 474; carry out, 458; behave, 596; do, 183, 287*, 289; **doð** *pres. ind. 3 sg.* (*representing another v.*) does, 125, 137, 176 etc.; performs, 268, 292; causes to, 374, 379; **dede** *pret. ind. sg.*, 150; **don** *pp.*, 598; **do** *imperat. pl.*, 176; *do we . . . in* let us subject . . . to, 151; *do we of* let us abandon, 592†; *doð . . . hire non oðer god see* **god** *n.* ².
dragunes *n.pl.* dragons, 559.
draȝen *v.* draw, 384; **draȝeð** *pres. ind. 3 sg.* drags, 5, 192; draws, 272; **draȝen** *pl.* draw out, 210; move, 345, 368.
dreccheð *pres. ind. 3 sg.* remains, stays, 77 [OE dreccan, 'vex'].
dred *n.* doubt, 275.
drem *n.* sound, 484.
drepeð *pres. ind. 3 sg.* kills, 327, 376.
dreueð *pres. ind. 3 sg.* vexes, 333†.
drie *adj.* dry, 552.
driȝten *n.* Lord, 20; **driȝtin**, 93; **driȝtinnes** *gen. sg.*, 211.
drink *n.* drink, 139.
drinken *v.* drink, 103, 224, 290 etc.; **drinkeð** *pres. ind. 3 sg.*, 106, 202, 327 etc.
driueð *pres. ind. 3 sg.* hastens, 7.
droui *adj.* stirred up, turbid, 359.
dun *adv.* down, 5*†, 7, 18, 47 etc.
dure *n. see* **kirke-dure.**
dure *pres. subj. sg. see* **dar.**
dust *n.* dust, 5, 6.

eche *adj.* eternal, 123, 124.
eft *adv.* again, 530.
eȝen *n. pl.* eyes, 13, 34, 45 etc.

elde *n.*¹ old age, 30, 96.
elde *n.*² hill, 318† [OE; cf. WS hylde].
elded *pp.* grown old ~ *art fro* have failed to attain, 124† [OA eldan].
eldere *n. pl.* ancestors, 150, 210.
elp *n.* elephant, 465, 490; **elpes** *pl.*, 423.
er *adv., conj. see* **or** *adv., conj.*
er *conj.*² or, 88, 112, 194 etc.; *on stalle ~ on stede see* **stalle**; *stille ~ lude see* **stille.**
eried *pp.* ploughed, 270.
ern *n.* eagle, 62; **ernes** *gen. sg.*, 27.
erö-chine *n.* crevice in the ground, 270.
erðe *n.* earth, 16; people of the earth, 130; *gen. sg.*, 566.
erðliche *adj.* of this world, 184*†.
es *see* **ben.**
eten *v.* eat, 171, 290; **heten**, 373.
euelike *adj.* spiritual, 184 [OE heofonlic].
euen-sterre *n.* evening star, 566.
euerilc *adj.* ~ *del* every bit, completely, 226*.
eure *adv.* all the time, 354; ever, 551.
eurilc *pron.* everyone, 251.

fader *n.* father, 11, 22, 494 etc.
faȝen *adj.* glad, 346, 367.
faier *adj.* fair, beautiful, 565; **fairere** *comp.*, 534.
falleð *pres. ind. 3 sg.* falls, 48, 82, 269 etc.; **fallen** fall, become trapped, 322; drop off, 46; come down, 274; **fel** *pret. ind. sg.*, 493; **falle** *pres. subj. sg.*, 443; **fallen** *pp.*, 512; *fallen . . . togaddre* collapse, 468.
faren *v.* go, travel, 532; **fareð** *pres. ind. 3 sg.* moves about, wanders, 520; **faren** *pl.* come, 322; **fare** *pres. subj. sg.* 88 (twice); **faren** *pp.*, 527; *fareð on* attacks, 114*†.
fast *adv.* firmly, 142†.
fasteð *pres. ind. 3 sg.* fasts, 97.
fat *see* **funt-fat.**
fecheð *pres. ind. 3 sg.* fetches, gets, 157; **feccheð** steals, 264; **fecchen** *pl.*, 233.
fede, fedeð *see* **fet** *pres. ind. 3 sg.*
feȝ *imperat. sg.* cleanse, 141.
fel *n.* skin, 97, 102, 137 etc.
felde *n. p.c.* field, 269.
fele *adj.* many, 261, 407.
feleð *pres. ind. 3 sg.* feels, 374; perceives, 276; **felen** *pl.*, 346; **fele** suffer, 494.
fen *n.* mud, dirt, 566.
fend *n.* fiend, devil, 307.

fer *adv.* far away, 233.
festeð *pres. ind. 3 sg.* fastens, attaches, 317; puts, 389; **festen** *pl.* moor, 369; **feste** *imperat. sg. reflex.* confirm yourself, 126; *feste ðe forðward* make a solemn promise, 141†.
fet *n. pl.* **fet steppes** *see* **steppes.**
fet *pres. ind. 3 sg.* feeds, 185, 296; *reflex.* feeds himself, eats, 542; **fedeð**, 540; **fede** *subj. sg.*, 186.
feðres *n. pl.* feathers, 46.
fiȝteð *pres. ind. 3 sg.* fights, offers resistance, 114†; **fiȝtande** *ppres.*, 114†.
fikeð *pres. ind. 3 sg.* struggles, 475 [?ON fikja: *see* OED *s.v.* fike *v.*¹].
fille *n.* fill, 280, 328.
fillen *v.* observe, 259†; **filleð** *pres. ind. 3 sg.* fills up, 4.
filstnede *pres. ind. sg.* helped, 22.
filðe *n.* filth, sinfulness, 137.
fin *adj.* excellent, perfect, 580†.
finden *v.* find, 6, 157, 282; **fint** *pres. ind. 3 sg.*, 180; **findeð**, 382; **finde** *pres. subj. sg.*, 165.
finnes *n. pl.* fins, 395.
fir *n.* fire, 109, 374.
firmest *adv. sup.* first of all, 142†.
firste *adj.* first, 494.
fis *n.* fish, 335, 341, 353 etc.; **fisses** *pl.*, 345, 350.
Fisiologet *n.* Physiologus 191 (?OF: cf. Ysopet).
fleȝes *n. pl.* flies, insects, 322.
fleȝeð *pres. ind. 3 sg.* flies, 38, 517, 520.
flen *v.* desert, 235; **fleð** *pres. ind. 3 sg.* flees, 109, 145.
flerd *n.* deceiver, 309.
fles *n.* flesh, body, 102, 386.
flet *pret. ind. sg.* floated, 338†.
fleð *see* **flen.**
fliȝt *n.* flight, flying, 33; wings, 44.
fo *adj.* hostile, 317† [OE fāh, fā-].
fode *n. p.c.* food, 54, 92, 157 etc.; **fod** *n. liues* ~ provisions, 178†.
folde *n. p.c.* flock, 24; sheepfold, 426.
folȝen *v.* follow, 390, 579; **foleȝeð** *pres. ind. 3 sg.*, 382, 557; **foleȝen** *pl.*, 237.
fondeð *pres. ind. 3 sg.* tries, 475.
for *conj.* for, 73, 102, 111 etc.; because, 450.
for *prep.* for the sake of, for the good of, 24; because of, 46, 262, 263 etc.; in spite of, 481; ~ *to* in order to, 270, 274, 531; to, 150.

forbedeð *pres. ind. sg.* forbids, 183.

forbisnede *pp.* given as an example, 408.

forbisne *n.* allegorical interpretation, 281; **forbisnes** *pl.*, 189.

forbredes *pres. ind. 2 sg.* become corrupted, 122; **forbroiden** *pp.* made monstrous, 96†.

forbroken *pp.* broken, enfeebled, 96.

fordon *v.* kill, 312.

fordriuen *pp.* beaten by storms, tossed about by wind or waves, 363.

forȝelues *pres. ind. 2 sg.* wither, 123†.

forȝeten *pres. ind. pl.* forget, 400.

forleteð *pres. ind. 3 sg.* abandons, 166.

forloren *pp.* lost completely, 59.

forsaket *pres. ind. 3 sg.* renounces, 70.

forð *adv.* forth, on, 99, 102, 168; forth, 548.

forðen *v.* achieve, 112, 476, 496; *pres. ind. pl.* provide for, 246.

forði *adv.* for that reason, 125*, 176, 266.

forðward *adv.* from now on, 143, 229†.

forðward *n. feste* ... ~ *see* **festeð** [OE foreweard, *?infl. by prec.*].

forwerpen *v.* cast off, 226.

forwurðes *pres. ind. 2 sg.* are lost, 123*; **forwurðe** *subj. sg.* decay, 171; **forwurden** *pp.* enfeebled, 96.

fox *n.* fox, 262, 301*†, 307, 309 etc.; **foxes** *gen. sg.*, 276, 293, 303.

foxing *n.* fox's trick, 292†.

frame *n.* benefit, good, 19, 282 [cf. ON frami & OE fremman, framian, *vv.* & OE fram, *adj.*, 'forward'; *see OED s.v.* frame, *n.*¹].

fret *pres. ind. 3 sg.* eats, 280, 328; **freteð**, 334.

fro *prep.* from, 22, 105, 109 (twice) etc.; *hire* ~ so that she loses it, 171†; *let* ... ~ *see* **leteð**; *elded* ... ~ *eche blis see* **elded**.

fro ... ward *prep.* away from, 526.

fuȝeles *see* **fules**.

ful *adj.* full, 126, 261; satisfied, 542; **fulle** whole, 97; *to* ~ *iȝewis, to* ~ *iwis see* **iwis** *n.*

ful *adv.* completely, 203; very, 567.

fules *n. pl.* birds, 267, 274; **fuȝeles**, 270.

fulle *see* **ful** *adj.*

funt-fat *n.* font, 82.

furȝ *n.* furrow, 269.

gaddreð *pres. ind. 3 sg.* gathers, 158.

galle *n.* malice, 589.

gandre *n.* gander, 265.

gangen *v.* move, crawl, 98; **gangeð** *pres. ind. 3 sg.*, 135; moves about, 155; **gangen** *pl.* wander, 127; go, 370; *cumeð* ~ comes walking, 473*†.

gapeð *pres. ind. 3 sg.* opens his mouth, 342.

Gast *n.* Ghost, Spirit, 386, 576; **Gost**, 185.

gin *n.* trick, trap, 464.

god *adj.* good, 271; **gode**, 585.

God *n.*¹ God, 256; **Gode** *p.c.*, 78, 90, 228; **Godes** *gen. sg.*, 138, 582.

god *n.*² what is good, 183; friendly words, 305; reward, 500; *doð* ... *hire non oðer* ~ helps herself in no other way, does herself no other kindness, 327; *to none gode* without any benefit, 55.

godcundhede *n.* pious talk, 411.

godcundnesse *n.* divine nature, 580.

Gode *see* **God**.

godspel *n.* gospel, 138.

golsipe *n.* lechery, 214*†, 430.

gon *v.* go, 136, 195; **goð** *pres. ind. 3 sg.*, 56, 269, 280; moves about, wanders, 517, 521; **gon** *pl.*, 26, 425; **gon** *subj. pl.*, 223; **go** *imperat. sg.*, 138; *ðermide* ~ carry it, 434.

gos *n.* female goose, 265.

Gost *see* **Gast**.

goð *see* **gon**.

grace *n.* grace, 93.

gredilike *adv.* greedily; thirstily, 202.

gres *n.* grass, 159; plant, 431 [cf. OFris gers].

grete *adj.* big, 352.

groning *n.* wailing, lamentation, 597.

grund *n.* bottom, 48, 359; **grunde** *p.c.*, 375; *water-* ~ *see* **water-grund**.

ȝe *pron. pers. 2 pl.* you, 63, 209; **ȝu** *obliq.*, 492, 516, 550 etc.

ȝe *pron. pers. 3 sg. fem.* she, 153, 157, 161 etc.; *hire obliq.*, 160, 162, 165 etc.; *ire*, 159†; *hire poss. adj.*, 157, 160, 163 etc.; *pron. reflex.*, 156, 524; *ȝet* = *ȝe it*, 170.

ȝef *see* **if**.

ȝelt *pres. ind. 3 sg.* pays back, 278; **ȝeld** *subj. sg.*, 297†.

ȝemen *v. reflex.* take heed, 229.

ȝer *n. pl.* years, 434, 435.

ȝet *adv.* yet, still 52, 85, 86 etc.; yet, 337.

ȝet = **ȝe** + **it** *see* **ȝe** *pron. pers. 3 sg. fem.*

ȝeuelic *adj.* equal to, 152; *o ȝeuelike* equally, 185; *o ȝeueliche*, 531*†.

3ing *adj.* young, 143.
3ingen *v. reflex.* be rejuvenated, 228†;
3ingiŏ *pres. ind. 3 sg.*, 208*.
3iscing *n.* covetousness, 214 [OE gitsian,
v.].
3iuernesse *n.* gluttony, 215 [OE gīfre,
adj.].
3iueŏ *pres. ind. 3 sg.* gives, 256.
3u *see* **3e** *pron. pers. 2 pl.*
3ungling *n.* young one, 486.
3uŏhede *n.* youth, 29.

hac *adv.* ? ruthlessly, without hesitation,
592† [cf. ON hak-r, *adj.*].
haleŏ *pres. ind. 3 sg.* drags, 160, 266.
half *adj.* half, 406 (twice).
haliweie *n.* sweet healing liquid, 549.
harde *adj.* severe, 175.
harde *n.* hard time, 442†.
harde *adv.* severely, 177.
hardilike *adv.* vigorously, 155.
harm-dedes *n. pl.* harmful acts, 263.
hatieŏ *pres. ind. 3 sg.* hates, 266; **haten** *pl.*,
263; **hatien**, 267.
hauen *n.* property, possessions, 159†.
hauen *v.* have, 134, 181, 500; experience,
175, 304†; **haue** *pres. ind. 1 sg.* (*aux. forming perfect*), 492, 558; **hauest** *2 sg.*, 122;
haueŏ *3 sg.*, 10, 59, 455; has, possesses,
8, 12, 162 etc.; feels, 148, 199; keeps, 522;
hauen *pl.*, 154, 187, 209 etc.; **haue** 260,
594; **haue** *pres. subj. sg.*, 149; ~ *in mode
see* **mod**; *of . . . haueŏ ŏrist see* **ŏrist.**
he *pron. pers. 3 sg. masc.* he, 1, 2, 3 etc.; **him**
obliq., 4, 10, 11 etc.; **his** *adj. poss. sg.*, 2, 5,
7 etc.; **hise** *pl.*, 4, 13, 31 etc.; **his**, 34;
him *pron. reflex.*, 7, 18, 54 etc.; *al his mi3t
see* **mi3t.**
he *pron. pers. 3 pl.* they, 232, 233, 234 etc.;
hem *obliq.*, 247, 278, 279 etc.; **here** *adj.
poss.*, 246, 278, 327 etc.; *mid here best ouel
see* **ouel.**
he3 *adj.* high, 143.
he3e *adv.* loudly, 504.
heil *adj.* healthy, well, 49, 245, 354.
helde, helden *see* **holden.**
helle *n. p.c.* hell, 223, 300, 390 etc.; *gen.*,
574.
helpe *n.* help, 470, 472, 481 etc.
helpen *v.* help, 255, 502; **helpeŏ** *pres. ind.
3 sg.*, 160; **helpen** *pl.* help, 243; **helpe**
imperat. sg., 127.
her *adv.* here, 16, 164, 209 etc.; **here**, 175.

here *adj. poss. see* **he** *pron. pers. 3 pl.*
heren *v.* hear, 138; **hereŏ** *pres. ind. 3 sg.*,
556; **here** *subj. sg.*, 1; **hereŏ** *imperat. pl.*,
35; ~ . . . *to pres. ind. pl.* obey, 26; **herd**
pp. herd told see **telleŏ.**
herien *v.* pull, drag, 243†.
herkne *imperat. sg.* listen, 449.
Herodes *n.* Herod, 309.
herof *adv.* of this, 260, 523.
hert *n.* hart, stag, 188, 227; **hertes** *gen. sg.*
(*or pl.?*), 249; **hertes** *pl.*, 230.
herte *n.* heart, 142, 522; *wit* ~ sincerely,
121.
herto *adv.* to this, 523.
heruest *n.* autumn, 155.
hete *n.* heat, 46.
heten *see* **eten.**
heued *n.* head, 116, 152.
heuekes *gen. sg.* hawk's, 599 [OA heafuc].
Heuen-Louerd *n.* Lord of Heaven, 149.
heuene *n.* heaven, 39, 41, 129 etc.; *gen. sg.*,
574.
Heuen-king *n.* King of Heaven, 506.
Heuenriche *n.* Kingdom of Heaven, 14,
257, 529; *gen. sg.*, 500.
hid *n.* skin, 107.
hi3tes *pret. ind. 2 sg.* promised, 120, 142;
hi3test, 118.
hil *n.* hill, 14; **hille** *p.c.*, 1.
hileŏ *pres. ind. 3 sg.* conceals, 461.
hille *see* **hil.**
him *see* **he** *pron. pers. 3 sg. masc.*
himself *pron. reflex.* to himself, 55;
himseluen, 463.
hirde *n.* shepherd, 24, 25.
hire *see* **3e** *pron. pers. 3 sg. fem.*
his, hise *see* **he** *pron. pers. 3 sg. masc.*
hitt *pres. ind. 3 sg. reflex.* hides, 321.
holden *v.* keep, 23; **helden** observe, 121;
helde *imperat. pl.* protect, 152†; **holdeŏ**
pres. ind. 3 sg. ~ *luue see* **luue; holde**
subj. sg. lif ~ *see* **lif.**
hole *n. p.c.* hole, 160, 321, 543 etc.; fox's
earth, 266; cleft, cavern, 601.
holi *adj.* holy, 121, 576; ~ *spel see* **spel.**
hope *n.* hope, 78; hope, trust, 602; trust,
389.
hopeŏ *pres. ind. 3 sg.* hopes, 472, 474.
hornes *n. pl.* horns, antlers, 206, 227; *gen.
sg.* horn's, 484.
houeŏ *pres. ind. 3 sg.* hovers, is poised, 43;
lingers, 361; **houen** *pl.*, 347 [? OE
hōfian].

hu *see* **wu** *adv.*
hule *n.* shelter, 163 [OE hulu, 'husk'].
hulen *pres. ind. pl.* pursue or chase away with shouting, 267† [cf. MDu hulen & AN ouler].
hundred *n.* hundred, 248, 435.
hunger *n.* hunger, starvation, 175, 268.
hungren *v.* feel hungry, 379; **hungreð** *pres. ind. 3 sg. reflex.*, 342 [OE hyngrian *with vowel of prec.*].
hunten *v.* hunt, 1; **hunte** *pres. subj. sg.*, 17†.
hunte *n.* hunter, 455; **huntes** *gen. sg.*, 491.
hus *n.* house, 138.
husebondes *n. pl.* householders, 263.
hus-rof *n.* roof of a house, 317.

I *pron. pers. 1 sg.* I, 27, 499, 518; **Ic**, 28, 166, 492 etc.
idel *adj.* idle, 294.
idiȝt *adj.* ready, 320 [OE gediht, *pp.*].
if *conj.* if, 26, 108, 110 etc.; **ȝef**, 242, 258, 338 etc.; *wat ~ see* **wat** *pron. interr.*
iȝewis *see* **iwis** *n.*
Ihesu *n.* Jesus, 72.
ikindled *pp.* born, 8 [ME kindel, *n. from* OE gecynd, 'offspring'].
ilc *see* **ilk** *adj.*
iliche, ilik, ilike *see* **like.**
ilk *adj.* each, every, 71, 523, 556; **ilc**, 225, 592.
ilk *pron.* everyone, each, 596.
ilkines *adj.* of every kind, 158.
ille *adj.* bad, 362; dangerous, 399.
illing *n.* injury, 278 [*from prec.*].
imene *adv.* together, 217†.
in *adv.* in, 350.
in *prep.* in, 18, 21, 43 etc.; into, 82, 163; to, 48; *bringeð ~ see* **bringeð**; *do ~ see* **don**; *~ ðoȝt see* **ðoȝt**; *~ wis see* **iwis** *adv.*
Inde *n.* India, 423.
inoȝ *n.* a great deal, 106.
into *prep.* into, 310, 580.
ire *see* **ȝe** *pron. pers. 3 sg. fem.*
is *pres. ind. 3 sg. see* **ben.**
is *pron. pers. 3 pl. obliq.* them, 6, 122, 266; **wes = we is**, 586 [*see MED s.v.* his *pron. (4)*].
it *pron. pers. 3 sg. neut.* it, 28, 68, 94 etc.; (*introductory*) 21, 343, 355; (*with pl. concord*) 399, 588; **itt**, 538.
iuel *adj.* evil, 284; **iuele**, 302.
iuel *n.* evil things, 306; harm, 334.

iuele *adj. see* **iuel** *adj.*
iuele *adv.* badly, scarcely, 98.
iwis *adv.* certainly, indeed, 307; **in wis**, 573.
iwis *n. to ful ~* very certainly, 395; *to ful iȝewis*, 451† [OE gewiss, *adj.*].

kam *see* **cumen.**
ket *n.* flesh, 295 [cf. ON kjöt].
kinde *n.* characteristić, property, 8, 230; nature, 27, 564, 587; **kindes** *pl.*, 188; *of ~* by nature, 429.
kindles *n.* young one, 439† [OE gecynd, 'offspring', + OE -els].
kirke *n.* church, 67, 121.
kirke-dure *n.* church-door, 119, 524.
kiðen *v.* show, tell about, 27; **kiðeð** *pres. ind. 3 sg.* shows, exercises, 99.
knoweð *pres. ind. 3 sg.* knows, 94; **knov** *imperat. sg.*, 118.
kolde *adj.* cold, 429; **cold**, 438.

laȝe *adj.* weak, 383† [ON lág-r, 'low'].
laȝe *n.* characteristic, property, 12; Law, Dispensation, 181, 183, 186 etc.; **laȝes** *pl.*, laws, precepts, 120.
laȝelike *adv.* in accordance with the law, faithfully, 514 [lOE lahlīce, *first element infl. by prec.*].
laȝt *n.* snatching, 591† [OE læccan, *v.*].
lai *see* **lið.**
late *adv.* late, 401.
lat, lateð *see* **leteð.**
ledeð *pres. ind. 3 sg.* leads, 300.
lef *adj.* (+ *obliq. of person*) pleasing to, 364; **leue** (+ *poss. adj. of person*), 532.
lefful *adj.* faithful, pious, 523*.
leȝeð *pres. ind. 3 sg.* speaks falsely, 308; is lying, 518; **leȝen** *pl.* deceive, 418.
leiȝeð *pres. ind. 3 sg.* places, lays, 240.
leiðe *adj.* hideous, 314.
lendbon *n.* haunch, 241.
lene *adj.* thin, emaciated, 98.
leneð *pres. ind. 3 sg. reflex.* leans, 453, 466.
lengðe *n.* length *on ~* in the end, 388.
lepeð *pres. ind. 3 sg.* rushes, runs, 200; leaps, 277.
leren *v.* learn, 89; **lereð** *pres. ind. 3 sg.*, 75, 79; teaches, 183; **lered** *pp.*, 209.
lesing *n.* lying, 422.
leteð *pres. ind. 3 sg.* leaves behind, 102; leaves, 593; **lat** pretends, 286, 287; **lateð** abandons, 239; **let** *pret. ind. sg.*, 578; **let** *imperat. sg.* let . . . *fro* cast . . . from, 137.

letteð *pres. ind. 3 sg.* prevents, 277.
leue *adj. see* **lef.**
leue *n.*[1] faith, 383†, 386.
leue *n.*[2] permission, 149.
leue *pres. subj. sg.* grant, 186†.
leuen *v.* believe, 120, 311; **leueð** *pres. ind. 3 sg.*, 74; **leuen** *pl.*, 314; **leue** *imperat. pl.*, 528, 529.
leun *n.* lion, 1, 9, 12 etc.
lic *see* **like.**
licham *n.* body, 185.
lides *n. pl.* lids, 13.
lieð *see* **lið** *pres. ind. 3 sg.*
lif *n.* life, 117, 123, 135†; manner of life, 513, 516; **liue** *p.c.* o ~ alive, 522; **liues** *gen. sg.* ~ *fod see* **fode**; ~ *holde* keeps alive, survives, 117; *to* ~ alive, 23.
lif-time *n.* lifetime, 514.
li3ten *v.* alight, come down, 16; relieve, 254.
li3tlike *adv.* lightly, quickly, 277.
like *adj.* like, 394; **iliche**, 424*†; **ilike**, 392; **lic**, 597†; **ilik** (+ *obliq.*) equivalent to, 301.
likede *pret. ind. 3 sg. impers.* (+ *obliq. of person*) it pleased, 16.
limes *n. pl.* limbs, 31, 53, 117.
list *n.*[1] dexterity, 200.
list *n.*[2] desire, 380 [OE lystan, *v.*].
listen *v.* listen, take heed, 63*†; **list** *imperat. sg.*, 523.
listneð *pres. ind. 3 sg.* listens to, 387; *imperat. pl.* hear, 268.
litel *adj. see* **little.**
litel *n.* a little thing, 84†; ~ *him is of* he cares little about, 117.
little *adj.* little, short, 173; small, 383; **litel** small, humble, 508.
lið *n.* joint, 445.
lið *pres. ind. 3 sg.* lies, 9; **lieð**, 12; **lai** *pret. ind. sg.*, 21, 569.
liuen *v.* live, 364; **liueð** *pres. ind. 3 sg.*, 15, 354, 529 etc.
liuenoðe *n.* provisions, 173.
liue, liues *see* **lif.**
liueð *see* **liuen.**
lodlike *adj.* horrible, fearsome, 314*†.
loken *v.* look, 128.
lond *n.* land, 270; dry land, 245; *o londe* on earth, 344, 554.
long *adj.* long-lasting, 173.
longe *adv.* for a long time, 569.
lore *n.* teaching, 75, 387, 594.

loð *adj.* (*with obliq. of person*) hateful to, 364; **loðe** (*with poss. adj. of person*), 532.
loð *n.* injury, harm, 287.
louerd *n.* Lord, 15, 74, 186 etc.; **louerdes** *gen. sg.*, 259.
lude *adv.* loud, 546; *stille er* ~ *see* **stille.**
luken *v.* close, 13; **lukeð** *pres. ind. 3 sg.*, 349.
luteð *pres. ind. 3 sg.* bends down, 487.
luue *n.* love, 79, 567, 584; loved one, 521, 528; *holdeð* ~ is faithful in love, 514.
luuelike *adv.* lovingly, 259.
luuen *v.* love, 251; **luuien**, 120; **luue** *imperat. pl.*, 525.

ma3t *see* **mi3t.**
ma3ti *adj.* strong, vigorous, 153.
mai *pres. ind. 3 sg.* can, 98, 144, 157 etc.; may, 460; **mai3**, 54, 352*, 384; **mu3en** *pl.*, 282, 446, 579; **mi3te** *pret. ind. sg.*, 17, 496, 498; **mi3ten** *pl.*, 502; **mu3e** *pret. subj. sg.*, 112, 163.
mainles *adj.* weak, 98.
make *n.* mate, 515, 517, 519.
maken *v. to ded* ~ *see* **ded**; *on stalle* ~ *see* **stalle**; **makeð** *pres. ind. 3 sg.*, makes, 11, 45, 116 etc.
man *n.* man, person, 1, 66, 108 etc.; (*generic*) one, people, 62, 94, 169 etc.; **mannes** *gen. sg.*, 131; **men** *pl.*, 127, 130, 267 etc.; **manne** *gen. pl.*, 19, 315.
mandragores *n.* mandrake, 432.
manhede *n.* human form, 509.
manie *adj.* many, 391, 398, 399 etc.; **mani**, 380.
manikines *adj. phr.* of many kinds, 315.
mankin *n.* mankind, the human race, 148, 212, 511.
manne *see* **man.**
Marie *n.* Mary, 19.
market *n.* market, 331.
meche *n.* mate, lover, 524.
mede *n.* reward, 73, 256.
meiden *n.* maiden, virgin, 18; young woman, 392.
men *see* **man.**
mene *pres. ind. 1 sg.* mean, 385.
mere *n.* mermaid, siren, 398†, 405.
mereman *n.* mermaid, siren, 392 [OE mere-men(n), *but cf.* OED *s.v.* mermin].
merk *see* **mirke.**
mete *n.* food, 61, 163, 172.

mid *prep.* with, 279, 371, 419 (twice) etc.; **miÐ**, 302, 395†, 536 etc.; **mit**, 11; ~ *here mi3t see* **mi3t**; ~ *here best ouel see* **ouel**.

middel-erd *n.* world, 310.

mide *adv.* along with them, 47; with him, 243.

mid-side *n.* the middle of the side, 441.

mi3t *n.* power, 204; **ma3t**, 377; **mi3te** *p.c. wiÐ mi3te* heartily, fervently, 525; *al his* ~ as hard as he can, 475; *mid here* ~ with all their might, 368†.

mi3te *pret. ind. sg.*, **mi3ten** *see* **mai**.

mikle *adj.* big, 384, 385, 479; great, 485; **mikel**, 200, 260, 377 etc.

mikel *adv.* greatly, hard, 153.

milce *n.* forgiveness, 134, 603.

mildelike *adv.* humbly, meekly, 130.

minde *adj.* (+ *obliq. of person*) in mind, 231, 430, 588.

mire *n.* ant, 153, 172, 180 [? *OE mīre; cf. MDu miere, MLG mire].

mirie *adv.* sweetly, 398.

mirke *adj.* dim, sightless, clouded, 69; **merk** dark, 300.

misdedes *n. pl.* sins, 134.

mist *n.* mist, dimness of sight, 76.

mit *see* **mid**.

mitte *prep.* + *def. art.* because of the, 402; with the, 489.

miÐ *see* **mid**.

mod *n.* pride, 131 (twice); anger, 218; **mod** mind, 306; **mode** *p.c.*, 232, 415; *hauen in mode* remember, 586.

moder *n.* mother, 595.

Moyses *n.* Moses, 495.

mone *n.* moon, 417.

more *adj. comp.* more, 436; greater, 169; **moste** *sup.* biggest, 336.

more *adv. comp.* again, in future, 520; **most** *sup.* most, 444.

mot *n.* meeting, 331.

moten *pres. ind. pl.* must, 181; **mote** *pres. subj. sg.* may, 134.

mu3e, mu3en *see* **mai**.

munen *v.* keep in mind, consider, 249; **muneÐ** *pres. ind. 3 sg.* admonishes, urges, 172; *imperat. pl.*, 516.

muÐ *n.* mouth, 85, 86, 91 etc.

naked *adj.* naked, 82, 108; *of* ... ~ deprived of, 107.

nakede *n.* naked man, 145.

name *n.* name, 19, 95, 303; *is hire to* ~ is her name, 262.

narwe *adj.* narrow, 101.

ne *adv.* not, 6, 26, 51 etc.

ne *conj.* nor, 9, 18, 131².

necke *n.* neck, 265.

neddre *n.* adder, serpent, 95, 107, 115 etc.

ned *n.* need, 260; **nede** 187, 246; *his nede* what is necessary for him, 89†; *at nede* in distress, 235, 239, 255; *it is te* ~ it is necessary for you, 125; *of* ... *haue* ~ need, 594.

nede *adv.* needs, of necessity, 115†.

nedeÐ *pres. ind. 3 sg.* troubles, oppresses, 144†; *reflex.* forces himself, 101.

ne33en *v.* approach, 108; **ne33e** *pres. subj. sg.*, 2.

neilond *n.* island, 339, 366.

nes *pres. ind. 3 sg.* is not, 461.

nese *n.* nose, 193; *gen. sg.* ~ *smel* sense of smell, 2†.

nest *n.* nest, 601.

net *n.* net, 325.

neuermor *adv.* never again, 437.

neure *adv.* never, 13, 17, 526.

newe *adj.* new, 181, 528; renewed, 53, 83, 143.

neweÐ *pres. ind. 3 sg.* renews, 29; *reflex.*, 35, 66, 95; **newe** *imperat. sg.*, 125.

ni3t *n.* night, 37, 133, 517 etc.; **ni3te** *p.c.*, 526.

nimeÐ *pres. ind. 3 sg.* goes, 67, 101, 325¹; seizes, 325²; takes, 541.

niÐ *n.* malice, 148, 213.

niÐer *adv.* down, 3, 443.

niÐerward *adv.* downwards, 394.

no *adj.* 131, 394, 430 etc.; **non**, 54, 204, 272 etc.; ~ *wi3t, non wi3t see* **no3t**; *to none gode see* **god** *n.*²; *doÐ hire non oÐer god see* **god** *n.*².

no3t *adv.* not, not at all, 108, 128, 144 (twice)†; **nout**, 9, 531; **nowt**, 167, 185; **no wi3t**, 476, 496; **non wi3t**, 205.

no3t *n.* none, 308.

nome *n.* snatching, seizing, 600 [OE niman, *v.*].

non, none *adj. see* **no**.

non *pron.* none, 235, 239, 250 etc.

norÐ *adv.* north, 88.

nos *n.* nose, beak, 265.

noster *see* **pater noster**

noten *pres. ind. pl.* eat, 431.

noule *n.* navel, 394.

nout *see* **no3t** *adv.*

nowor *adv.* nowhere, 26.

nowt *see* **noȝt** *adv.*
nu *adv.* now, 187, 209, 268; (*emphasizing exhortation*) 63.
nummor *adv.* no more, 402; **nummore** no longer, 179.

o *prep. see* **on**.
oc *adv.* also, 45, 189.
oc *conj.* but, 104, 109, 130 etc.
of *adv.* away, 174; *don* . . . ~ *see* **don**.
of *prep.* of, 13, 121, 126² etc.; about, concerning, 79, 169, 308 etc.; in, 126¹, 136, 601; (out) of, 116; because of, 198; away from, 244; off, of, 76; **off**, 93, 210, 232 etc.; *bare* ~ *see* **bare**; *cumeð ut* ~ *see* **cumen**; ~ . . . *kinde see* **kinde**; *litel him is* ~ *see* **litel** *n.*; ~ . . . *naked see* **naked**; *swic* ~ *see* **swiken**; ~ . . . *haueð ðrist see* **ðrist**; *vt* ~ *see* **vt of**.
offriȝt *adj.* afraid, frightened, 562.
ofte *adv.* often, 154, 218, 264 etc.
oȝ *pres. ind. 3 sg.* (+ *poss. of person*) ought to, 231, 250; **oȝen** *pl.*, 181, 249, 586.
oȝt *see* **out**.
old *adj.* old, 64; **olde** old, Mosaic, 181; old, former, 521.
on *adv.* on it, 369.
on *prep.* on, 1, 16, 177 etc.; in, 74, 100 (*postponed*), 120, 190 etc.; at, 295, 363, 415; towards, 146 (twice); **o**, 28, 94, 124 etc.; according to, 319; into, 425; during, 517 (twice); *one*, 293, 340, 372; *fareð* ~ *see* **faren**; *o ȝeuelike see* **ȝeuelic**; ~ *lengðe see* **lengðe**; *o liue see* **lif**; *o londe see* **lond**; ~ *stalle see* **stalle**; ~ *stede er* ~ *stalle see* **stede**; *wullen* ~ *see* **wille** *v.*
on *pron.* one, 236, 433, 473.
onde *n.* breath, 272, 343, 381 etc.
one *adj.* one, 232; **ore**, 503*† [OE ān, *dat. sg. fem.* ānre].
one *adv.* alone, 520, 521 (twice); only, 559.
ones *adv.* once, 515.
oni *adj.* any, 331.
onon *adv.* at once, 193; continuously, 571; **anon**, 325.
or *adv.* before, 104, 140, 150; **er**, 166, 206, 499.
or *conj.* before, 65, 68; **er**, 171.
ore *see* **one** *adj.*
otwinne *adv.* in two, 170, 182.
oðer *adj.* second, 8; other, 166, 331, 380 etc.; **oðre**, 274, 345; *doð* . . . *hire non* ~ *god see* **god** *n.* ².

oðer *conj.* or, 2, 484; ~ . . . ~ either . . . or, 6.
oðer *pron.* another, 235, 239, 250 etc.; someone else, 305, 329; other, 477, 521; **oðres** *gen. sg.*, 241; **oðre** others, 237, 243, 428.
ouel *n. mid here best* ~ with all the strength they have, 404*† [OE afol].
ouer *prep.* above, 565, 566; across, 234.
oueral *adv.* in every direction, everywhere, 548.
ouercumeð *pres. ind. 3 sg.* surpasses, 549.
ouerwene *n.* presumption, 216.
ouese *n.* eaves, 318 [OE *ofes].
out *adv.* in any respect, at all, 464; **ovt**, 518; **oȝt**, 502*†, 560.

panter *n.* panther, 533, 539, 560.
pater noster *n.* the Lord's prayer, 87.
pine *n.* torment, suffering, 574.
pit *n.* pit, 561.
poure *adj.* poor, 127.
prest *n.* priest, 140; **prestes** *gen. sg.*, 75.
pride *n.* pride, 216, 226.
prophetes *n. pl.* prophets, 497.
puteð *pres. ind. 3 sg.* puts, 488.

qual *n.* whale, 535†.
quenchet *pres. ind. 3 sg.* extinguishes, suppresses, 225.
quenching *n.* quenching, suppression, 139.
quike *adj.* swift, running, living, 222.
qwemeð *pres. ind. 3 sg.* is pleasing to, 165.
qweðsipe *n.* wickedness, 262.

rapelike *adv.* hurriedly, quickly, 156, 324.
raðe *adv.* at once, 278, 487; quickly, 292.
rauen *n.* raven, 273.
reche *imperat. sg.* take thought, take heed, 523.
reden *v.* advise, 516; **rede** *pres. ind. 1 sg.* read, 28.
redi *adj.* ready, 111, 273; prepared, 324.
reisen *v.* raise, 495; **reiseð** *pres. ind. 3 sg.* wakes, raises, 11; **reisede** *pret. ind. sg.*, 511; ~ *on stalle see* **stalle**.
rem *n.* cry, 11, 483, 548.
remeð *pres. ind. 3 sg.* cries out, roars, 470, 471, 478 etc.; **remen** *pl.* utter, 483; **remede** *pret. ind. sg.*, 573; **remeden** *pl.*, 503.
reming *n.* roaring, bellowing, 485.

rennen *v.* run, 221; **renneð** *pres. ind. 3 sg.,*
156, 324; **rennande** *ppres.,* 486.
resteð *pres. ind. 3 sg. reflex.* rests, 156, 447.
reufulike *adv.* pitifully, 471.
rewen *v.* grieve, 388; **rewe** *pres. subj. sg.,*
177.
riche *adj.* rich, 423.
riche *n.* kingdom, 532.
riȝt *adv.* straight in front, 42.
riȝte *adj.* straight, 60; right, 386.
riȝten *v.* make straight, 91; *up . . . riȝteð*
pres. ind. 3 sg. reflex., assumes an upright
position, 111.
rime *n.* rhymed verse, 513.
risen *v.* rise, get up, 446, 472; **riseð** *pres.*
ind. 3 sg., 546; **ros** *pret.,* 22, 573.
robbinge *n.* robbing, stealing, 592.
rode *n. p.c.* Cross, 416.
rof *n.* roof, 318.
ros *see* **risen.**
rotieð *pres. ind. 3 sg.* is rotting, 273.

sadue *n.* shade, 467.
saȝe *n.* words, 419.
saȝeð *pres. ind. 3 sg.* saws through, 459.
saken *v. cume ~* come walking, 479*†;
sakeð *pres. ind. 3 sg.* moves, passes, 168.
salt *pres. ind. 2 sg.* must (denoting necessity), 136; **sal** *3 sg.,* 89, 115, 388 etc.; will
(denoting future), 73, 177, 474; is bound
to (denoting necessity), 530; will
(denoting habit), 13; **sulen** *pl.,* 175, 257,
428 etc.; **sulde** *pret. ind. sg.,* 109.
same *n.* something to be ashamed of, 168;
disgrace, 298, 304.
sampnen *pres. ind. pl. reflex.* come
together, 427.
sapen *see* **sop.**
sarpe *adj.* sharp, 279.
satanas *n.* Satan, 70.
scaðe *n.* suffering, injury, 397.
scrifte *n. p.c.* confession, 140.
se *pres subj. sg. see* **seð.**
se *n.* sea, 356, 363, 391; **sees** *gen. sg.,* 359.
sed *n.* seed, 158, 166†, 593.
seftes *n. pl.* creatures, 313.
se-grund *n.* bottom of the sea, 353.
seien *v.* say, 337; **seie** *pres. ind. 1 sg.,* 499,
518, 550; **seieð** *3 sg.,* tells, 305; **seit,** 518;
seide *pret. ind. sg.,* 311; mentioned, 166;
sei *imperat. sg.,* 140; **seid** *pp.,* 492.
sekeð *pres. ind. 3 sg.* seeks, 36, 100, 451;
seke *imperat. pl.,* 178.

selcuðes *n. pl.* marvels, 391.
seld *n.* shield, 116.
seldum *adv.* seldom, rarely, 156.
selleð *pres. ind. 3 sg.* gives, inflicts, 332†.
sen *see* **seð.**
senden *see* **ben.**
sending *n.* disgrace, 298.
sene *adj.* evident, 313.
sepes *n. gen. sg.* sheep's, 409*†; *pl.* sheep,
25, 426.
Seppande *n.* Creator, 313.
se-sond *n.* bottom of the sea, 340.
set *pp.* set down, 190.
sete *see* **sit.**
seð *pres. ind. 3 sg.* sees, 39; **sen** *pl.,* 365;
se *pres. subj. sg.,* 108, 110; **soȝe** *pret. subj.*
sg., 338; **sen** *pp.,* 154.
seuene *adj.* seven, 587; *ðurȝ skies sexe & ~*
see **sexe.**
sexe *adj.* six *ðurȝ skies ~ and seuene*
through whatever clouds may chance to
come his way, 40†.
side *n.* side, 466.
siȝte *n.* sight, 81; view, sight, 527.
siker *adj.* safe, 178.
sikerlike *adv.* certainly, 80, 203.
silden *v.* shield, protect, 25; **sildeð** *pres.*
ind. 3 sg., 116.
sille *n.* sonorous, resonant, 399.
simple *adj.* free from guile, honest, 590.
siniȝing *n.* sinning, 225; **sineȝinge** *p.c.,*
132.
sinen *pp.* shone, 10.
sinful *adj.* sinful, 71, 380; **sinfule,** 299.
sinfule *n.* sinful man, 147.
singeð *pres. ind. 3 sg.* sings, 398.
sineȝinge *see* **siniȝing.**
sinken *v.* sink, 374; **sinkeð** *pres. ind. 3 sg.,*
397†; subsides, 396; **sinken** *pl.,* 402.
sinne *n.* 183, 288, 296; **sinnes** *gen. sg.,* 139;
pl. sins, 64, 140, 146
sipes *n. pl.* ships, 369, 397, 402; ships'
crews, 363†.
sipmen *n. pl.* sailors, 400.
sit *pres. ind. 3 sg.* sits, 463, 517, 521; **sete**
pret. subj. sg. rested, 340.
siðen *adv.* then, 60, 106, 160 etc.
siðen *conj.* when, 31, 32, 33 etc.
skemting *n.* enjoyment, 291.
skies *n. pl.* clouds, 40†.
slakeð *pres. ind. 3 sg.* grows slack, grows
loose, 97.
slep *see* **slepen.**

slepe *n. p.c.* sleep, 9.

slepen *v.* sleep, 544; **slepeŏ** *pres. ind. 3 sg.*, 467; **slepen** *pl.*, 401; **slep** *pret. ind. sg.*, 571; *to* ~ sleeping, 12.

sloŏ *pres. ind. 3 sg.* slays, kills, 288.

slumeren *pres. ind. pl.* slumber, 401.

smake *pres. subj. sg.* perceive by scent, 2† [OE smæc, *n.*].

smale *adj.* small, 351.

smel *n.* smell, 547, 577*; *nese* ~ *see* **nese**.

smelleŏ *pres. ind. 3 sg.* smells, 551.

smit *pres. ind. 3 sg.* rushes, 343.

snute *n.* snout, 488.

so *adv.* so, 92, 359, 362 etc.; in the same way, 309; in this way, 468; like, 484; **swo**, 22; *weŏer* ~ *see* **weŏer so**; *wilc . . . ~ see* **wilc . . . so**; *wo* ~ *see* **wo so**; *wor ~ see* **wor so**.

so *conj.* as, 24 (twice), 124, 125 etc.; as if, 168, 219, 272 etc.; as . . . as, 546; ~ . . . ~ as . . . as, 42; *al . . . ~ see* **al** *conj.*; *als ~ see* **also** *conj.*

softe *adj.* mild, 154; gentle, 590.

soȝe *see* **seŏ**.

sonde *n.* disgrace, 382.

sone *adv.* at once, 277, 375; soon, 418.

song *n.* song, singing, 419†, 597.

sop *pret. ind. sg.* created, 313; **sapen** *pp.*, 536.

sore *adv.* sorely, bitterly, 388.

sorȝeden *pret. ind. pl.* grieved, felt anxious, 501.

soule *n.* soul, 151, 422; **sowle**, 524; **sowles** *gen. sg.*, 92; **soule** 139, 525.

spekeŏ *pres. ind. 3 sg.* speaks, 414; **speken** *pl.* utter, 411.

spel *n.* story, 294; *holi* ~ Gospel, 568, 578.

speweŏ *pres. ind. 3 sg.* spits out, throws up, 104.

spinnere *n.* spider, 316.

spottes *n. pl.* spots, 536.

springeŏ *pres. ind. 3 sg.* wells up, 36.

spuse *n.* spouse, 525.

stalle *n. on* ~ on his feet, 499; *cumen on* ~ get back to his feet, 482; *on* ~ *maken* put back on his feet, 480†; *maken on* ~, 498; *reisen on* ~, 490; *on stede er on* ~ *see* **stede**.

standen *v.* stand, 474; **stonden**, 440; **stant** *pres. ind. 3 sg.*, 1; **stod** *pret. ind. sg.*, 499.

stede *n.* place, spot, 271; place, 396; *on* ~ *er on stalle* everywhere, continually, 330.

stedefast *adj.* steadfast, 385; (+ *obliq. of person*) steadfast towards, 253; firmly rooted, 452.

stedefastnesse *n. p.c.* steadfastness, constancy, 126.

stefnes *see* **steuene**.

stefninge *n. p.c.* singing, 400† [*from* OE stefn, 'voice'].

steȝ *pret. ind. sg.* rose, ascended, 575.

stel *n.* steel, 371.

steppes *n. pl.* steps *fet* ~ footprints, 4.

steppeŏ *pres. ind. 3 sg.* steps, treads, 5.

stereŏ *see* **stiren**.

steringe *n.* steering, 400.

stert *n.* tail, 5.

steuene *n. p.c.* voice, 503†; **stefnes** *pl.*, 398.

sti *n.* path, 135.

stille *adv.* still, without moving, 9, 21, 328 etc.; ~ *er lude* at any time, 330.

stiren *v.* stir, move, 583; **stireŏ** *pres. ind. 3 sg.*, 9, 356, 361; **stereŏ**, 271; **stiren** *pl.*, 559.

stoc *n.* tree trunk, 194.

stod *see* **standen**.

ston *n.* stone, 56, 100, 136 etc.; sepulchre hewn in stone, 21.

stonden *see* **standen**.

storm *n.* storm, 356.

strenen *v.* beget, 428.

strong *adj.* strong, 53, 452.

stund *n.* time, while, 271, 360.

suggeden *pret. ind. pl.* sighed, 501.

suk *n.* sucking action, 402.

sukeŏ *pres. ind. 3 sg.* sucks, 350.

sulde, sulen *see* **salt**.

sum *adj.* some, 406.

sumer *n.* summer, 154, 357.

sund *adj.* healthy, sound, 49, 245, 354.

sundren *pres. ind. pl.* part, 518.

sunen *v.* shun, avoid, 181, 250; **suneŏ** *pres. ind. 3 sg.* 168, 180.

sunne *n.* sun, 10, 43, 44 etc.

sures *n. pl.* showers, attacks of pain, 175.

suŏ *adv.* south, 88.

sweleŏ *pres. ind. 3 sg.* swallows, 196†.

sweren *pres. ind. pl.* swear, 416.

swet *adj.* fresh, 201; **swete** sweet, 551, 577; **swetteste** *sup.*, 344.

swetnesse *n.* sweetness, fragrance, 550, 553, 558.

swetteste *see* **swet**.

swic *see* **swiken**.

swik *n.* treachery, 302; **swike** treacherous intent, 348.

swiken *v.* deceive, trap, 456; *pres. ind. pl.* deceive, betray, 420; **swic** *imperat. sg. swic of* stop, 132.

swiking *n.* deceit, 421.

swilc *adj.* such, 217; **swilk**, 297.

swimmeð *pres. ind. sg.* swims, 236, 238.

swinkeð *pres. ind. 3 sg.* labours, toils, 153.

swiðe *adv.* quickly, 196, 316*†; very, 367, 538; entirely, 273.

swiðeð *pres. ind. 3 sg.* scorches, singes, 44*.

swo *see* **so** *adv.*

takeð *pres. ind. 3 sg.* takes, seizes, 61; *reflex.* devotes himself, 72.

tanne *conj. see* **ðanne** *conj.*

tat *adj. demons. see* **ðat** *adj. demons.*

tat *pron. demons. see* **ðat** *pron. demons.*

taunede *pres. ind. sg.* showed, 567 [see *OED s.v.* tawne, taune *v.* ¹: *aphetic form of* ME *at-awne(n) from* OE *æt-awnian; cf. MLG, MDu t-ônen].

te *def. art. see* **ðe** *def. art.*

te *pron. pers. see* **ðu.**

telleð *pres. ind. 3 sg.* tells, 294; says, 164; **told** *pp.* mentioned, 558; expounded, 564; *herd told* heard tell, 405†..

ten *adj.* ten, 97.

ten *pres. ind. pl. see* **teð** *pres. ind. 3 sg.*

ter *adv. demons. see* **ðer** *adv. demons.*

tetireð *pres. ind. 3 sg.* tears to pieces, 279.

tetoggeð *pres. ind. 3 sg.* pulls to pieces, 279 [OE tō- + eME toggen: *see OED s.v.* tug *v.*].

teð *n. pl.* teeth, 279.

teð *pres. ind. 3 sg.* goes, 38, 242; **ten** *pl.*, 234.

tide *pres. subj. sg.* (+ *obliq. of person*) happen, 442†.

til *conj.* till, 10, 21, 41 etc.; ~ *ðat*, 39, 322.

tilen *v.* procure, gain, 54, 92, 172; **tileð** *pres. ind. 3 sg.* labours, 164, 179.

time *n.* time, 355; opportunity, 164.

tin, tine *see* **ðu.**

tireð *pres. ind. 3 sg.* tears, 295.

tirȝen *v.* grow tired, 242 [OE tyrgan, 'vex'].

tis *adj. demons. see* **ðis** *adj. demons.*

tis *pron. demons. see* **ðis** *pron. demons.*

to *adv.* too, 401.

to *prep.* to, 3, 7, 16 etc.; 506 (postponed); for, 19 282; as, for, 159, 315, 524; up to, 441; into, 512; *cumeð* ~ *see* **cumen;** *for* ~ *see* **for;** ~ *none gode see* **god** *n.* ²; *heren* ~ *see* **heren;** ~ *ful iȝewis*, ~ *ful iwis see* **iwis** *n.*; ~ *lif see* **lif;** ~ *name see* **name;** ~ *slepen see* **slepen;** ~ *... ward see* **to ... ward;** *eche lif* ~ *wolden see* **wolden.**

togaddre *adv.* together, 425; **togiddre,** 248; *fallen ...* ~ *see* **fallen.**

tokneð *pres. ind. 3 sg.* is meant, is symbolized, 406; **tokned** *pp.* meant, symbolized, 563.

tokning *n.* mark, 407.

told *see* **telleð.**

tolleð *pres. ind. 3 sg.* attracts, entices, 381.

to ... ward *prep.* towards, 78, 103, 129 etc.

tre *n.* tree, 451, 467, 493.

trendled *adj.* rounded, 537 [OE trendel, *n.*, 'circle, ring'].

trewe *adj.* true, steadfast, 143; (+ *obliq. of person*) true to, 527.

trostlike *adv.* confidently, 453* [OE trust, *n.*].

tu *see* **ðu.**

tun *n.* farm-yard, 264.

tunder *n.* tinder, 371.

turtres *n. gen. sg.* turtle-dove's, 513.

tus *see* **ðus.**

twifold *adj.* twofold, double, 281; deceitful, 415.

two *adj.* two, 189, 434.

ðan *adv. see* **ðanne** *adv.*

ðan *conj. see* **ðanne** *conj.* ¹.

ðanne *adv.* then, 11, 56, 103 etc.; **ðan,** 138, 280, 477 etc.

ðanne *conj.* ¹ when, 12, 67, 96 etc.; **ðan,** 179, 332, 334; **tanne,** 187.

ðanne *conj.* ² than, 169.

ðar *adv. demons. see* **ðer** *adv. demons.*

ðar *adv. rel. see* **ðer** *adv. rel.*

ðar *conj. see* **ðer** *conj.*

ðarinne *see* **ðerinne.**

ðarto *see* **ðerto.**

ðarwiles *conj.* while, 164.

ðarwið *adv.* about this, 260.

ðat *adj. demons.* that, 18, 49, 177 etc.; **tat,** 14.

ðat *compound rel.* what, that which, 142, 160, 414.

ðat *conj.* 2, 22, 339 etc.; in order that, so that, 6, 26†, 134 etc.; so that, 98; in order that, 223; (introducing exhortation) 260; *til* ~ *see* **til.**

ðat *pron. demons.* that, 139, 337, 494; **tat**, 84.

ðat *pron. rel.* that, which, 11, 14, 36 etc.

ðe *adj. demons.* this, 12¹.

ðe *def. art.* the, 1, 11, 12² etc.; **te**, 11, 15, 80 etc.; **ðat** (tending to **ðat** *adj. dem.*) 18, 48, 244 etc.

ðe *pron. pers. see* **ðu.**

ðe *pron. rel.* who, that, 15, 19, 127 etc.; that, 173, 558.

ðenkeð *pres. ind. 3 sg.* thinks, 306; **ðoʒte** *pret. ind. sg.*, 312.

ðer *adv. demons.* there, 102, 322, 354 etc.; **ðore**, 70, 77, 178*†; **ðar**, 161†; **ter**, 288; **ðere**, 325.

ðer *adv. rel.* where, 49, 396, 499; **ðar**, 119.

ðer *conj.* where, 5, 157, 280; **ðar**, 7.

ðerabuuen *adv.* above, in heaven, 15.

ðerbi *adv.* against it, 453.

ðere *see* **ðer** *adv. demons.*

ðerfore *adv.* for that, 256; because of that, 345.

ðerimong *adv.* meanwhile, 420.

ðerinne *adv.* into it, 322; on it, 358; **ðarinne**, 269.

ðermide *adv.* ~ *gon see* **gon.**

ðerof *adv.* because of it, 197; because of this, 367; of this, 260.

ðeron *adv.* on it, 57.

ðerouer *adv.* above it, 38.

ðerto *adv.* there, to that place, 462; **ðarto** to it, 368.

ðerðurʒ *adv.* because of this, 212.

ðerunder *adv.* under it, 195.

ðerwile *conj.* while, 584.

ðeðen *adv.* from that place, 320, 530.

ðewes *n. pl.* virtues, 126.

ði, ðin, ðine *see* **ðu.**

ðing *n.* thing, 344, 406, 408; creature, thing, 198; *pl.*, 315.

ðirl *n.* hole, 100, 136*.

ðis *adj. dem.* this, 114, 115, 124 etc.; **tis**, 62, 268; **ðise** *pl.*, 350.

ðis *pron. demons.* this, 135, 308, 406 etc.

ðo *adv.* then, 22, 334, 503.

ðo *conj.* when, 16, 20, 310 etc.

ðo *pron. demons. pl.* those, 383, 541.

ðoʒ *conj.* although, 17, 53, 527; even if, 248, 435.

ðoʒt *n.* thought, mind, 444; *in* ~ anxious, 501.

ðoʒte *see* **ðenkeð.**

ðolen *v.* suffer, 570; **ðolede** *pret. ind. sg.*, 509.

ðore *see* **ðer** *adv. demons.*

ðornes *n. pl.* thorns, thorn-bushes, 207.

ðre *adj.* three, 435, 544, 571.

ðredes *n. pl.* threads, 317*†.

ðridde *adj.* third, 12, 21*†, 545.

ðries *adv.* thrice, three times, 10.

ðrist *n.* thirst, 379; *of . . . haueð* ~ thirsts after, 201.

ðrote *n.* throat, 343, 547.

ðrowing *n.* suffering, tribulation, 509*† [OE þrōwian, *v.*].

ðu *pron. pers. 2 sg.* you, 119, 120, 122 (twice) etc.; **tu**, 118, 128, 133 etc.; **ðe** *obliq.* 27, 144 (twice) etc.; **te**, 125; **ðe** *reflex.*, 125, 126, 128 etc.; for yourself, 133; **ðine** *adj. poss.*, 134; **ðin**, 137, 421; tine, 140; **tin**, 142; **ði**, 141, 422.

ðurʒ *adv.* through, 101.

ðurʒ *prep.* through, 2, 40, 93 etc.; because of, 211, 493; by, 563.

ðus *adv.* thus, so, 81, 95, 99 etc.; **tus**, 66, 91, 106 etc.; *al* ~ just so, 393.

uenim *n.* venom, 104, 204.

vncost *n.* evil nature, 131.

uncuð *adj.* unaware, 348; **vnkuð** unacquainted, 86; **vncuð**, 413.

under *prep.* under, 488 (postponed).

underʒede *pret. ind. sg.* went under, passed under, 510.

underset *pres. ind. 3 sg.* props up, 459.

uniemete *adj.* immeasurable, grotesque, 405†.

unkuð *see* **uncuð.**

vnneðes *adv.* with difficulty, 101.

vnride *adj.* enormous, 341; unwieldy, 450; **unride**, 465 [OE ungerȳde, 'rough, violent'].

unskil *n.* want of reason; *wið* ~ excessively, 290.

unstrong *adj.* feeble, 33.

untrewe *adj.* not straight, crooked, 51, 85.

unwelde *adj.* weak, infirm, 31.

up *adv.* up, 38, 129, 193 etc.; to the surface, 361, 402; ashore, 370; against it, 466; **vp**, 573; ~ . . . *riʒteð see* **riʒten.**

upon *prep.* on high in, 529; **upone** on, 557.

up to *prep.* as high as, 504.

ure, vre, us *see* **we.**

ut *adv.* out, 323.

ut of *prep.* out of, 343, 426, 547; *cumeð* ~ *see* **cumen.**

vuemast *adj. sup.* highest, 575*†.

wadeð *pres. ind. 3 sg.* wades, 238.

wakeð *pres. ind. 3 sg.* keeps watch, 24; **waken** *pl.* wake up, 401.

walke *n.* walking, 454.

walkeð *pres. ind. 3 sg.* moves, 103; journeys, moves, 448, 554, 555; **walke** *imperat. sg.* go about, live, 130.

wan *conj. see* **wanne.**

wan *pret. ind. sg. see* **winnen.**

wankel *adj.* insecure, 396.

wanne *conj.* when, 8, 333, 442; **wan**, 338, 346, 568.

war *adj.* cautious, prudent, 175; aware of, 461; **warre**, 403; ~ *wurðe* should become aware, cautious, 113.

ward *see* **fro . . . ward**; **to . . . ward.**

warmen *v. reflex.* warm themselves, 372.

warre *see* **war.**

warsipe *n.* prudence, 283.

was *see* **ben.**

wat *compound rel.* what, 118.

wat *pron. interr.* what, 84†; ~ *if* what happens if, 113, 149.

water *n.* water, 103, 201, 202 etc.

water-grund *n.* bottom of the river, 244.

waxeð *pres. ind. 3 sg.* grows, 110; **waxe** *pres. subj. sg.* sprout, 171; **waxen** *pp.*, 395.

we *pron. pers. 1 pl.* we, 25, 26 (twice), 154 etc.; **us** *obliq.* 25, 150, 172 etc.; **vs**, 23; **ur** *poss.*, 250, 596; **us** *reflex.*, 258; **ure** *adj. poss.*, 20, 74, 149 etc.; **vre**, 15, 186.

web *n.* web, 316*†, 319, 323.

wed *n.* weed, 158.

weder *n.* weather, 154, 362.

weie *n. p.c.* way, 3.

wel *adj.* well, recovered, 203; (+ *obliq. of person*) ~ *he* may good fortune befall him (*OED s.v.* well *a* sense 1), 570.

wel *adv.* well, 94, 461, 538 etc.; fully, completely, 86, 276, 567; very, 196, 399; thoroughly, 373; **welle**, 14.

wel *n.* wheel, 537.

welle *adv. see* **wel** *adv.*

welle *n.* well, spring, 36, 222; *gen. sg.*, 48 [OA wella, welle: *see OED s.v.* well *sb.* ¹].

wenden *v.* go, 3; go, get, 323; *pres. ind. pl.*, 174; **wende** *imperat. sg.*, 526.

weneð *pres. ind. 3 sg.* thinks, supposes, 169, 273; **wenen** *pl.*, 275, 366; hope, expect, 480.

were, weren *see* **ben.**

weren *v. reflex.* defend himself, 113 [OE werian¹].

wereð *pres. ind. 3 sg.* wears, fades away, 76†; **weren** *pl.*, 409 [OE werian²].

weri *adj.* weary, 454.

werk *n.* behaviour, 299.

werkeð *pres. ind. 3 sg.* does, 334; causes, 397.

werld *n.* world, 124, 173; **werlde** *n. p.c.*, 94, 313, 436 etc.

werpeð *pres. ind. 3 sg.* casts, 206, 319.

wes = **we is** *see* **is** *proń. pers. 3 pl. obliq.*

wete *adj.* wet, 552.

wete *n.* ¹ wheat, 165, 180.

wete *n.* ² wet, water, 47.

weðer *conj.* whether, 464; ~ *so*, 238.

weueð *pres. ind. 3 sg.* weaves, 319; **weveð**, 316.

wicches *n. pl.* witches, 378.

wide *adv.* wide, 342; far, 448.

widue *n.* widow, 519.

wiȝt *n.* **no wiȝt, non wiȝt** *see* **noȝt** *adv.*

wikke *adj.* wicked, 412 [? OE wicca, 'wizzard': *see OED s.v.* wick *adj.*].

wil *n.* craft, deceit, 377; **wiles** *pl.* wiles, tricks (? ON *wihl: *see OED s.v.* wile *sb.*].

wilc . . . so *adj. interr.* whichever, whatever, 3.

wilde *adj.* wild, 208, 261, 533.

wile *n.* while, time, 173.

wile *pres. ind. 3 sg., subj. sg.*, **wilen** *ind. pl. see* **wille** *pres. ind. 1 sg.*

wiles *conj.* while, 77, 362, 560.

wiles *n. pl. see* **wil.**

wille *adv.* astray, 26.

wille *n.* will, 20, 24, 289; **willen** *pl.* inclinations, 458†.

wille *pres. ind. 1 sg.* will, want to, 27; *3 sg.*, 7, 25, 171 etc.; is accustomed to, 544; **wile**, 103, 195, 286; is accustomed to, 108, 147, 161 etc.; wants, 541; wants to go, 515; **wilen** *pl.*, 323; **wile** *subj. sg.*, 3; **wuldes** *pret. ind. 2 sg.*, 337; **wulde** *3 sg.*, 311, 312, 495 &c.; **wulde** *pret. subj. sg.*, 63; *wullen on* wish to land on, 276†.

willen *see* **wille** *n.*

wimmen *n. pl.* women, 516.

win *n.* animosity, 148, 213.

wine *n.* friend, 253†.

winnen *v.* obtain, 274; *pres. ind. pl.* contend, 357; **wan** *pret. ind. sg.* won, redeemed, 568.

winter *n.* winter, 161, 162, 174 etc.; ~ *aȝen see* **aȝen.**

wirm *n.* serpent, 94, 114, 124 etc.; insect, 169, 179, 329 etc.

wis *adj.* aware, 599; **wise** wise, 403.

wis *in* ~ *see* **iwis** *adv.*

wise *adj. see* **wis** *adj.*

wise *n.* way, 331, 460, 471; habit, 319.

wisedom *n.* wisdom, 283.

wissing *n.*[1] (evil) desire, concupiscence, 215 [OE wyscan, *v.*].

wissing *n.*[2] guidance, 224, 315 [OE wissian, *v.*].

wit *adj.* white, 537; **wite**, 536.

wit *prep. see* **wið.**

wite *see* **wit** *adj.*

witen *v.* know, 17.

wið *prep.* with, 5, 60, 87 etc.; 446 (postponed); against, 114, 284 (twice), 600; towards, 148, 596; in, 377, 550; among, 130; on, 353; *wit herte see* **herte**; ~ *miȝte see* **miȝt**; ~ *unskil see* **unskil.**

wiðeren *pres. ind. pl.* struggle, 323.

wiðerwine *n.* enemy, 581.

wiðinnen *adv.* inside, within, 199, 410.

wiðuten *adv.* outside, 409.

wiðuten *prep.* without, 275, 376.

wod *adj.* mad, 219.

wold *n.* earth, 557; **wolde** *p.c.* open country, 425.

wolden *v.* possess *eche lif to* ~ 'as far as the attainment of eternal life is concerned' (Hall), 123†.

woning *n.* lamentation, moaning, 597.

wor *adv. rel.* where, 457; ~ *so see* **wor so.**

word *n.* word, 26, 211, 582.

wore *see* **ben.**

wor so *adv. indef.* wherever, 539, 554, 555 (twice) etc.

worður3 *adv. rel.* through which, 579.

wos *pron. rel. gen. sg.* whose, 564.

wo so *pron. indef.* whoever, 294, 296, 305 etc.

wrengöe *n.* crookedness, 59.

writen *pp.* set down, recorded, 513.

wrong *adj.* crooked, twisted, 32†, 52.

wrong *n. don* ~ done wrong, sinned, 598.

wu *adv. interr.* how, 18, 29, 35 etc.; what, 449; **hu**, 18, 30.

wu *int.* (expressing surprise, admiration, exultation), 16† [cf. OE hu *int. and see* OED *s.v.* who *int. and s.v.* ho *int.*[2]].

wude *n.* wood, tree, 158, 207.

wulde, wuldes, wullen *see* **wille** *pres. ind. 1 sg.*

wulues *n. pl.* wolves, 410.

wunde *n. p.c.* wound, 376.

wunder *n.* marvel, 169, 268, 372 etc.

wune *n.* habit, practice, 247; opportunity, 457.

wunen *v.* dwell, live, 358, 360; **wuneð** *pres. ind. 3 sg.*, 353, 396, 539 etc.; **wunen** *pl.*, 173; **wuneden** *pret. subj. pl.*, 436.

wurðeð *pres. ind. 3 sg.* grows, becomes, 49*; becomes, 326; **wurðen** *pl.*, 219, 253; **wurðe** *pres. subj. sg. war* ~ *see* **war**; **wurð** *pres. ind. sg.*, 508.

wurði *adj.* worthy, 128*, 304.

wurðlic *adv.* worthily, as it deserves, 152.